THE BRITISH
BONAPARTES

Dedicated to my mother and grandmother:
Maria Eugenie Michèle
and
Michele Jeanne Marie
and in memory of my third and fourth great-grandfathers.

THE BRITISH BONAPARTES

NAPOLEON'S FAMILY IN BRITAIN

Edward Hilary Davis

PEN & SWORD HISTORY

AN IMPRINT OF PEN & SWORD BOOKS LTD.
YORKSHIRE - PHILADELPHIA

First published in Great Britain in 2022 by
PEN AND SWORD HISTORY
An imprint of
Pen & Sword Books Ltd
Yorkshire – Philadelphia

ISBN 978 1 39908 852 7

A CIP catalogue record for this book is available from the British Library.

Typeset in Times New Roman 11.5/14 by SJmagic DESIGN SERVICES, India.
Printed and bound in the UK by CPI Group (UK) Ltd.

Pen & Sword Books Limited incorporates the imprints of Atlas, Archaeology,
Aviation, Discovery, Family History, Fiction, History, Maritime, Military,
Military Classics, Politics, Select, Transport, True Crime, Air World, Frontline
Publishing, Leo Cooper, Remember When, Seaforth Publishing, The Praetorian
Press, Wharncliffe Local History, Wharncliffe Transport, Wharncliffe True Crime
and White Owl.

For a complete list of Pen & Sword titles please contact
PEN & SWORD BOOKS LIMITED
47 Church Street, Barnsley, South Yorkshire, S70 2AS, England
E-mail: enquiries@pen-and-sword.co.uk
Website: www.pen-and-sword.co.uk

Or

PEN AND SWORD BOOKS
1950 Lawrence Rd, Havertown, PA 19083, USA
E-mail: Uspen-and-sword@casematepublishers.com
Website: www.penandswordbooks.com

Contents

Acknowledgements

I am grateful to many friends for their help and support in the creation of this book, particularly Ashley Coates, Peter Barnes, Dr Helen Scott, Prince Jean-Christophe Napoleon and his family, and, of course, my own long-suffering family. (My profound apologies to anyone I sat next to at a dinner party while I was writing this book.) As this book was written during my Master of Studies degree at the University of Cambridge Faculty of Architecture, I am particularly grateful to my supervisors Adrian Tinniswood OBE and Dr Adam Menuge for their continued patience and for letting me research and write alongside my other studies. I am also indebted to Professor Kate Williams for her advice and encouragement for getting the book off the ground.

As this work has been created partly in support of the Royal Versailles Ball (a charity event taking place at the palace of Versailles celebrating the anniversary of the 1855 State Visits of Queen Victoria and Napoleon III), I would like to take this opportunity to thank all my fellow volunteers, committee members and patrons of the Ball, for their support of this book and their continued generosity to its charities: HRH Prince Michael of Kent, TIH Prince and Princess Napoleon, Sir Rodney Williams, GCMG, the Duke of Rutland, the Duke of Fife, the Marquess of Reading, Lord Winston, Lord Lyon King of Arms, Sir Ranulph Fiennes Bt, OBE, Lady Huntington-Whiteley, Julia Carrick OBE, Debbie Wiseman OBE, Antonia Da Silva, Stephanie von Oppell, Emma Murray-Jones, Charlie Oliver, Maddy Everington, Leonora Service and many more. Additionally, I should also like to thank, Roan Hackney, Richard Black, Charles Mundy, Sonya Ebermann, Anastassia Dimmek, Nicholas Morton and the late Helen Morton for their assistance.

Foreword
Written by HIH Prince Napoleon

His Imperial Highness Prince Jean-Christophe Napoleon Bonaparte

Since the time of my four-times great-uncle, Napoleon Bonaparte, my family has had an interesting relationship with the United Kingdom. Between the events of the invasion force gathering at Boulogne in 1803–1805, and the state visit of Queen Victoria to Versailles in 1855, Britain and the Bonapartes evolved from the greatest of adversaries to the closest of friends.

Following the Battles of Trafalgar and Waterloo, Bonaparte family members went from being prisoners in Britain to welcome guests, and some even became lifelong residents. Many of the wider family (some lesser known than others) made lives for themselves in Britain and, in some instances, were able to make their own small contribution to its history. We must also not forget that the last emperor of the French remains interred in England to this day.

For almost two centuries, Britain and France have been staunch friends and allies. Given their ancient warring history, this is an achievement to be celebrated. The close bonds of friendship formed between members of the British Royal Family and members of the Bonaparte family, such as Napoleon III, Empress Eugenie and others, greatly contributed towards the growing cooperation of the two great nations and sowed the seeds of lasting peace.

As a London resident of some years, I am delighted to continue the close relationship my family has with the British Isles, and that research into the lives of my earlier Bonaparte relatives here has been undertaken. I commend Edward Hilary Davis for his work and research into the family, and for his excellent regaling of lesser-known Bonaparte stories. I thoroughly recommend this book.

Jean-Christophe Prince Napoleon

Preface

The Eagle has Flown (to England)

For many years I have been fascinated by the way we compartmentalise history. It is a useful tool when teaching children; however; we must understand that there are no blank spots, no gaps between phases of history. Nor should history be viewed solely from one nation's perspective. The Middle Ages did not end at Bosworth Field. The Renaissance did not start there either. The Hundred Years War was not 100 years, it is a grouping of several wars, and the English lost them. The British Empire did not start in 1815 and end in 1997. When Napoleon I or Napoleon III fell, the Bonaparte family did not disappear with them. The Second World War is part two of the First World War. The First World War is part two of the Franco-Prussian War. The Franco-Prussian War is arguably part two of the power struggles in Europe in the mid-nineteenth century, following the Napoleonic Wars – which in turn are a consequence of the French Revolutionary Wars. If viewed through the eyes of one family and several of its generations, the gaps and blank spots of history (caused by our subconscious compartmentalisation) can be filled, and shed more human light on the times.

This book aims to shed light on a particular family which ordinarily is most famous for being connected to one (or two) great men and one particular country: France. What may be a surprise to many is how big the Bonaparte family was, and how many of its members lived in or made homes for themselves in Britain – their traditional enemy. Through surprisingly amusing anecdotes and stories of the Bonapartes, I have tried to show the vibrant and colourful history of this family with the running theme of Great Britain (and her (former) empire)) running throughout. The focus is particularly on those families with a strong interaction with the British Isles and its dominions, including the US and Ireland. Admittedly, the layout of the family is difficult to initially comprehend, mostly owing to overlapping marriages of step-nieces and cousins. I also hope that by working through some of the various branches of the family that these will be made clearer.

The inspiration for this book came from two sources. As I child, thanks to my mother and grandmother, I became particularly fascinated in history, genealogy and heraldry – which ultimately led to my working at the College of Arms for several years. I was brought up on stories of the family's connection to the Bonapartes through 'the wrong side of the blanket'. Emperor Napoleon III had many formally recognised bastards throughout his life which he begat in France, Britain and probably other countries of the world. He paid for the education of several of my family, and, after his death, support continued from the Bonaparte family. This, of course, has led to a lifelong fascination with the Bonapartes and their lesser-known members, especially those dwelling in Britain.

The second source of inspiration came in 2019 when I was invited to be on the organising board of the Royal Versailles Ball as head of sponsorship but also as resident historian. As such, I began writing historical content for its programme and online platforms – mostly regarding the 1855 State Visits of Napoleon III and Queen Victoria. While writing these articles, I could not contain my excitement or enthusiasm, and began adding anecdotes and stories that I had collected about the Bonaparte family over the years. Before I knew it, I was well beyond the allotted word count. From then on, I decided to compile the many anecdotes I have collected, and construct the history of the Bonaparte family in Britain. All this I put into a book. This book.

As chance would have it, while writing this book, a Napoleonic eagle fell into my lap. Having worked for several years in the world of London auction houses, in 2020 a fellow dealer and collector of militaria asked me to come to his West End shop to view an item he had recently acquired at auction. The item in question turned out to be a French naval imperial eagle. Many will be familiar with the golden eagles carried into battle by French Napoleonic soldiers, some of which were captured by the British, perhaps most famously by Bernard Cornwell's fictional hero, Sharpe. This, however, was a naval eagle. Much bigger and far rarer. The naval eagles were presented by Napoleon in 1804 to the French admiralty. Each one was ceremonially kissed by the emperor himself, and later placed near the prow of battleships. Thirty-eight in total were made. My excitement on handling this object was palpable. Sotheby's were engaged. Their research found that this was one of only four known surviving naval eagles – the other three being in museums in France and Spain. Furthermore, this eagle, with signs of having been broken and then carefully fixed, was most likely the eagle from the *Bucentaure* – the French 86-gun ship which was Admiral Villeneuve's flagship at the Battle of Trafalgar in 1805. During the battle, Lord Nelson's own flagship, HMS *Victory* raked the stern of *Bucentaure* rendering her incapacitated for the rest of the battle. She surrendered a few hours later to the aptly named HMS *Conqueror*. Napoleon's orders in the event of capture were to break the eagle and throw it over the side. It seems likely that the French sailors only carried out half of these instructions. The eagle never made it to the deep but was likely pocketed by a British sailor and brought home to England. Tracing the item's provenance, it only re-emerged in the mid-twentieth century. It was for sale in a Camden Market junk shop, described as a probable church lectern. By that time, the broken wings had been expertly soldered back on. It was acquired for a few quid. It is thought that the value of the item now runs to seven or maybe even eight figures!

Introduction

Royal Exiles to Britain: Bourbons and Bonapartes

It is surprising to think that the last five undisputed monarchs of France, at one time or another, lived in exile on British soil. Accompanying these monarchs were their wider family. Some not only lived in Britain but died (and are buried) there. France and Britain have for most of the last millennium been the closest of adversaries yet French kings and emperors have spent many of their non-ruling years on the shores of Great Britain. In the case of the Bonapartes, they have assimilated into Britain reasonably seamlessly, becoming British aristocrats, holders of civil office, soldiers and even volunteer policemen in the Westminster Constabulary. To this day (2021), Napoleon's heir dwells among us in London.

For centuries, Britain has been famed as a home or temporary home for exiled monarchs. These have come from many countries – not just France. Being one of the world's oldest and strongest monarchies, the rulers of the United Kingdom have shown hospitality, of varying degrees, to other (foreign) monarchs who have had the misfortune to be deposed or exiled, or who have fled or abdicated. This has been particularly true during the course of the nineteenth and twentieth centuries when many monarchies both rose and fell. In the wake of the First and Second World wars, many ancient European monarchies gave way to republicanism, or indeed in less fortunate instances, communism. The former premier families of these countries in many cases were, for political reasons, banished from their former homes and needed to seek shelter in a different country. Britain was, of course, a favourite destination for such families – based on its existing strong monarchy but also its safety. As an island, and based on historical form, Britain was very unlikely to be successfully invaded by any enemy power that might wish to haul the royal family in question back to their former lands.

In this, the third decade of the twenty-first century, when we think of exiled monarchs who resided or still reside in England, we are inclined to think of recent examples such as the king of Norway, Haakon VII, who was in exile during the German occupation of his home from 1940 to 1945; or Queen Wilhelmina of the Netherlands or King Zog of Albania for similar reasons. Many of these such royals stayed long stretches in London hotels such as the Ritz, or were lent grace-and-favour houses on the Windsor estate by the Crown. Naturally, the British royal family has shared close kinship with many other European royal houses, most especially since the reign of Queen Victoria. However, one also remembers those monarchs from more exotic lands such as Emperor Haile Selassie who, like King Zog, had lost his lands to an occupying Italian force. He initially stayed in Warne's Hotel in the seaside town of Worthing in Sussex before eventually settling in Bath. (Old Worthing residents remember him taking his lions for a walk on leashes on the promenade.) Kings, princes and rajahs connected to the British Empire also frequently found themselves exiled to mainland Britain – willingly or unwillingly. Duleep Singh, Maharaja of the Sikh Empire is one example. He succeeded, aged only 5, in 1844, but a few years later Britain annexed the Punjab and he was effectively held a captive and dethroned. He was brought to England and 'converted' to Christianity. He was a resident at Claridge's Hotel before he was provided with a house in Roehampton – ironically supplied by the East India Company. Duleep later moved to Castle Menzies in Scotland and threw large parties – earning the title of 'Black Prince of Perth'. The Maharaja also owned a hunting estate in Norfolk.

There were many Indian rulers who at one time or another were 'moved' to the United Kingdom during the days of the British Raj. Some even came to England following India's independence. Other unfortunate rulers (or would-be rulers), such as the Zulu kings, would spend time effectively incarcerated. King Cetshwayo, responsible for the initial defeat of the British at Isandlwana (1879) in the Anglo-Zulu War, was taken prisoner, dethroned, taken to Cape Town and then to London. For a brief time, he lived on Melbury Road in Kensington. His son, Dinuzulu, succeeded his father as king of the Zulu Nation but was not officially recognised by the British. He was captured and exiled for seven years to St Helena – the same British territory where Napoleon was exiled.

There are some foreign royals who have been exiled to London for so long they are thought of as part of the furniture or part of the establishment. The Greek royal family has long lived in Hampstead Garden Suburb in London since the abolition of the Greek monarchy. King Constantine II (king of the Hellenes) ruled from 1964–1973 and has only recently (2013) been allowed to return to Greece. It cannot be forgotten, however, that he too is connected to the British royal family through his cousin the late Prince Philip (of Greece and Denmark). He is also godfather to Prince William, Duke of Cambridge.

As with Cetshwayo, even monarchs who had formerly been Britain's adversary were offered asylum in the United Kingdom. In May 1940, Germany invaded the Netherlands, where former Emperor of Germany, Kaiser Wilhelm II, was living out his days in exile at Huis Doorn. Winston Churchill, perhaps with the thought of using the Kaiser as a symbol against Nazi rule in Germany, offered him asylum in Great Britain. Additionally, Wilhelm was first-cousin-once-removed of the British king, George VI. Proud to the end, the Kaiser refused. He died a year later.

It is perceivably ironic that perhaps the most famous royals associated with tragedy or exile to Britain are the ones who sadly never made it. Over 100 years on, we know that plans had been made between King George V and the Cabinet Office to house the Tsar of Russia, Nicholas II, and his family in Britain if they could be successfully extracted – possibly at a spare royal residence, possibly in Scotland. Both the Tsar and Tsarina were first cousins of George, and he famously had a close attachment to Nicholas – not least of which because of their striking resemblance. Despite this, it was George himself who took the political decision not to rescue the Romanovs and house them in Britain lest they spark a communist or anti-monarchist revolution in the United Kingdom. The decision may well have led to the circumstances of their eventual murder by the Bolsheviks in 1917. Though this may seem bloodless, George V did arguably protect the British monarchy and is often hailed as the father of the modern monarchy. One must remember that his oath was to protect the country and the Crown – not his wider family.

Arguably, it is politically safer to have a defeated former adversary as a royal guest than any other king or royal exile. Notably, this is where the French come in! That said, the tradition of English kings and French kings seeking sanctuary in each other's lands goes back to the Middle Ages.

Perhaps French exiled royals are less well known in Britain because there have been so many of them over the centuries. However, many English ex-monarchs, future monarchs or would-be monarchs have settled in exile in France – usually for their safety. The deposed James II, his son and famed grandson, Bonnie Prince Charlie, all spent their long exiles in France with the blessing of their Bourbon cousins. In the Middle Ages, great figures of the Wars of the Roses seem to have regularly used France as a bolthole or place to gain support, most notably Queen Margaret (of Anjou) and Edward Prince of Wales, Edward IV (in Flanders) and Henry VII (in Brittany for fourteen years). Even Richard Cromwell, Oliver Cromwell's son and successor as Lord Protector, went into exile in France in 1659 in the face of the return of Charles II – himself returning from exile in both France and the Netherlands. The most recent monarch to serve a kind of exile in France was Edward VIII – the Duke of Windsor. Following his abdication in 1936, he married Wallis Simpson at Chateau de Chande in France. At various times throughout their lives, they lived in France. Intriguingly, George VI banned any royal family from attending the wedding; however, Randolph Churchill (Sir Winston's son) attended. During the Second World War, when Edward refused to come back to Britain (from Portugal), Winston Churchill threatened him with a court martial. The Duke and Duchess of Windsor both died in Paris – in 1972 and 1986 respectively.

Rulers have more often been resident in Britain by either force or out of necessity. In the Middle Ages, at the Battle of Poitiers in 1356, the English, commanded by Edward the Black Prince of Wales, defeated a French force of nearly twice the size. Towards the end of the battle, with the French forces being encircled, the French king, John II (confusingly known in France as 'John the Good'), was captured, taken back to England and held for ransom. He was four years a captive in England and housed at various residences such as the Savoy Palace, Windsor Castle, the Tower of London and in a house in East Sussex, known ever since as King John's Lodge. It is now a nursery. The ransom money paid to the English greatly weakened the stability of France and its monarchy, while giving greater influence to England and her possessions, such as Gascony, in France.

As we will later see, following both the French Revolution and the rise of Napoleon, the would-be Bourbon king, Louis XVIII (younger brother of Louis XVI), spent many years holding a miniature Bourbon Royal French Court at Hartwell House in Buckinghamshire from 1809 to 1814. After Napoleon's exile to Elba, Louis was restored to the throne of France in Paris in May 1814 only to flee less than a year later when the escaped Napoleon approached with a growing force. Louis fled to the Netherlands – perhaps he was too embarrassed to return to Buckinghamshire! He was reinstated as king by the allied victors months later, following Napoleon's final defeat at Waterloo in 1815.

After Waterloo, Napoleon's surrender was taken on a Royal Navy ship and he was taken to Torbay and Plymouth Sound but not permitted to disembark on British soil – though there are many local tales of the emperor sneaking ashore in the evenings to visit the occasional innkeeper's daughter! Napoleon was soon taken to his enforced exile on the British island of St Helena in the South Atlantic where he remained until his death in 1821. Meanwhile, several of his family made their homes in Britain and led interesting lives amongst the gentry and nobility of the day.

King Louis XVIII was in turn succeeded by his younger brother Charles X. Charles, like his brother, had spent much of the Revolutionary Wars in exile in Britain. He was given a hefty allowance by a sympathetic King George III and permitted him to live in Edinburgh and also in London (with his mistress), in Mayfair. After succeeding his brother, Charles reigned until the July Revolution deposed him in 1830. His fifth cousin, Louis-Philippe Duke of Orleans (a descendant of Louis XIII), was proclaimed king of the French instead. Fleeing a hostile mob, Charles X and his family sailed for England. The Duke of Wellington, then prime minister, required them to travel as private citizens, so they arrived under pseudonyms. They were first housed at the secluded Lulworth Castle in Dorset, and then Holyrood Palace in Edinburgh. They left after being offered a better option in Prague in 1832.

The new (and last) king of the French did not last long either. As a young, minor royal during the Revolution, Louis-Philippe had travelled much of the world during the times of the republic and Napoleonic regime. He travelled to the US where he met George Washington and Alexander Hamilton. While in Nova Scotia, he met Prince Edward the Duke of Kent (Queen Victoria's father). He struck up a close friendship with the duke and they travelled together back to England where Louis-Philippe remained for fifteen years. For some of this time he became a teacher of mathematics at the Great Ealing School. Such was his closeness with the

British royals, Louis-Philippe proposed marriage to King George III's daughter, Princess Elizabeth, the Duke of Kent's sister. The offer had to be reluctantly turned down based on Louis's Catholicism. During his years as France's monarch, his former friendship with the Duke of Kent proved a useful asset as he was invested as a member of the Order of the Garter by Queen Victoria. Following the 1848 Revolution in France and his subsequent deposition, Louis-Philippe spent the remainder of his years in exile in Claremont in Surrey. He was a frequent visitor to St Leonards and to Brighton. He died at Claremont in 1850 and was buried in Weybridge in Surrey, although his body was moved to the Royal Chapel of Dreux in France in 1876.

The 1848 Revolution saw the removal of a Bourbon from power and the installation of a Bonaparte. At roughly the same time Louis-Philippe arrived in exile in England, Prince Louis-Napoleon was preparing to leave for France. He was elected the first president of France later that year. A few years later, in a coup d'état, he was declared emperor of the French as Napoleon III and reigned for more years than his famous uncle Napoleon I. As this book will show, Napoleon III spent much of his time in Britain amongst English and Scottish society during three different periods of exile and a state visit. He, like so many of the Bonapartes, had many links to Britain through family, friends, and love interests.

To this day, Napoleon III, his wife, his son, and many cousins and fellow Bonapartes lie buried in British burial grounds or churches from Hampshire to Midlothian – which is perhaps a testament of how surprisingly British many of them became.

Chapter 1

Bonaparte Origins: Corsica, Italy, and Ethiopia

We instantly recognise Bonaparte as one of the great names of history. It is synonymous with suggestions of power and grandeur as well as cunning and military excellence. This is mostly thanks to Emperor Napoleon I.

Behind every great man, however, there is a wider family: brothers, sisters, nephews and nieces and their descendants. These too bear the weight of the prominent name. Although not a particularly ancient dynasty, like the Habsburgs, Bourbons or Romanovs spanning the previous centuries, the name still ranks alongside these such houses and other older families. Though the Bonapartes were able to form marriage alliances with great houses, and have many descendants living today in many countries of Europe, including Britain, they sprang on to the stage of history relatively out of the blue and achieved enormous power and influence within a matter of a few years. Napoleon went from a mere second lieutenant to emperor of the French in roughly nineteen years. Bonapartes were, arguably, great influencers in the courts of Europe from 1799 until as late as 1920. Two men of this family, through feats of arms, political cunning and luck, became emperors of the French, and their siblings or relatives became heads of state in their own right too, or achieved other heights in art and science. Many of them ended up living in Britain and some made their home there. But where did these people come from? What kind of family could achieve so much in such a short space of time?

Most will be aware that the Bonapartes hailed from Corsica. An island in the Mediterranean that is now French, it was one time briefly independent and, even more briefly, British. However, from 1284, Corsica was ruled by the Republic of Genoa, until 1755, when it experimented as an independent republic and then as a piece of the

1

Family Tree

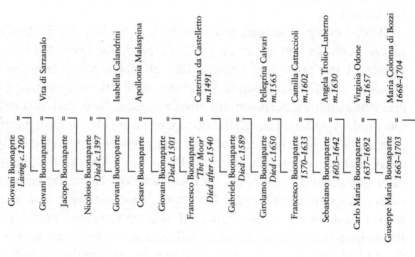

Giovani Buonaprte
Living c.1200
=
Vita di Sarzanalo

Giovani Buonaparte
=
Jacopo Buonaparte

Nicoloso Buonaparte
Died c.1397
=
Isabella Calandrini

Giovani Buonoparte
=
Apollonia Malaspina

Cesare Buonaparte

Giovani Buonaparte
Died c.1501
=
Caterina da Castelletto
m.1491

Francesco Buonaparte
'The Moor'
Died after c.1540

Gabriele Buonaparte
Died c.1589
=
Pellegrina Calvari
m.1565

Girolamo Buonaparte
Died c.1650
=
Camilla Cattaccioli
m.1602

Francesco Buonaparte
1570–1633
=
Angela Trolio–Luberno
m.1630

Sebastiano Buonaparte
1603–1642
=
Virginia Odone
m.1657

Carlo Maria Buonaparte
1637–1692
=
Maria Colonna di Bozzi
1668–1704

Giuseppe Maria Buonaparte
1663–1703

Bonaparte Origins: Corsica, Italy, and Ethiopia

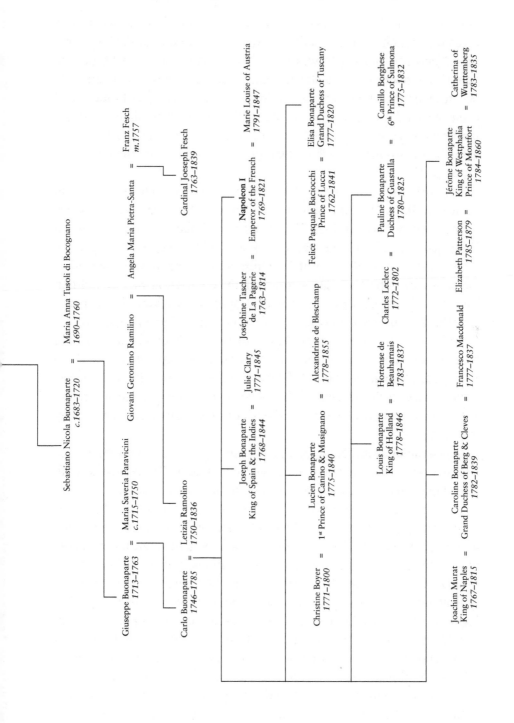

British Crown. It was ceded to France with unpaid debts that Genoa owed the French Crown. Corsica became part of France around the same time Napoleon Bonaparte was born. Napoleon's father, Carlo, despite being a member of the resistance against French occupation, eventually became Corsica's representative to the court of Louis XVI of France and even received a patent of nobility in 1771. Though by then Corsican, the Bonapartes were in fact Italian in origin, and Italian speakers. The name being originally spelt as *Buonaparte*, deriving from the Italian for 'good part'.

The origins of the family have been traced to Sarzana, a town in Liguria in Italy. Near the border with Tuscany, Sarzana changed hands over the years between Pisa, Florence and ultimately Genoa. Gandolfo Buonaparte is one of the earliest known of the family, living there around the year 1200. One of Gandolfo's descendants was married to the cousin of Pope Nicholas V, although the connection was very slight. The nine-times-great-grandfather of Napoleon, Giovani Buonaparte, was the first to leave Sarzana for Corsica. Both Sarzana and Corsica were by now ruled by Genoa. Many of Giovani's descendants would be town councillors in Ajaccio as far down the generations as Carlo Bonaparte (Napoleon's father). However, Giovani's son, Francesco, was a mercenary in the service of the Genoese republic in Ajaccio around 1490. He was known locally as 'The Moor of Sarzana'. The reason why is fascinating.

A genetic study into Napoleon's DNA through his maternal and paternal ancestry was conducted and published in 2010 and 2012 respectively in *Investigate Genetics* and in the *Journal of Molecular Biology Research*. These were conducted by Gerard Lucotte of the Institute of Molecular Anthropology in Paris. According to the research, Napoleon, belonged to Y-haplogroup E1b1b1c1. A haplogroup is a genetic group of people who share a common ancestor either patrilineally or matrilineally. To this day, Bonaparte men belong to the same Y-haplogroup. Their DNA is typical of those with Moorish ancestry. The study shows that the specific haplogroup has its highest concentration among Ethiopian Amhara, Ethiopian Jews, Ethiopian Wolayta, Ethiopian Oromo, Yemenis and Jordanians. It is likely that Francesco Buonaparte may have been north African or almost Arabic in appearance – hence his nickname. Many medieval Italian merchants and mercenaries were engaged in commerce with North Africa and the Middle East and some married people from

4

other ethnic backgrounds. Indeed, many Italians to this day have darker complexions. Napoleon was aware of the stories of Francesco the Moor and found them rather amusing – adding an exotic layer to his Corsican background. Coincidently, the flag of Corsica to this day is a Moor's head! As early as the twelfth century, Ethiopia was ruled by emperors, it is perhaps fitting that a family of Ethiopian descent should be the first emperors of the French.

Aside from the Sarzana Buonapartes, there were other Buonapartes living in San Miniato in Tuscany, and it is probable that there was another branch living in Florence in the late Middle Ages, although the exact links are sometimes vague. Jacopo Buonaparte was of the San Miniato branch of the family. He was a friend and adviser to Giulio de Medici – a member of the ruling family of Florence. In 1523, Giulio become Pope Clement VIII and went on to commission Michelangelo to paint the Sistine Chapel as well as preside over the Church during the English king Henry VIII's divorce and subsequent break with the Roman Catholic Church in 1527. Famously, Jacopo, as an eyewitness, wrote an account of the Sacking of Rome, which took place that same year. Pope Clement had to surrender the Castel St Angelo and pay a ransom in exchange for his life. Jacopo only survived by hiding with the Pope's staff. During the Sacking of Rome, a rebellion took place in Florence. Two of Jacopo's nephews were involved and were subsequently banished, but their citizenship was restored by the first Duke of Florence, Alessandro de Medici. The San Miniato branch of the Buonapartes died with Jacopo *c.*1550. The Florentine branch died with Abbot Gregorio Buonaparte. He had the good fortune to meet his distant cousin, Napoleon. Gregorio died in 1803 – supposedly leaving Napoleon as heir (although the latter had an elder brother, Joseph).

In view of the heritage of the Bonaparte family, and in part due to the last wishes of his uncle, Cardinal Fesch, the Emperor Napoleon III built the Chapelle Imperiale in Ajaccio in 1857. The chapel is the burial site of ten members of the Bonaparte family, including Napoleon I's parents Carlo and Letizia, but not of either of the two Bonapartes who became emperors.

Although the Bonapartes came from France, Corsica, Italy and (further back), Ethiopia or the Middle East, many of them, willingly or not, were destined, either for a long or short period, to end up on the shores of Great Britain. Arguably, some of them became British.

Chapter 2

Napoleon I: Plymouth to Prometheus

History will remember Napoleon as long as Europe exists. The man stands shoulder to shoulder with other epic men of military history, such as Alexander, Hannibal, Caesar, or Charlemagne. In many ways he exceeded some of their achievements. Born in Corsica in 1769 (then part of Italy) he was effectively an immigrant to France; Napoleon was commissioned a second lieutenant in 1785. Just fourteen years (and a revolution) later, he was the first consul and effective ruler of France, aged 30. In 1804, backed by a public referendum and the blessing of the Pope, he crowned himself emperor of the French. Through his wars and politics, Napoleon became known as the 'master of Europe' as he steadily built a road of conquest from Madrid to Moscow.

In Britain at least, we sometimes see Napoleon as the arch-nemesis of Britannia in the late eighteenth and early nineteenth centuries. This is partly due to the rendering of him in the British press as a monster or dwarf, hungry to carve up Europe for his dinner and delight. Even as recently as a few decades ago, English children were threatened with '*Old Boney the Ogre*' coming to get them if they did not behave. Throughout his career, Napoleon himself was proud to have been the British Empire's greatest enemy. He was, in fact, enamoured of the plucky strength of this island nation. Being from an island nation himself, he could sympathise better than most other Frenchman with the points of view of the British. He is attributed with calling Britain a nation of shopkeepers, perhaps as an insult towards Britain's military strength. However, Barry Edward O'Meara, who was surgeon to Napoleon during his St Helena captivity (and a founder of the Reform Club), claimed that Napoleon clarified this comment to him and that he meant it more as a compliment to Britain's merchants and growing wealth and influence from trade and not necessarily conquest or large population. Whether Napoleon actually made either of the comments is unknown.

Family Tree

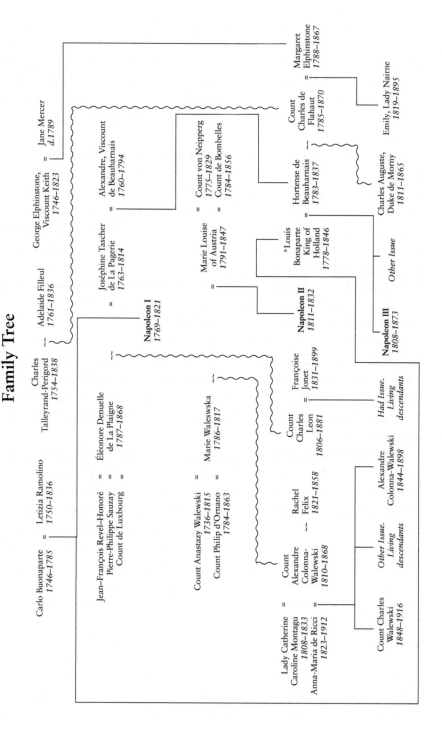

Despite his conquests, successes and reforms (which we will not concern ourselves with in this book), his epic life ended in an equally legendary way. Twice Napoleon was completely defeated, and twice sent into exile – first on Elba and secondly St Helena. Despite an impressive and meteoric comeback, the second of these was as a captive on British (overseas) soil – and he died under the watchful guard of English, Irish and Scotsmen.

Napoleon's captivity can be likened to the fate of Prometheus, the Greek titan who stole fire from the gods of Olympus and gifted it to man. As punishment for this, he was chained to a rock and Zeus sent his eagle to peck out his liver. Each night it would grow back, only to be pecked out the next day. Such was the fate of Napoleon – to languish far away from a continent he once dominated with his energy, charisma and reforming zeal. The fires he left behind are arguably the ideas of the French Revolution, helped spread from country to country by corps of French soldiers. There is perhaps poetic coincidence in that Napoleon selected the imperial eagle as his standard.

Metaphors aside, in the last years of his life, Napoleon had much interaction between himself, Britain and Britons. These small interactions fade into obscurity behind the colossal achievements and failures of his life; they are nonetheless worthy of note. Also worthy of marking are the lives of his sons who also briefly made their lives on British shores. More on them later.

The love/hate relationship between Napoleon and Britain began when he was young. After travelling from his island home to France and completing his military training, one of Napoleon's earliest encounters with Britain was at Toulon. In 1793, just a few years after the Revolution had begun, and only months since the guillotining of Louis XVI, Toulon was overrun by royalists, who, with the help of the British and Spanish navies, secured the vital port city and proclaimed Louis XVII as king of France (although he was only 8 and a prisoner in Paris). This was a potentially deadly blow for the Revolution: if the royalists were able to gain a foothold in the south of France, belief in, and support for the republic might collapse. The republic sent the army to take back the city and lay siege to the small forts the British had constructed around the town protecting the harbour. It is during this siege that young artillery captain, Napoleon Bonaparte, first made a name for himself. Though irritating his senior officers at times, he was instrumental in capturing some of these positions. He understood that if he could capture some of the forts – including one nicknamed Little Gibraltar – he could cut off the city from being resupplied by sea. Eventually, Napoleon led an assault on Little Gibraltar, successfully capturing the fort. The fighting lasted all night and Napoleon was nearly killed by a British sergeant who stabbed him in the thigh with a bayonet. Had the sergeant's aim been higher, history would doubtless be very different. It was during these operations that Napoleon captured a British general. Napoleon formally accepted the surrender of Charles O'Hara who was then held in a Paris jail for two years before being released in an exchange. O'Hara had the dubious privilege of being the only man to have personally been taken prisoner by both Napoleon and George Washington; twelve years earlier, O'Hara had presented Lord Cornwallis's sword to Washington at the British Surrender at Yorktown, thus ending the American War of Independence. Napoleon must have been amused that this British officer was humbled by a republican for a second time.

Reports of Napoleon's ingenuity and bravery were reported back to Paris. He was promoted to brigadier general and given command of the French army of Italy's artillery. The British meanwhile, evacuated from Toulon and the French royalists left in the town were massacred by republican forces.

Although Napoleon's earliest connections to Britain were in fire and blood at the siege of Toulon, we should not forget that, arguably, for two years, Napoleon himself was, in effect, British! By 1793, Corsica had only been part of France for two decades. The president of the Corsican Department, Pasquale Paoli, fell out with the National Assembly in Paris over the execution of Louis XVI. He was not anti-monarchy like the Jacobins, and he may well have acted as a British agent. He was a Corsican patriot more than a revolutionary. In 1793, he and the Corsican Assembly formally seceded from republican France. After requesting help and protection from the British government, in 1794 Admiral Samuel Hood arrived off the Corsican coast with a fleet of Royal Navy ships. The same fleet had just been forced out of Toulon thanks to the plans of a plucky young Corsican/French officer – Napoleon himself!

French forces were systematically pushed out of Corsica by the British, who were hoping to acquire a Mediterranean base of their own, and by Corsican patriots. The Bonaparte family, prominent and powerful on the island, were driven out by Paoli and his followers as they were mostly pro-French or Jacobins. Napoleon could do nothing – he was leading the French army of Italy. Calvi was the last remaining French stronghold on Corsica. The British launched a joint military and naval siege of the fortress. The military expedition was led by General Sir Charles Stuart (1753–1801). Little could Sir Charles have known that his own nephew would go on to marry Napoleon's niece thirty years later! (Lord and Lady Dudley Stuart). Sir Charles's forces were escorted by HMS *Armageddon*, captained by Horatio Nelson, then aged 35. During the bombardment, a shot that may have hit a sandbag as well as the deck struck debris towards Nelson and caused his famous loss of sight in his right eye.

For just over two years (1794–1796), Corsica was added to the list of dominions of King George III as a client kingdom. The Anglo-Corsican kingdom was given a democratic constitution, a viceroy (the 1st Earl of Minto) and a president of the Council of State. George III's coat of arms was used alongside those of Corsica as a symbol of this new British dominion. This effectively meant that, for a short period of time at least, the place and country of Napoleon's birth and of his siblings' birth, was British – indirectly making them British themselves (although, they certainly would not have seen it that way). By late 1796, France had gained more allies in the Mediterranean and it was obvious that the Anglo-Corsican kingdom could not last. The British forces tactfully retreated to Gibraltar and Corsica became part of France again. Perhaps the events in Corsica during those years heightened Napoleon's loathing of the British – who invaded and caused betrayal and fragmentation on his island home. Despite Napoleon trying, he was never able to return the insult.

Because of his doubtless skill and bravery at Toulon, Napoleon was a brigadier general at the age of 24. Ten years later he was emperor of the French; much of his career and life was quick-paced and impressive. From his first rise to prominence at Toulon, to his downfall and abdication in 1814, Napoleon's military and political ambitions were usually anti-British. Britain, being an island north-west of the mainland, and having a strong navy, was able to effectively hover around Europe and meddle in the affairs of most of the continental countries. Napoleon took exception to this. The Napoleonic Wars featured many battles between French and British forces on land and sea in many parts of the globe, and, at one time Napoleon had planned to invade Britain from

Boulogne where he gathered his forces. This was avoided, partly due to the events of Trafalgar. His anti-British policy was underlined further by the Continental System, a ban on all trade with Britain (and even mail) throughout all France's European dominions, satellite countries and allies – effectively nearly all Europe. In time, however, after a dazzling career, and meteoric reversal in fortunes, Napoleon would find himself a 'guest' of the British more than once, and like much of his family, spend his last remaining years on British soil.

As well as Napoleon being temporarily British by birth (though only technically), his first wife and longest of lovers, Empress Joséphine, may also have been British. Marie-Josèphe-Rose Tascher de La Pagerie (later known as Joséphine) daughter of a minor French noble and sugarcane plantation owner, is usually cited as being born in Martinique, a French Caribbean colony, in 1763. However, the actual location of her birth is missing from her birth records. Her family's estates stretched between the islands of both Martinique and St Lucia. The island of St Lucia had been changing hands between the French and the British for nearly 100 years by the time of Joséphine's birth. It is possible, and indeed likely, that though she was baptised in Martinique, she was born on St Lucia were there were no civil registers at the time. A few months before Joséphine was born, St Lucia was handed back to the French by the British in the Treaty of Paris; however, the British occupied the island again from 1778 for six years and again finally seized it for good in 1794 in the wake of the French Revolution and slave uprisings, gaining complete control of the island in around 1803. This, again, by technicality, would make the empress (and emperor) of the French British by birth. Perhaps that is why the history books (and the French) prefer to cite the place of Joséphine's birth as Martinique!

Napoleon was defeated in 1814 by the sixth coalition. Austria, Russia, Prussia, Sweden and other German states had invaded France from the east, resulting in the battle of Paris, while the British had led an invasion across the Pyrenees together with Spanish and Portuguese allies, resulting in the Battle of Toulouse. Napoleon had retreated to his palace at Fontainebleau outside Paris; there the emperor waited for the old monarchies of Europe to give him terms. He watched as many of his servants and marshals began to trickle away, offering their services to the coalition or to the Bourbons. Napoleon eventually signed the Treaty of Fontainebleau, in which he abdicated the throne, but was given sovereignty of the island of Elba in the Mediterranean. He and his second wife, Marie-Louise, were permitted to keep their titles of emperor and empress, but he and the Bonaparte family and their descendants were barred from ever holding power or office in France again. Napoleon at one point tried to commit suicide while at Fontainebleau. However, he used an old vial of poison he kept with him, one that he had had made for him years before in case he was captured on campaign. Its potency had diminished over time and though it made Napoleon unwell, the potion was no longer fatal.

Meanwhile, in England, the would-be king, Louis XVIII, waited alarmingly patiently for his throne to be 'returned' to him – the divine right of kings theory, if applied here, would suggest he had actually been king of France ever since the death of the 10-year-old Louis XVII in captivity during the Revolution in 1795. Louis had been in exile in England since 1807. Before that, he had been away from France since 1791. After travelling with his wife, Marie Joséphine of Savoy, from Stockholm to Great Yarmouth in England, he acquired Hartwell House in Buckinghamshire (near Aylesbury) in 1809 – which was rented to him by Sir Charles Lee, from a prominent gentry family, and a kinsman of Sir Christopher Lee CBE (of Dracula and Scaramanga fame). Over 100 courtiers followed Louis, then Count of Provence, to Hartwell. One can imagine the Lees must have had mixed feelings about that. Louis waited patiently in the Buckinghamshire countryside for Napoleon to make a mistake and for the obliging British to ship him back to France and his throne. He had waited many years and was in no rush to leave the English countryside. He would not agree to make the journey until the French Senate had formally invited him to be king and until Napoleon was truly finished. Both happened in 1814.

Before his exile to an island which he was to be sovereign of, Napoleon eventually made peace with his decision to abdicate from the throne and politics – or so it appeared. He received British ministers and gentlemen, all of whom were curiously testing him to see if he could be trusted and what his intentions for the future might be. The British were the most opposed to his 'detainment' on Elba, claiming it was too close to the continent and he had too much autonomy – being allowed a small court and a personal bodyguard/small army. The Mediterranean islands were also still full of Jacobins, revolutionaries and pirates. Ministers Lord Castlereagh and Lord Bathurst met with the fallen emperor as did Colonel Sir Neil Campbell, who was able to speak with Napoleon about his illustrious career and also discuss the future. Napoleon is alleged to have remarked that Britain was the greatest of nations. This was probably because he wanted to be sent into exile in England, as his brother had been permitted to do. Maybe he hoped to utilise his brother Lucien's house in Worcestershire – Dinham. He would feel less cut off from the world there. The British, however, were concerned he might cause trouble in the United Kingdom. Napoleon's fame and celebrity would certainly have outshone the Prince Regent – which would not be cricket! Had Napoleon been given asylum in England, history would be very different indeed.

Napoleon expressed a desire to travel to Elba via a British navy vessel. This was for safety. Firstly because of barbary pirates from northern Africa – prone to raiding the island waters. Secondly, he suspected that if he went on a French ship, any royalist officers or sailors on board might be tempted to assassinate him. The British agreed with this line of thought. Alternative arrangements were made and Napoleon's convoy of carriages and cavalry escort travelled south to the sea. At Fréjus, on 28 April 1814, Napoleon boarded HMS *Undaunted,* a fifth-rate 38-gun sailing frigate. and met with the commander Rear-Admiral Sir Thomas Ussher, KCH, CB (then only a captain). It must have been a strange experience for the emperor to come face to face with a foe that had decimated any naval ambitions France might have had at Trafalgar, just nine years earlier. It must have been a slight insult that the Royal Navy sent a mere captain and not an admiral to meet with Britain's greatest foe; nevertheless, Napoleon got his own back. Despite the insult, Napoleon insisted on a full 21-gun salute as they left port – a privilege only afforded to sovereigns. Though he was no longer the ruler of France, he was the Sovereign of Elba, and still an emperor to boot. He insisted and got his way, despite the Royal Navy's tradition of not firing salutes after nightfall. The Royal Navy, Nelson's navy, gave Napoleon a 21-gun salute as it ferried him to his new home.

After just a month, news reached Napoleon that Joséphine, his first wife, the former empress and Duchess of Navarre, had died. To add insult to the tragedy, she had reportedly caught a chill and died of pneumonia after a stroll with Tsar Alexander I of Russia in her own gardens at Malmaison – the man who had arguably broken Napoleon's confidence and chased him from Moscow to the gates of Paris. Napoleon learnt of her passing through French newspapers and was inconsolable; he retreated to his rooms for several days. This must have cast a shadow over the rest of Napoleon's exile. One of the ways he entertained himself was to agree to give interviews to prominent individuals who were 'passing through' Elba. Many of these gentlemen were British. These included several peers and MPs, including Lord John Russell (who would become prime minister from 1846 and see Napoleon's nephew reign France as Napoleon III). Of course, any British interviewer was keen to know Napoleon's opinion of the British and the Duke of Wellington – who had been a constant thorn in his side. The emperor did much to praise the bravery of British soldiers and the ability of Arthur Wellesley, and was at pains to make clear he had resigned from the pages of history and had no further plans. He may have still been hoping for a move to England. That said, he was keen for news, and perhaps once too often asked for news of developments on the continent, particularly in France. While other European powers at the Congress of Vienna (Austria, Russia, Prussia, Spain et al.) concentrated on restoring the old monarchies and territories, the British had growing suspicions about Napoleon's curiosity.

Elba was now Napoleon's mini kingdom. Most would have been delighted with its climate, its hardy people and its tranquillity – especially after years of difficult military campaigning – but Napoleon felt it rather restrictive. After all, he was used to ruling most of Europe, several countries, whole armies and being master of his own destiny. Here he could do none of those things. There was also the issue of money. Though he had brought a vast treasury with him and been promised a generous allowance from the new Bourbon administration, it was clear only one of these would be reliable. The Bourbons were reluctant to pay for the upkeep of their enemy's court. Napoleon's funds might well run dry in a few years. This fact, held over Napoleon like the sword of Damocles, was coupled with rumours of worse to come. The British, concerned about Napoleon's curiosity and the close distance between Elba and the mainland, were considering moving him to Botany Bay in Australia or to St Helena in the South Atlantic.

Napoleon was used to being a man of action. In his glorious campaigns of earlier years, he had always seized the initiative. Strike first. Strike before you yourself are struck. Not wanting to wait for his circumstances to get worse, and, taking advantage of the reinstated Bourbon regime's unpopularity in France, Napoleon made his move. Arguably, the allure of a second rise to power against all the odds was too tempting for him. He may have felt that destiny was giving him a second chance, or that he would rather go down fighting than be king of a pebble in the Mediterranean for life. It is also thought that his health may have already been ailing at this point. He had long suffered from haemorrhoids and by early 1815 may have also been suffering from retention of urine. These would undoubtedly affect his progress in the coming campaign.

Using the brig at his disposal, *Inconstant*, and collecting his small force of roughly one thousand men, Napoleon was able to slip past the British patrol ships and arrive at the French coast. Famously, he gathered support as he went along, eventually entering Paris 20 March 1815 – Louis XVIII and the Bourbons leaving the city shortly beforehand. The great powers of Europe had been distracted. While they sat at the Congress of Vienna carving up his empire and redrawing the map of Europe, Napoleon effectively took them by surprise and returned to the head of the French government.

This marked the beginning of the One Hundred Days of Napoleon's return which ended with the disastrous Waterloo campaign which will not we will not concern ourselves with too closely. For the uninitiated, however ...

In March 1815, the Bourbon regime sent men to meet Napoleon's force on the road with the objective of arresting or killing the former emperor. Michael Ney, formerly one of Napoleon's marshals, commanded the royalist forces and had suggested that the emperor be brought back in an iron cage. When he came face to face with his old master, however, Ney quickly changed sides and Napoleon's followers grew. With news of Napoleon's imminent return to power in Paris, the great powers of Europe: Britain, Prussia, Russia and Austria, declared him an outlaw and enemy of peace, each nation pledging 150,000 men towards the coming conflict. Britain was unable to commit to this large number, not having a large standing army, and with most of its forces spread throughout the globe. (Many military units were still in Canada having not long ago completed the war of 1812 – when British burned the White House down.) Britain instead sponsored other smaller European states to provide extra forces which would contribute to the massed British forces.

Napoleon, seizing the initiative, as was his way, attempted to carve a wedge between the Prussian and British armies in modern-day Belgium. Numerically, he could not defeat them simultaneously but he hoped to keep the two separate so he could defeat them one at a time. On 16 June, the French, under Marshal Ney, engaged the Allied Forces under the Duke of Wellington at Quatre Bras, which led to the British making a tactical withdrawal. Meanwhile, a few miles away, Napoleon defeated a large part of the Prussian army under von Blücher; however, the majority of the Prussian army retreated and survived. Two days later, Napoleon went toe to toe with Wellington, hoping to finish off the British and their allies at the infamous Battle of Waterloo. Not for nothing does the phrase 'met his Waterloo' exist. Everything began to unravel for him. The weather had made the field of battle too muddy for effective artillery; battle orders were confused or misinterpreted by commanders; bad decisions were made, such as dividing his forces; and, halfway through the battle, Napoleon was so unwell that he missed several key moments, leaving the decisions to lesser men. The British had not been as easy to crush as he had optimistically hoped. It had taken too long, and when the Prussian army finally arrived to join battle, the French forces began to falter. Hoping to deal a surprise knockout blow to Wellington's centre position, Napoleon sent in the Old Guard. This imperial infantry guard was made up of some of the finest soldiers in the French army, an elite infantry that hitherto was undefeated in all of Napoleon's campaigns. They had gained a legendary significance in the French armed forces. However, when they were pushed back by impressive volley fire from the British front lines, who had been lying down until the last moment, the guard began to falter and subsequently retreat. The sight of the guard retreating (followed by a British bayonet charge) demoralised the French forces and prompted panic. The battle was lost. In Napoleon's hurry to flee the battlefield to escape capture he left behind his carriage. It contained his personal copy of Machiavelli's *The Prince* as well as several diamonds which found their way into the crown jewels of Prussia.

After the failure and defeat at Waterloo became known, the French people's support for the empire melted away almost as quickly as it had fired up. (A similar phenomenon would befall his eventual successor Napoleon III after the Battle of Sedan in 1870.) Napoleon had hoped to rally more support from the capital and believed, perhaps naively, that he could yet turn things around, even writing 'all is not lost'. But the trickle of disarmed soldiers retreating/streaming back into the capital told Parisians all they needed to know of the Waterloo campaign. In his career, Napoleon had often manipulated the truth about his wars in order to retain popular support from the people, but ultimately this was not a defeat he could live down.

Napoleon abdicated in favour of his son (Napoleon II) on 22 June 1815 – just four days after Waterloo. He had been in this position before. So one would think Napoleon knew the drill. Abdication. Enforced exile. It was, however, his intention to become a private citizen in the United States of America. Far enough away from Europe to be safe, and European enough to be palatable. But it was not to be. Ultimately the British put an end to that idea, but it was also due to the fact that Napoleon, uncharacteristically, dallied with his next moves. He hesitated.

Napoleon retired to the palace of Malmaison outside Paris, the house of his late first wife Joséphine, on 25 June. Hostilities between the French military and the allies were not strictly over and in the following days Prussian forces were within a mile of Malmaison, hoping to capture him. Having been alerted to the danger, Napoleon left the palace for the coast at Rochefort where the provisional government had put two small frigates, *Meduse* and *Saale,* at his disposal for his voyage to America. They had sought safe a safe conduct passport for Napoleon from the allies, but the Prussians ignored it and the British mused about it. While at Rochefort, Napoleon dithered for days and worried how these two ships could slip past the large British ship blockading the port, HMS *Bellerophon*, a 74-gun Arrogant-class ship of the line.

By now it was the 5 July. Napoleon's elder brother, Joseph, arrived and, seeing as the two looked fairly alike, offered to swap identities so that Napoleon might get safe passage to America. Napoleon proudly refused and continued to dither. (It was to be Joseph who would manage to make a successful life for himself in the US.) This time wasting was costly. A few days later, the Bourbon monarchy was restored once more and the two frigates were no longer under Napoleon's control – they belonged to the Bourbon government. Save for daring schemes of escape unbecoming for an emperor, the possibility of evading capture became extremely doubtful.

Napoleon was lodging on board the *Saale* which was anchored only a short distance from HMS *Bellerophon*. Perhaps weary of running, perhaps in genuine fear of being captured by the Austrians (his backstabbing Habsburg in-laws) or worse, the royalists or the Prussians (who might well have killed him), the emperor reconsidered his options and decided it would be far safer and more sensible to surrender voluntarily to the British – not that he had much choice. He had been well treated by them when they had couriered him to Elba a year earlier, and he would need their protection from French royalists and other European enemies. He sent messengers over to the *Bellerophon* to negotiate his capitulation with her captain, Frederick Lewis Maitland.

Maitland was from a military and noble family. His grandfather was the 6th Earl of Lauderdale and his father, also Frederick, was named after his godfather, Frederick, Prince of Wales. The Maitlands included several senior military officers such as General Sir Thomas Maitland, GCB, GCH who had served in the Peninsular War against Napoleon. The young captain of the *Bellerophon* was only 38 when his blockade duty was interrupted by messengers from Napoleon. Though young in years he had seen action at the naval battles of Alexandria and the Fourth Battle of Ushant (among others) and was not unaware of how important his position now was regarding the ending of the Napoleonic Wars.

There followed days of negotiations between the two vessels. Maitland was obviously keen that Napoleon should surrender to him, for it would be a huge achievement in his career. In his keenness he may have unknowingly fibbed. Maitland assured Napoleon that English weather was not as bad as he had probably heard, and that Napoleon would be well treated in England. This was probably interpreted by Napoleon and his small group of loyal followers as an offer of asylum in England. They jumped to that conclusion. Despite there being chances of escaping to another port in France, Napoleon preferred to end his career with dignity rather than risk arrest or the perils of the sea. He earnestly hoped for a quiet exile in England, rather like the one his younger brother Lucien had experienced years before in Worcestershire (See Chapter 7). Napoleon signalled his intent to surrender to Maitland and *Bellerophon* was prepared for its imperial 'guest'.

Napoleon probably did not know, but surely found out later, that the *Bellerophon* had played an impressive part in harassing his career over the years. Known as 'Billy Ruffian' by many of its crew (out of affection or maybe quaint ignorance) and launched in 1786, the ageing ship had seen service throughout the French Revolutionary and Napoleonic Wars. Most notably it had been among Lord Nelson's fleet at the Battle of the Nile in 1798 where Napoleon's fleet was dealt a deadly blow, effectively trapping him in Egypt. *Bellerophon* successfully took out the French flagship, *Orient*. In 1805, *Bellerophon* was the fifth ship in Admiral Collingwood's column as it took on the combined Spanish and French fleets at the Battle of Trafalgar. On board was midshipman and future arctic explorer, Sir John Franklin, KCH, who, from the deck of *Bellerophon,* recorded Nelson's famous message, 'England expects that every man will do his duty'. Though badly damaged during the battle, *Bellerophon* was given the honour of escorting HMS *Victory* and Nelson's body back to England. After further service in the Baltic, Caribbean and Atlantic, the rather tired ship was put on blockade duty along the French Atlantic ports – including Rochefort.

Napoleon boarded *Bellerophon* on the morning of 15 July 1815, less than a month after Waterloo. Anxious that his superior officer, Rear-Admiral Hotham (Vice-Admiral The Honourable Sir Henry Hotham KCB GCMG, son of Lord Hotham) should not turn up in his ship, HMS *Superb*, and steal the glory by 'encountering' Napoleon before him, Maitland sent out his barge to meet Napoleon halfway – not the glamorous symbolic affair one might have imagined! At roughly 8 a.m., when Napoleon came aboard *Bellerophon* – a ship that had defeated his navies at both the Nile and Trafalgar – his defeat must have felt complete. The Marines stood to attention but did not salute. Such a thing was not done that early in the morning. Taking off his hat, Napoleon surrendered to Captain Maitland throwing himself on the protection of him and the Prince Regent (whom Napoleon had described as his most constant and generous of enemies).

This truly was the end of the war. Following that special moment on a wooden ship in Quiberon Bay, Britain and France were not to fight each other in war again. It marked an end to centuries of battles between the neighbours in all parts of the world; what Winston Churchill identified as the *real* First World War. It did not, however, mark an end to their rivalry. Both still commanded large colonial empires, but the Napoleonic Wars had a clear victor, Great Britain. As a direct consequence, the British Empire can be recognised as the first world superpower. However, the nation of shopkeepers, whose only lust was for trade, knew that France, as a fellow colonial partner was a necessary partner; justifying their colonialism as well as colonial trade monopolies. The partnership became a reality when the two countries took on the Crimean War against Russia as allies, and Queen Victoria was invited to a state visit to France by Napoleon's successor and nephew, Napoleon III, in

1855. (The first time a British monarch had been to Paris in an official capacity since Henry VI.) This new relationship led to the world's first international trade treaty a few years later, the Cobden-Chevalier Treaty, and in turn ultimately led to the forming of the *entente cordiale*. So in fact, Napoleon and the Bonapartes unknowingly caused the triumphant rise of the British Empire throughout the nineteenth century, as well as causing it to partner with France and stand together through the Crimea, the First and Second World wars and beyond. Over 200 years of peace between the old adversaries. It was all made possible because of what happened on *Bellerophon* in 1815 – arguably!

As was customary for such a distinguished guest, Maitland afforded Napoleon the captain's great cabin. That evening, the officers of the *Bellerophon* and the *Superb*, including Admiral Hotham, dined with Napoleon in the great cabin. Napoleon also visited the *Superb* at Hotham's invitation, doubtlessly because Hotham was trying to steal some of the prestige for himself. The two ships set sail for England with the emperor comfortably accommodated in Maitland's cabin on *Bellerophon*. In his memoirs, Maitland records how strange it was. He liked Napoleon, as did many others. Napoleon had very likeable qualities. He joked and teased the young midshipman and, Maitland records, that he did not show the signs of defeatism or depression you might expect from one who had reached the heights that he had reached in his life and career. He was still active, taking daily exercise on deck and conversing with the officers. Nevertheless, Maitland felt pity for the former emperor. In terrible English, Napoleon confessed that he believed if it had not been for the English, he would still be an emperor. His high spirits and polite manners may have been genuine but we must not forget that here was a man hoping to be granted formal asylum in England and therefore needed to show his personal qualities to his hosts and that he was no longer a threat.

On 23 July, the ship passed the last piece of France, Ushant, an island at the south-west entrance to the English Channel. Napoleon stood on deck and took one last look at France; stoic and silent, he would never see France again. Within a day they were in sight of England and made for Torbay. The bay gives its name to the modern-day Borough of Torbay (1968) which includes the fishing towns of Brixham, Paignton and Torquay. Maitland dropped anchor in the bay awaiting instructions from the admiralty. *Bellerophon* was just off Brixham. It did not take long for word to spread in the town and the surrounding countryside that Britain's greatest adversary had been captured and was in a British ship in a Devon harbour. Locals took to their own small boats and rowed out to get a glimpse of 'the ogre'. Maitland had received orders that not a single person was to come aboard for any reason whatsoever. A sensible measure; the *Bellerophon's* crew had a hard job pushing away curious 'tourists'. Whether or not you agreed with his politics or actions, he was still a man who had achieved absolute greatness and had dominated his era; to the British people, this gave him mystique and a magnetic power. Ultimately, most were just curious to see him. Napoleon graciously waved to the seemingly affectionate crowds, doffing his famous hat to the ladies. He is rumoured to have remarked that the town reminded him of Portoferraio on Elba; I think the residents of Brixham today would have a hard time understanding that! Other rumours (or local legends) have it that, during the mere day or two the ship was in the bay, Napoleon, having certain needs, got permission to go ashore at night to Torquay to find an inn where he might find a woman to fulfil those needs, and that a child (or even children) was born of this 'meeting'. Of course, it cannot be true. It may have been a tale of fancy by a local Torquay tavern keeper, or possibly been started many years later in an effort to help the town's growing tourist industry. One wonders if father and son, Napoleon III and the Prince Imperial were familiar with the Torquay story when they visited in 1871.

The Cabinet Office in London debated Napoleon's future. The admiralty did not want Napoleon to wait around in Torbay long, mostly for reasons of security. No one wanted over-passionate crowds to overpower *Bellerophon* nor a Bonapartist rescue to take place. There was also the unfortunate historical significance of Torbay. In the Glorious Revolution of 1688, William of Orange (later King William III) landed at Brixham, and went on to successfully depose King James II. Had Napoleon been allowed to disembark at Brixham, it would have been a stain on the area's history (not that it had any particular influence on the government's decision). Orders found their way to Maitland telling him to head west and make for Plymouth. A far more secure location with a huge naval presence supported by multiple fortifications.

Plymouth must have been a hopeful destination for Napoleon. Five years earlier, his younger brother, Lucien Bonaparte, had also been taken to Plymouth after being captured by the Royal Navy while aboard a ship, hoping to emigrate to the US. He too had originally been incarcerated on a Mediterranean island but was moved to England for security. Lucien and his family were kept at the port of Plymouth for several days before going into their comfortable exile in Shropshire and later Worcestershire. They lived like landed gentry. No doubt Napoleon hoped that Plymouth was a sign that similar treatment was to be afforded to him. Like his brother, he hoped to be an English country gentleman. However, as the chief architect of so much death and inconvenience to the British Empire, as well as having a magnetic power and presence over people, it is difficult to imagine the British government considering this. The prime minister, Lord Liverpool, was certainly against it.

When *Bellerophon* arrived at Plymouth on 27 July, the interest in him and curiosity of the British public became obvious. It is reported that at least 1,000 vessels went out into Plymouth Sound just to catch a glimpse of him. With an average of eight people to a boat, roughly 10,000 took to the water, some reportedly travelling from as far as Scotland for the opportunity. This phenomenon continued for five days. From Mount Edgcumbe in the west, to Mount Batten in the east, all Plymouth Sound was alive with activity. Napoleon, in a polite manner, waved or doffed his famous hat to swooning ladies – so much so that Maitland noted that he often had to take long naps on the sofa in his cabin. Again, no one was allowed on board, so one can imagine the tedium and frustration of the emperor – surrounded by Devon and Cornish countryside, and not able to set foot on it. Sir Charles Lock Eastlake (a famous artist who would one day go on to be president of the Royal Academy), was himself a 'Plymothian'. Like many locals, he paid a man to row him out to the *Bellerophon* so that he might have the opportunity of sketching the great man. His completed painting survives in the National Maritime museum. Napoleon was reportedly impressed by the fortifications, dockyard and harbour, and must have been hoping to be put up at the same tavern his brother Lucien had stayed at on his first night in England, but Plymouth Sound was the closest Napoleon would get to Britain's shores.

Having been waiting for days in the Sound, Captain Maitland and his special guest received a visit on board from Admiral Viscount Keith, GCB, who was commander-in-chief of the English Channel, and Sir Henry Bunbury Bt, KCB, Under Secretary of State for War and the Colonies. Together the two men informed Napoleon of his fate; that he was not to enter Britain but instead be taken into permanent exile on the island of St Helena in the South Atlantic. To make matters worse, he was to be given no personal guard (as at Elba), but was only permitted three officers and a dozen domestic staff. Napoleon was understandably deflated and furious. He had given himself up to the English in good faith, assuming that he would be treated as a guest, but the reality was he was too dangerous to be treated as such and, if held in England, far too close to Europe (or even America) – an escape risk. There was no longer any ambiguity. He was a glorified prisoner of the British. The emperor and his officers who had accompanied him on the *Bellerophon* raged, believing to be sent out to the Atlantic to die was very dishonourable – they considered going down fighting right there in Plymouth. Fortunately, they were dissuaded.

Lord Keith (Admiral George Keith Elphinstone, 1st Viscount Keith, GCB 1746–1823), was an ageing, seasoned commander, who, like Maitland was a member of the Scottish aristocracy – the fifth son of the 10th Lord Elphinstone. He had served the Royal Navy with distinction since 1761. A hardened navy man, Keith did not mince his words. He was a straight-talking officer. He did not appreciate the airs and graces Napoleon and his lackeys had. Admiral Keith addressed Napoleon as General Bonaparte: not Imperial Majesty nor emperor. He stated the intentions of the British government regarding the general and St Helena to the letter, and, having done so, brushed aside any wild Gallic emotions or objections retorting that he was merely following orders. (This did not lessen the blow to Napoleon and his small band of retainers. In fact, that evening, one of the wives of one of Napoleon's staff even tried to drown herself in Plymouth Sound – so upset from the news was she.)

Yet, of all the great men on deck that day, Admiral Lord Keith (the bringer of bad news), had the strongest connection to the Bonapartes. Just two years after the meeting in Plymouth Sound, his daughter Margaret, married Napoleon's former aide-de-camp, General Auguste-Charles-Joseph de Flahaut, Comte de Flahaut (1785–1870). Not only was Keith's new son-in-law a Bonapartist but he was also known to be the illegitimate son of Napoleon's famous former foreign minister, Talleyrand – whom the emperor described as 'sh*t in a silk stocking'. The Comte de Flahaut went on to have a successful political career, becoming French ambassador to Britain under Napoleon's eventual successor, Napoleon III. However, he had a disreputable past. He had been the known as the lover of Hortense de Beauharnais, Queen of Holland, Napoleon's stepdaughter, and wife of Napoleon's brother Louis. They had at least one illegitimate son together in 1811. Some have questioned if he might be the real father of Emperor Napoleon III. Flahaut and Margaret Keith, eventually inheriting one of her father's titles as Baroness Keith, had several children including Emily Jane, Marchioness of Lansdowne (born 1819). Emily's son, the 5th Marquess of Lansdowne, became Viceroy of India in 1888. It is strange to think that the grandfather of a British viceroy stood side by side with Napoleon as his ADC at the Battle of Waterloo. We none of us choose our family!

Napoleon sent letters of protestation to anyone he could, including the Prince Regent. These were, of course, ignored. In early August, Napoleon was transferred from *Bellerophon* on to another ship, HMS *Northumberland*. He had spent more than three weeks on the *Bellerophon*. The admiralty believed it unwise to risk the old battleship in the South Atlantic all the way to St Helena, hence the younger *Northumberland* was used. Like her special guest, *Bellerophon* had a diminished end. She was refitted as a prison hulk and served as a prison for boys for several years. Her name was given to another battleship and she was aptly renamed *Captivity*, either in reference to her new job, or to her most famous cargo. She was sold as scrap in Plymouth in 1836 and her timber and parts were auctioned off. Captain Maitland bought her figurehead. It found its way into the Royal Navy Museum. A pitiful end for a ship that had seen such historic events and played its own special part; that said, she outlived her most prestigious captive, Napoleon.

On hearing the news of his imminent transportation and incarceration, Napoleon is said to have declared to Lord Keith that he would rather die on the *Bellerophon* than go to St Helena. Perhaps Keith did not mind either way. Despite a letter of protestation to the Prince Regent, the emperor and his selected entourage of twenty-six were transferred to HMS *Northumberland* on 7 August 1815. Napoleon's own surgeon refused to make the journey, and thus it was that Barry O'Meara, the *Bellerophon's* surgeon, who volunteered to accompany the emperor. The ship sailed away for the South Atlantic, much to the disappointment of the Napoleonic tourists – not to mention Napoleon himself. One can only imagine his thoughts as England passed out of sight.

Napoleon suffered more insult at the choice of ship. The *Northumberland* was another veteran ship that had also been instrumental in the Napoleonic Wars. She was a flagship at the Battle of San Domingo (1806) – a decisive British naval victory and the last fleet engagement of the war between France and Britain. All of the major French Ships of the Line were captured or destroyed – the British suffered minimal losses. Those figures must have been bitter pills to swallow for Napoleon on his seasick-plagued journey south aboard such a vessel. His new captor, and commander of the ship, was Admiral Sir George Cockburn Bt, GCB. Cockburn was a seasoned officer having served as a captain at the Battle of Cape St Vincent (1797) along with Nelson, but he was more famous for his role in the war of 1812 with America. It was under his command that British forces invaded the US capital and set Washington ablaze, including the White House. (The only time a foreign power has occupied part of the US.) Cockburn was clearly a deliverer of Britain's revenge (in this case, on the Americans for their raids into Canada, but also to remind them that, though the US had recently acquired independence, the British still dominated the world stage and could do as it pleased). Perhaps Cockburn, now in command of the *Northumberland*, was to once more to exact Britain's revenge, this time on Napoleon, for the years of war and turmoil he had caused.

After a journey of months of card games, English lessons, dinners, putting on weight, and an offering of coin to the gods of the sea (as he crossed the Equator), Napoleon, his captors and entourage, came within sight of their destination in October that year. A small British island, over 1,000 miles from Africa and over 2,000 from South America. A windswept, volcanic landscape lashed by the sea and rain – a promethean prison indeed. The nearest island was British-held Ascension Island. Though hundreds of miles away, it was garrisoned with troops to remove any hope of Napoleon making a break for it, or being rescued, both of which must have seemed depressingly impossible to Napoleon and his companions.

Though by now British, St Helena was 'discovered' by Portuguese traders and explorers in the sixteenth century. Accounts vary of exactly when and who was responsible, but it was named after St Helena of Constantinople. They did not form a settlement there, but the island became a useful stopping point on voyages between Europe and Asia – which would go around the Cape of Good Hope. Sir Francis Drake located the island on his circumnavigation of the globe, after which English sailors used it as a good location to ambush Portuguese trade ships. Dutch merchants also used the island and claimed it as their own in 1633 but did not colonise it, instead preferring to use their other colony at the Cape of Good Hope in South Africa. Within a few years, Oliver Cromwell and later King James II, granted royal charters to the East India Company giving them permission to fortify the island. The government sent Britons to settle the island as farmers. The capital was naturally called Jamestown. The East India Company continued to govern the island through the following centuries as an important station on the trade routes to India and the Far East (pre-Suez Canal). Captain James Cook even stopped off there on his way back from 'discovering' Australia. Coincidently, the Duke of Wellington, the man who made Napoleon meet his Waterloo, had visited the island in 1805 while returning from India. The British government came to an arrangement with the East India Company, where the company would still govern the island but Crown troops would occupy and patrol the territory with a garrison, signal posts, and two war ships circling the island.

It is said that news took so long to reach St Helena that, by the time a letter had made it to the island officials, they were told not only of Napoleon's escape from Elba, his Hundred Days Campaign, Waterloo and capture, but that the dreaded emperor was being sent to them as a 'guest'. St Helena's people must have shuddered. No sooner had they fully learnt of this troublesome news, did their troublesome guest arrive.

Northumberland made port at Jamestown, and Napoleon disembarked amid the tropical weather, making his way through the British town sandwiched between soaring cliffs on either side. A slightly different setting to the one he had doubtless hoped for back at Plymouth. He was not to be housed in the town – the British were not comfortable with that, and, besides, there was only really one building large enough to accommodate him and his entourage: Longwood House.

Longwood, an old, long, barn-like structure, had previously been the summer residence of St Helena's lieutenant governor. Though perhaps the second grandest residence on the island at the time (the first being the governor's house), it was not used nor designed for permanent occupancy. The weather there was terrible. While Jamestown was by the sea and enjoyed warm, tropical, Caribbean-like weather, Longwood had an entirely different microclimate. High on an outcrop about 1,500 feet above the sea, the house was covered and surrounded by cloud for nearly the whole year. With humidity sometimes 100 per cent, it meant that everything from timbers to furniture and wallpaper was almost constantly damp. To make matters worse it was infested with rats, termites and cockroaches. However, as Napoleon's arrival had not been long behind the warning messages, Longwood was not yet ready for habitation, so for his first few months Napoleon was a guest of the Balcombe family at their home, The Briars, just outside of Jamestown, until Longwood was refurbished and fit for permanent residency.

William Balcombe was a Sussex gentleman, originally from Rottingdean, who had become an East India Company colonial administrator. He and his family took in the exiled emperor after it was discovered that he rather conveniently had a one-bedroom pavilion at the end of his garden. Through strange twists of fate, while on his travels, the Duke of Wellington had stayed at The Briars ten years earlier. It was at this bungalow that Napoleon struck up a special friendship – arguably his last – with one of Balcombe's children. Betsy Balcombe was 14 when she met the emperor, and, like all British children, had been taught that Napoleon was a raging ogre with red eyes and ate children for dinner. So she was rather pleasantly surprised when she met 'Boney the Ogre' in the flesh. She had some grasp of French and he, by now, had some grasp of English. They soon formed a very sweet, innocent friendship. Napoleon tested Betsy on her geography, history and French, while Betsy tested Napoleon's English and teased him for not being able to sing, and the two of them played children's games in the garden. She was the subject of jealousy from many of the French and British officers as she had a special connection with him that no one else on the island had. It seems that, now fully free of responsibilities or cares, Napoleon was able to stumble into a second (albeit part-time) childhood, reportedly racing his carriage up and down St Helena's only couple of roads, playing blind man's bluff and other games. The children were even able to get away with calling him Boney too! Captivity among children was a happy time for Napoleon, which made his eventual move up the hill to Longwood all the more difficult. His lifetime of great successes and calamitous blunders had made him wise; he knew that he would die there.

Shortly before Christmas of 1815, Napoleon moved in at Longwood. Though damp, it had been made as comfortable as possible with reception rooms, a billiard room, library, servants' quarters and a private study for Napoleon to compile his memoirs. He ran the residence as if it was one of his courts: there was a dinner each day where officers were expected to wear full military dress, and ladies expected to wear jewels. Napoleon was able to ride to anywhere on the island (with British escort), and allowed to help create the gardens surrounding Longwood – though the wind blew nearly everything over. The exiled emperor gave dinner parties and was even invited to balls by British neighbours. Betsy continued to visit the emperor regularly – for tea and doubtless more teasing. For a short time, the arrangements must have seemed similar to the bliss 'captivity' of Elba – only smaller, less scenic and with even worse weather – but still reasonably pleasant and bearable to a point.

Napoleon's time as a resident of British soil is understood to have taken a sour turn upon the arrival of St Helena's new governor, Hudson Lowe, in April 1816. Major General Sir Hudson Lowe, originally from Galway, had seen service in Napoleon's old home in Corsica, while it was a British protectorate, and had even lodged in the Bonapartes' former house. He had been attached to the allied armies during the subsequent Napoleonic Wars and it was he who had been sent to formally bring news to London of Napoleon's total defeat and first abdication in 1814. That said, he was described by Wellington as under-educated and by others as outwardly unfeeling and regulations-obsessed. Wellington and others lamented that he was a very poor choice as Napoleon's jailer. His personality as well as his previous military exploits on Corsica were bound to cause tension.

From the start, it was obvious that Lowe was tactless. According to Lord Bathurst's instructions for Napoleon's incarceration, the emperor was only to be referred to as General Bonaparte; the titles of Emperor, Imperial Majesty, Sire and others, were not to be recognised lest the British indirectly offend the newly restored Bourbon monarchy. Many on the island were aware of such rules; however, as a small island community far from anywhere else, many thought it did no harm to humour the ex-emperor and his mini court. (He at least had earned his grand titles to a degree.) Hudson Lowe insisted on 'General Bonaparte' which caused offence. In his career liaising with Britain's military allies, he also personally knew and admired Tsar Alexander and Gebhard Leberecht von Blücher, both of whom had at one time humiliated or betrayed Napoleon. Lowe may also have been bitter since, owing to other orders, he missed taking part in the Battle of Waterloo. Though he had seen great things and met great men, Lowe had never really held a major command. All this meant that the emperor was faced with a jailer already prone to be embittered and hostile to him. Napoleon is thought to have told him he was more of a clerk than a general.

For the rest of Napoleon's life on the island, a battle of personalities raged between the two in a strange echo of wars between France and England over the last century. Napoleon refused to receive Lowe (they actually only met fewer than a dozen times); Lowe seems to have found ways to make Napoleon's life difficult, such as reducing his firewood allowance, stopping him from receiving any new books, stopping him from giving or receiving certain gifts (including vegetables from his garden), and attempted to reduce the living allowance afforded to the miniature court. On the other hand, Napoleon famously removed all the chairs when he did receive Lowe for meetings, forcing him to stand as though Napoleon was his senior.

Slight respite came in the form of the many interviews he gave to visitors to the islands from all over the world, curious about the former master of Europe. One particularly enjoyable occasion was when Admiral Cockburn was relieved of military command by his replacement, Admiral Sir Pulteney Malcolm. His wife Clementina Elphinstone was the niece of Lord Keith and therefore a cousin-in-law of Napoleon's old ADC, Flahaut. The emperor and the Malcolms reportedly got on very well at dinner; they updated him on London and European gossip. Other than small events such as these, life on the island was dull and repetitive. His daily routine involved walking, long baths, and sometimes rat catching. Highlights were visits from Betsy.

Less than a year at Longwood had passed before Napoleon started to show signs of poor health. Both he and his staff at various times had suffered from bronchitis owing to the dampness of Longwood, and Napoleon's habit of not eating vegetables did not help. The damp was so bad that playing cards needed to be warmed in an oven to dry them out and prevent them from sticking together. Owing to the battle with Lowe, he exercised less and less, preferring not be watched by Lowe's men, to keep them guessing at possible escape plans, but this only meant more hours spent in the damp air at Longwood. Various unpleasant and sometimes painful symptoms lead Napoleon's British doctor, O'Meara, to diagnose possible hepatitis. O'Meara, owing to Napoleon's declining health, had to remove one of Napoleon's teeth. It is surprising to think that despite all the wars and major battles the emperor had fought in from Europe to Africa and Asia and back, this is the first and only known operation of his life. Lowe was unsympathetic to General Bonaparte's condition or health.

By 1818, the European press had heard of Napoleon's friendship with Betsy and made unpleasant insinuations. Lowe disliked the Balcombe family and suspected that they were smuggling messages for Napoleon; he attempted to limit Betsy's visits and reprimanded her for her closeness to the emperor. However, by March, Lowe got what he had been hoping for: the Balcombes, together with Betsy, left for England. This may have been to mend her reputation. Nevertheless, it meant that Napoleon would never see her again, which was depressing for him. Betsy married three years later and published her tales from St Helena in *Recollections of Emperor Napoleon* in 1844. The same year, O'Meara was also sent away. He had fallen out with Lowe over his treatment of the emperor. He had warned London that harsh treatment was causing Napoleon ill health He published his version of events on St Helena shortly after Napoleon's death.

Napoleon entered a state of depression, having lost friends and knowing he would never see his son or family again. He believed that the British government was trying to hasten his death, and that Lowe was the designated executioner. It cost the British millions to keep the emperor at St Helena, and doubtless there must have been concern that he might live for several more decades. However, it is unlikely that such a thing was planned by the government, although Lowe may have wished for it, hoping to return to 'civilisation' sooner rather than later. Though unkind to Bonaparte, Lowe was principled at least: he freed all the slaves on the island, long before British anti-slavery legislation came into effect.

As the world moved on, the life of the emperor stood still. He became more reclusive and less active, despite a see-saw being placed in the billiard room. Eventually, he barely left the house. Napoleon finally died on 5 May 1821 aged just 55, a French-Corsican on British island thousands of miles from a continent he had once ruled. The autopsy, conducted in the billiard room at Longwood, concluded that he had died of stomach cancer (the same disease that had reportedly killed his father), as well as a stomach ulcer. Instantly, there was outrage in many parts of the world that he should have died so young and in such conditions. Rumours of the British poisoning Napoleon with arsenic started and some continue to this day. In 2007, a study into Napoleon's hair found high levels of arsenic in it. However, arsenic was a commonplace substance in the nineteenth century, and at Longwood it was even in the wall plaster. Furthermore, there copious amounts of rat poison were used at the house. In a similar scientific study, King George III's hair was found to have more arsenic in it than Napoleon's body, which would indicate that we should not read too much into the presence of arsenic. Though the conditions at Longwood certainly did not help, and nor did the depression, it was Napoleon's stomach that finally brought the eagle down. Napoleon is sometimes credited with the saying 'an army marches on its stomach'; neither of his would march any more.

Even in death, Napoleon could not be rid of Hudson Lowe, nor could the British shed their fear of Napoleon. He expressed a desire that his body be taken back to France, to the banks of the Seine. Sir Hudson Lowe, insisted that he be buried on St Helena at Torbett's Spring. The funeral procession went along a sheep path to the site of burial. Napoleon was buried with military honours, but the coffin was borne by British soldiers of the 66th and 20th regiments. Their colours bore the names of military victories they had won against Napoleon's forces. The irony was lost on no one. Lowe would only permit a gravestone to say Napoleon Bonaparte, rather than any other imperial titles. The French officers, in disgust, preferred there to be no headstone at all rather than suffer the insult.

Allegedly, while conducting the autopsy, Dr Francesco Antommarchi took a rib as a souvenir but also cut off the emperor's penis. The reasons for this are unclear, though one theory is that he may have been bribed by Napoleon's chaplain to do it, as revenge for the emperor calling the chaplain impotent. The object passed through several hands over the following two centuries, and was at one time on display in a New York museum and was reportedly unsuccessfully entered into an auction at Christies. Whether real or not, the item allegedly was freely offered to the French government, who were not interested. An American urologist, John Latimer (who had given medical evidence after the assassination of John F. Kennedy), purchased the 'artefact' in 1977 and is retained by his family. Reportedly, only ten people have seen it and it has never been recorded on camera. Although an amusing tale, it seems unlikely to be true given that there were over a dozen witnesses to Napoleon's autopsy – one would think that all the witnesses would have repeated such a story; however, it is rather fun to think that a piece of 'Boney' (however small) got to America in the end!

Objects or relics associated with Napoleon have spread throughout the world. In Britain there are such items in abundance. Many curious items are in private as well as public hands, such as his campaign chair (currently the office chair of the present Duke of Richmond), and his horse, Marengo (currently on display at the National Army Museum, Chelsea).

It was not until 1840 that Napoleon's remains were moved, with permission of the British, to Paris for a full state funeral on 2 December – the anniversary of both Austerlitz and his coronation. He was buried in the Cathedral of St Louis des Invalides in a magnificent sarcophagus beneath the dome – which is a curious echo of the final resting place of his old enemy, Lord Nelson, at St Paul's Cathedral. Interestingly, when a list of Napoleon's library books at Longwood was compiled, a biography of Nelson was discovered. Soon after Napoleon's death. Longwood House returned to the East India Company and subsequently the Crown when it formally took control of the island. The house was put to agricultural purposes and was effectively a barn for livestock. Years later, Napoleon's eventual successor, Napoleon III, who was good friends with Queen Victoria, managed to persuade Britain to part with the property for £7,100. He wished to protect the legacy of his uncle, and perhaps brush over the shame of his demise. To this day, Longwood (as well as The Briars) is the property of the French government which has restored Longwood and continues to upkeep it as a museum. A little piece of France on a remote, but British, island.

Chapter 3

Napoleon's sons: Prometheus's Progeny

As this book hopes to show, the tale does not end with Napoleon's death, nor is the story of the Bonapartes' relationship with Britain limited to just one man. Napoleon had children. Historians occasionally disagree about how many, but three sons everyone now agrees on: one legitimate, one illegitimate but recognised, and one illegitimate whom Napoleon never recognised but thanks to DNA (and popular belief) we can be sure was his. Respectively these were: the king of Rome also known as Napoleon II (1811–1832), Charles Count Léon (1806–1881), and Alexandre Count Walewski (1810–1868). There may well have been, and probably were, other unrecognised illegitimate offspring of the emperor; there were around a dozen or so confirmed mistresses. One such mistress, Marguerite Georges, a French actress, is said to have also had an affair with the Duke of Wellington – which would make the two gentlemen and old adversaries brothers in arms to a degree. Marguerite went on to have a child by none other than Tsar Alexander I. The other woman who can claim to have known both Napoleon and Wellington is Giuseppina Grassini, an Italian opera singer. Having seen her perform, Napoleon enlisted her as one of his lovers in 1800, and she was later appointed as chief virtuoso to Napoleon's imperial court. After Napoleon's downfall and the Bourbon restoration, she became the lover of Wellington, who had been made British ambassador to France following the war. His house is still the British ambassador's residence to this day.

It is possible that Napoleon fathered a child with one of his officer's wives, Albine de Montholon, while in exile on St Helena. (To be fair to the man, there was little else to do at Longwood!) Albine gave birth to a child on St Helena, imaginatively called Hélène, and she is often assumed to be Napoleon's. By technicality of location of birth, that

Family Tree

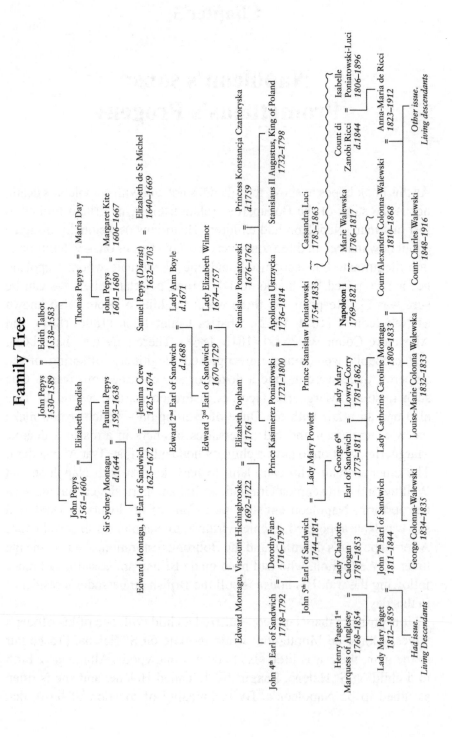

would make one of his children British. However, of the emperor's three (universally recognised) children, it was the elder two who were to go on to have a close connection with their father's old adversary: Britain.

The first of Napoleon's sons was neither legitimate nor an accident, but was the beginning of the end for one of Europe's most famous marriages and romances. Arguably, the birth of Charles Léon was of more historical significance than the birth of his half-brother, Napoleon II.

Soon after becoming emperor, Napoleon began an affair with Eléonore Denuelle de La Plaigne, an old classmate of Napoleon's sister, Caroline, and Napoleon's adopted daughter, Stephanie de Beauharnais. Thanks to her closeness to the family, she was appointed lady-in-waiting to Caroline, who was by now Princess Murat as her husband was Marshal Murat (who would go on to briefly be the ill-fated king of Naples). It was Caroline who put Eléonore and her brother the emperor together. This backstairs' matchmaking may have had two motives: firstly, Eléonore may have already have been sleeping with Murat, and Caroline hoped to separate the two any way she could. Secondly, and much more widely accepted, this was a plot by the Bonaparte family to prove to their stubborn brother that the only reason he and the Empress Joséphine could not sire heirs was because she was too old – not because of anything his end. The problem was Joséphine not Napoleon. The Bonapartes had long hated Joséphine and her hold over their brother. They thought her beneath him, believed she had ensnared him with her immoral charms and did not like how her family also benefited from the match. Crucially, Joséphine was older than Napoleon, had already had two children, several lovers and at least one rumoured abortion. Not a useful match if one is founding a dynasty. Hopes of a divorce had been shattered when Napoleon had crowned Joséphine empress at his coronation – a sight which his mother could not bear and therefore did not attend. The introduction of Eléonore to Napoleon by Caroline, was calculative family politics at its height – probably!

Less than nine months after a divorce from her estranged husband (who had served time in a prison), Eléonore gave birth to a boy on 13 December 1806. Charles – after Napoleon's father; Léon – half of Napoleon. (Napoleon did not want this illegitimate boy to have his name.) Charles was made Count Léon. The emperor finally had a son; not a son who could technically inherit the empire, but proof to Napoleon that he was capable of starting the dynasty he had imagined.

The seed had been planted. Just a few years later, Napoleon divorced Joséphine so as to marry the far younger Marie-Louise of Austria and sire a legitimate heir.

Charles Léon, though acknowledged by his imperial father, grew up estranged from his parents. Napoleon had his campaigns, while Eléonore was rebuilding her life with the allowance Napoleon had granted in gratitude – she had a further two husbands. That said, Napoleon ordered that the name of Charles's father, who was originally recorded as absent, should be rerecorded as General Macon – who had rather conveniently died earlier in October that year. Charles Macon, as he was to initially be known, was brought up close to the household of Caroline and Murat, at arm's length but with the same nannies and staff as his cousins. His mother lost interest in him and his father the emperor kept his distance but, not able to entirely cover his pride at having a son at last, compensated in large allowances and occasionally allowed visits and reportedly bounced him on his knee, delighting in their mutual likeness. Years later, when a small boy, Charles's aunt (and half adopted sister), Hortense, was introduced to him by Napoleon and she noted that he was the living image of the emperor and the king of Rome, but that he also seemed unaware of his true identity.

Though Charles had been a useful tool in the Bonaparte family schemes, he was always on the fringes of the family. He was cared for by old friends of the Murats. Unlike other Bonaparte clan members, he was not included in the list of those to be banished from France after the second Bourbon restoration following Napoleon's ultimate defeat at Waterloo in 1815. From an early age, Charles showed signs of brashness; he absconded from his tutors, travelling instead to a reunion with his scandalous mother whom he had not known as a child – she was perhaps more interested in his allowance than maternal affection. When Napoleon died on St Helena in 1821, his will mentioned that he wanted Charles to enter the legal profession – but Charles, now fully aware and proud of his patrilineage, had grander ideas. He now paraded himself as Count Léon, and sought a military role for himself, perhaps with a view to a great career like that of his father. With not much skill in study, living in Paris as a well-off bachelor, and getting through his money like water, he eventually joined the National Guard.

On the fringes of polite Parisian society, and entangled with some unsavoury types, Léon was often getting into trouble or needless squabbles in the way that all young men who feel hard done by or overlooked do. Léon's first crossing of swords with an Englishman, the enemy of his late father (who in fact was Prussian born), took place in 1832. Léon had yet again lost some money while gambling. Rather bewildered, Charles wrote an IOU for the sum of 16,000 francs. Soon after, he changed his mind and withdrew the IOU, insinuating that there had been foul play. Accusations of watering down the wine and cheating at the table were hurled. Honour had been compromised and inevitably a duel was challenged. Count Léon's opponent was Captain Charles Hesse – a man of reputation.

Hesse was supposedly the son of a Berlin banker or merchant; however, from an early age, rumours persisted that he was in fact the illegitimate offspring of Prince Frederick, Duke of York, the second son of King George III of Great Britain and the Prince Regent's younger brother. Hesse never denied this and he was indeed sponsored by members of the extended Hanoverian family. He swiftly became a lieutenant in 1809 in the 18th Light Dragoons, which must have been easy given that the Duke of York was at that time commander-in-chief. While stationed at Bognor, the handsome and dashing Hesse engaged in an opportunistic liaison with the Prince Regent's only daughter and heiress presumptive to the throne, Princess Charlotte – who was probably his cousin. Bognor by that time had been converted to a fashionable seaside resort by Sir Richard Hotham. Letters were exchanged between the couple by none other than Margaret Elphinstone (who went on to marry Napoleon's ADC, the Comte de Flahaut).

While taking part in the Peninsular Wars, Hesse had been told to return Charlotte's letters and portrait for she was entering the royal European marriage market, and their continued liaison would be scandalous. Distraught, he initially refused; however, Admiral Lord Keith was instructed to take the letters off him. Hesse then attended on Caroline Princess of Wales as equerry on her tour of the continent; however, when war broke out again in 1815, he was able to be present with his regiment at the Battle of Waterloo where he sustained some war wounds. Consequently, Hesse's résumé included royal parentage, royal dalliances, royal appointments, and a string of military engagements from Vitoria to Waterloo – a daunting prospect for any duelling opponent, one would assume.

So it was, that in 1832 the two men met in the Bois de Vincennes in the east of Paris. One the son of Napoleon; the other, the (probable) grandson of George III and nephew of the Prince Regent. Perhaps Léon romantically felt that he was somehow avenging his father's downfall at the hands of the meddlesome British. He was, in fact, accompanied by some of Napoleon's loyal retainers from St Helena days. Pistols were the agreed weapon. Backs to one another, the two took ten paces each. Upon the command they turned to face each other and prepared to fire. Hesse chose to fire immediately and missed; Léon, as was his right, walked forward five paces, fired, and hit Hesse square in the chest. Hesse died soon after from the wound, aged roughly 40. The brash 26-year-old Léon walked from the field. He was accused of manslaughter but quickly acquitted. He never paid the debt. Perhaps he had derived satisfaction from dispatching a British officer who had so proudly worn the Waterloo medal.

Léon continued in his less than successful career in the National Guard but ended up embarking on a European trip to various relatives – mostly for the purpose of asking for money. These included Napoleon's mother (his grandmother) in Rome as well as Cardinal Fesch. Next on his list was his uncle Joseph who had made his new home in England. It was a short visit. Joseph Bonaparte, former king of Spain and the Indies, Napoleon's elder brother and *de facto* head of the family, was renting Denham Place in Buckinghamshire – a house once visited by Captain Cook. When Léon arrived, Joseph was also entertaining his brother Lucien Bonaparte, Prince of Canino. It is curious to think of Napoleon's son and brothers relaxing together in the Buckinghamshire countryside. Lucien had met Léon previously in Italy and was able to warn Joseph against him. Joseph was impressed by the young man and his likeness to the emperor, and sympathised about his plight about still being owed some money from the will of Napoleon, but ultimately, he did not furnish Léon with any great fortunes. On the same trip, while in London, Léon met Napoleon's former physician, Dr O'Meara. The young count, typical to his brash character, blew his mouth off and made embittered and unsavoury comments about his uncle Joseph – which were to come back to haunt him. The young Count Léon returned to Paris to dabble in local politics.

The count's world spiralled downhill from here on. He basked in his assumed grandeur and attempted to get favours from sympathetic or nostalgic Bonapartists. In Paris, he fell out with fellow officers in the National Guard and was demoted. He bought things on credit with no intention of repaying. He moved from gullible landlord to gullible landlord sometimes minutes ahead of the bailiffs. He lived under the fantasy that, by virtue of his birth, the fortunes willed to him by his dead father would one day be bestowed on him; at one point he even believed the Pope was soon to promote him to a bishop. From 1837, Léon was in and out of debtors' prison. At one point he mysteriously managed to pay off all of his debts, probably thanks to yet another relative or duped supporters; however, within months he was having rent trouble. Léon became a friend and supporter of François-Guillaume Coëssin, the inventor and philosopher, who generously allowed Léon to lodge with him. Shortly after this, Count Charles Léon made another visit to England in 1840, this time to another exiled relative: Prince Louis-Napoleon.

The purpose of this visit could be one of three reasons. Léon himself insisted that it was to help his friend Coëssin in his efforts to sell the rights to a new lamp he had invented; however, it seems likely that this trip was yet another attempt at securing more money from one of the more richly endowed Bonaparte relatives, in this case, Prince Louis-Napoleon, the heir presumptive to the headship of the family and future Emperor Napoleon III. At the time, more cynically minded supporters of the prince suspected that Léon had been allowed out of debtors' prison by the French authorities purely so he could spy on the prince – who had already attempted a coup against the government. Nevertheless, armed with letters of introduction, the count made his way to London and acquired lodgings at Fenton's Hotel in St James's.

While in town, Léon had another attempt at approaching his uncle Joseph. The former king of Spain had taken up residence not far away, in Cavendish Square. Unfortunately, Joseph had been made aware of Léon's unsavoury comments about him through Dr O'Meara following Léon's last trip. Joseph openly refused to have anything to do with his ruffian nephew. Undeterred (needs must), Charles Léon stayed on in London hoping to attract investment, funding or just charity – but he was not as clever as his relatives.

While in London, and having been approached by another exiled Bonapartist called Montauban, Léon was introduced to some German arms manufacturers. They told him they had invented a new naval weapon capable of immense destruction – a special fireball. Knowing that Léon had intentions to visit his Beauharnais step-cousins in

St Petersburg (by then the princes and dukes of Leuchtenberg), they suggested he present the invention to the Tsar. Selling to the Russians would be more honourable than selling to the English – for a Frenchman! Léon was enormously excited; however, it soon became apparent to him that Montauban was in fact on his cousin Prince Louis-Napoleon's staff, and the German invention had been a mere ploy to compromise him. Disgruntled, the count marched round to 1 Carlton Gardens, the house his princely cousin was renting, but was not received. He attempted this a further three times but to no avail. Angry letters from the count to the prince followed, but the prince was too intelligent to respond except to send a man to Fenton's informing the count that communication written or otherwise was out of the question. Léon's last-ditch attempt at seeing his cousin was to send a challenge to a duel. Despite being first cousins, honour dictated that Prince Louis-Napoleon accept, which he did.

Charles Léon found himself in yet another duel, this time with his own cousin. Near to a clearing by a windmill on Wimbledon Common, the two men and their seconds met. The events of the duel were a farce. (See Chapter 6 for details.) In effect, the combatants could not agree on weapons. The prince favoured sword, the count favoured pistols – having good form in that department. At about the same moment as pistols were eventually agreed upon, and before anyone took a shot, the Scotland Yard Constabulary emerged from behind the bushes, in true Gilbert and Sullivan fashion, and arrested all parties concerned. Duelling was, of course, technically illegal, though it did go on, and Scotland Yard had been watching both Charles and Louis-Napoleon ever since their entry into England, for political and security reasons. At Bow Street Magistrates' Court, the two cousins were released on bail; however, where the prince was easily able to afford his bail, Léon had to charge his bail to his hotel, Fenton's. Having miserably failed in his purpose, humiliated and unable to bay his hotel bill, he quietly slipped away to some humble lodgings in Bloomsbury where he laid low until he could raise enough money for a crossing back to France. He returned to his Paris life, one step ahead of the bailiffs, later that year.

By 1849, Léon's cousin and former adversary, Prince Louis-Napoleon, had been elected the first president of the French Republic. Many old Bonapartes were returning to France in anticipation of money, office and other gifts. Sadly, for Léon, the president had not forgotten their meeting on Wimbledon Common, and he received neither bounty nor an audience. The Bonapartes were finally back in power, but to this child of Napoleon, it was of no benefit. Years later, after the coup d'état of 1851, the new Emperor Napoleon III began to take a different stance and became more paternalistic to extended members of his clan. There were several outstanding monies from Napoleon I's will which the Bourbon administrations had refused to pay out. The emperor paid off his cousin Léon's debts and granted over a quarter of a million francs, although, owing to Léon being useless with money, it was held in trust and he was to live off the interest for life. He continued, however, to fritter this away on outlandish business ideas and trying to get elected to a seat in the Assembly, unsuccessfully.

His life continued in much the same way as it had before. He did marry, but far from a dynastic allegiance his father would have been proud of he married his gardener's daughter, Françoise Jonet, but not before he had already had a son by her. Bastardy seems to be hereditary in the Bonaparte clan. He had four other surviving (legitimate) children; his grandson, Daniel died in 1917 on the Western Front in the First World War. The fifth and last Count Léon died in 1994. Charles Léon died 1881 at the age of 74; he had outlived his cousin the emperor, seen the collapse of the second empire and defeat of France in the Franco-Prussian War. If he had had better character, he might well have had a different story and been allowed to become a statesman, or the founder of a cadet branch of the dynasty. Such was the case with his younger half-brother – Napoleon's other bastard son – who had far more direct dealings with Great Britain.

The year 1810 was a busy year for Emperor Napoleon. He was finally divorced from the barren and scandalous Joséphine in January, and months later married the daughter of his former enemy, Emperor Francis of Austria, the Archduchess Marie-Louise in March (by proxy) and in April (in person). His political marriage was complete; married to one of the oldest dynasties in Europe, Napoleon could now start his own. However, another event happened that year: Napoleon became a father again, and not with his imperial bride. A month later, Napoleon's second (known) son was born. He was neither French nor Austrian but Polish, and was named Alexandre Florian Joseph Colonna-Walewski.

Alexandre was the product of a relationship between Napoleon and Countess Marie Walewska, a beautiful and very learned Polish aristocrat. Her tutor had been the composer Frederic Chopin's father.

41

She had married another wealthy aristocrat, Count Anastazy Walewski in 1805 – a man who had been close to Stanislaus II Augustus, a member of the Poniatowski family and the last king of Poland. She was 17, he was approaching 70! After a very swift meeting with Marie while he and his armies marched through Prussia and Russian-occupied Poland, Napoleon remembered her and ardently hoped to start an affair with her. She was initially very reluctant, but it is widely accepted that she was persuaded by Polish courtiers, including the former royal family and perhaps even by her own family, that a relationship with the emperor might be one way of helping Poland obtain independence from its Prussian, Russian and Austrian neighbours. The affair, be it political or romantic, was a badly kept secret, many knew of its existence; however, the couple seemed to get on very well and certainly did so for some time. Today their affair has become legendary and is highly romanticised in film and literature. One could say there was a benefit to be had for both parties – she: nationalism, he: another feather in his bonnet. Marie journeyed with the emperor to Vienna in 1809 – sometime during which she became pregnant. Alexandre was born the following year in Poland; Marie's husband, Count Walewski, dutifully and officially acknowledged him as his own, though he was undoubtedly Napoleon's son. Arguably, the affair did not ultimately advance the cause of Polish nationalism; Napoleon did not help reinstate its kings; however, Polish patriotism and indeed diplomacy was to become a part of his new son's life. The news of becoming a father again must have boosted Napoleon's ego and vigour, for before the year 1810 was out, Empress Marie-Louise was also pregnant with his true heir.

With his new high-born wife and expecting his first legitimate son, Napoleon was embarrassed by his former affairs, and brushed them under the carpet. He rarely saw Marie but did confer money, estates and the title of count on Alexandre. The young Alexandre grew up never publicly acknowledging or proclaiming his relationship to Napoleon, but this was probably because he eventually inherited a lot of his wealth from his legal father, Count Anastazy Walewski, who died just a few years after he was born. When Alexandre was a toddler, however, the British and her allies permitted Marie and Alexandre to visit Napoleon in captivity on Elba. He reportedly told his real father that he knew their true connection – children are very perceptive.

After his mother died in 1817 (aged only 31), Alexandre was brought up by an uncle on his feudal estates in Poland and was sent to a boarding school in Switzerland. He was, however, no anonymous aristocrat. The story of his real lineage and his being born out of a desire to express Polish independence had not been forgotten by the great powers. There was a chance the boy could have ambitions to match his father's. The Tsar of Russia felt uncomfortable with Alexandre being near France, preferring him to be watched in nearby Poland. Alexandre was confined within Polish borders; however, by the time he was a young man, the rebellious Bonaparte manifested in him. Using a fake passport, he managed to escape first to St Petersburg, where he was discovered by imperial police, and then, having evaded the authorities, he stealthily boarded a ship to London. This was probably because he knew he would be forced to join the Russian army. He was probably the first of Napoleon's children to visit the old enemy's capital in Great Britain. However, it was a short trip – a means to an end. He soon travelled to Paris where, thanks to useful connections, and the fact that he looked the spitting image of the emperor, the French refused to let him be extradited to Russia and he glided easily into some of the highest sections of society. His friends were from both new and very ancient noble families alike. He was one of the first members elected to the Cercle de l'Union Club in Paris. A clubhouse inspired by the English gentlemen's clubs of Pall Mall, Mayfair and St James.

In 1830, the new Orleanist king of France, Louis-Philippe, dispatched Alexandre back to his nominal homeland of Poland. In 1831, a Polish revolt against their Russian overlords began deposing Tsar Nicholas I. The young Alexandre was desperate to be involved, despite the Russians who were clearly watching him. He was arrested by border guards but made a daring escape through snowy forests and across freezing rivers back to Warsaw where he joined the free Polish army as an officer. Alexandre saw brave action at the Battle of Olszynka Grochowska, where a horse was shot from under him and he was subsequently decorated. He was entrusted by the revolutionary Poles to lead a diplomatic mission to London to ask for support from both Britain and France. Journeying secretly through Prussia, he had to pretend to be an actor to get through border police. He even had to give a performance in a local theatre just to prove his credentials. After making it to Paris he was sent to London. The very fact that Napoleon's natural son was now presenting himself officially at the Court of St James less than ten years after the ogre's death, must have been strange for the government of the day – the Leader of the Opposition was at that time the Duke of Wellington! One can only imagine what they talked to each other about, if they spoke at all. Lord Palmerston, then foreign secretary, and Prime Minister Earl Grey (now famous for tea and his affair with the Duchess of Devonshire) met with Alexandre and were brutally honest, explaining that since Russia was a natural ally of Britain they could not be seen to meddle. They were unable or unwilling to help Poland.

Undeterred, Alexandre visited the French ambassador in London, Charles-Maurice de Talleyrand. Talleyrand, whom Napoleon had described as faecal matter in fine hosiery, was now serving as the Bourbons' and the July Monarchy's representative in London. The Travellers Club on Pall Mall installed a handrail up the main staircase in order to accommodate him – he had a troublesome limp from birth. Talleyrand made diplomatic suggestions about Poland and recommended the help of his illegitimate son, Charles Count de Flahaut, who was by now married to Scottish aristocracy, a peer of France and equerry to the king's heir, the Duke of Orleans – not bad for Napoleon's former ADC. Despite seeking help in both Paris and London, Alexandre's efforts did not achieve an independent Poland. The British government was too occupied in installing Leopold of Saxe-Coburg-Saalfeld (widower of Princess Charlotte of Wales) as king of the Belgians, and were mistrustful of the French and did not want to intervene in her ally Russia's back yard. Warsaw eventually fell to Russia later that year. The Tsar took away any remaining Polish autonomy and formally made it part of his empire; he garrisoned Warsaw and closed the university.

Though Alexandre was bitterly disappointed by his own efforts, he could count himself lucky he had not been captured by the Russians. Many captured Polish leaders were sent to Siberia or executed. Instead, he was able to bask in the romanticism that surrounded him in London. An exiled revolutionary aristocrat who had lost his 'homeland' who also was rumoured to be Napoleon's son, was sure to be popular amongst London society, especially with the ladies. On 1 December 1831, he married Lady Caroline Montagu at St George's Hanover Square (the same church Theodore Roosevelt would eventually marry in). Napoleon's own son had married into the English aristocracy just sixteen years after Waterloo.

Caroline was the daughter of George Montagu, 6th Earl of Sandwich. The Montagu family remains one of the oldest families in the English peerage stretching back to the battle of Crecy and possibly even as far as the Doomsday Book. The first Earl of Sandwich was involved in the Restoration of Charles II who subsequently made him an earl. The first earl's cousin, Samuel Pepys, owed much of his career and advancement to him. John, the fourth earl, is the most famous of the clan for being the eponymous inventor and namesake of the sandwich. At his club (or one of the Hellfire clubs), reluctant to leave the gambling table to eat, he would have meats brought to him between slices of bread (supposedly in order to avoid getting the cards or his cuffs greasy). Subsequently, 'the sandwich' was ordered by friends and other club members and thus the dish was invented – or so the story goes. One can only guess whether sandwiches were served and Alexandre and Caroline's wedding breakfast! Nevertheless, the bride brought tens of thousands as a dowry and the couple moved to Paris. They were on friendly terms with another Franco-British couple, Flahaut and his wife Margaret Elphinstone – Baroness Keith and Lady Nairne. Alexandre continued to move in high Parisian circles during which he met Charles Auguste de Morny, his stepsister Hortense's bastard by none other than Flahaut, but also half-brother to the future Napoleon III – whom Alexandre would serve and also share a mistress.

Alexandre's in-laws may have been a peculiar prospect to a Bonaparte in all but name. His brother-in-law, the 7th Earl of Sandwich, went on to marry Lady Mary Paget, daughter of Henry Paget, 1st Marquess of Anglesey – who had been second in command at Waterloo and had lost a leg to a French cannonball. Paget, like Léon and Napoleon III, had also fought a duel on Wimbledon Common following his elopement with Lady Charlotte Cadogan, the wife of Henry Wellesley, 1st Lord Cowley, who happened to be the younger brother of the Duke of Wellington. Charlotte's brother, Henry Cadogan, challenged Paget to a duel in 1809. Despite firing off their pistols in Wimbledon, neither was injured and they were reconciled. Paget's marriage to Charlotte was eventually accepted and they had many children. Through a series of marriages, Alexandre was very nearly related to this grandee of Waterloo and even the Duke of Wellington himself; however, Caroline died in Paris just two years after they were wed. Their two children sadly did not see adulthood. The Anglo-Bonaparte dynasty did not materialise.

There followed a long period of mourning, a stint in the French Foreign Legion in Africa, a decline in political success, becoming a playwright and the siring of an illegitimate son with famous actress of the day, Rachel Felix. His actress lover, who rose to greatness both as an actor and as a lady in French society, came from humble Jewish heritage. She performed to great acclaim throughout Europe in the 1830s and 1840s. It is supposed that, after seeing her perform in London, Charlotte Brontë based the character of Vashti (from Villette) on Rachel. In her time, Rachel was mistress to three Bonapartes: Alexandre, Napoleon III and Prince Napoleon (Jerome's son). She was also a close friend of Victor Hugo. Alexandre and Rachel's son was born in 1844 and Alexandre recognised him and, years later, formally adopted him. The late Napoleon could now add a grandchild of Jewish heritage to his list of descendants. However, Alexandre believed he now needed a second wife with a pedigree to match his own and that of his late wife's. He married Anna-Maria de Ricci, daughter of a papal noble, in 1846 in Florence. On her father's side she was supposedly descended from Machiavelli, but on her mother's side she was a Poniatowski and a great-great-grandniece of the last king of Poland, Stanislaus II. Evidently, she met Alexandre's requirements.

The rise of Alexandre's cousin, Prince Louis-Napoleon, who became president in 1848, brought both blessings and problems. It did advance his diplomatic career which had hitherto been fairly unsuccessful; Napoleon made him French ambassador to Florence, Naples, Madrid and London in 1851 – unsurprising given his history with the place. Alexandre represented Emperor Napoleon III and France at the state funeral of the Duke of Wellington at St Paul's Cathedral in London. A real sign of reconciliation between the two countries. He managed to obtain British recognition of the second empire following his cousin's coup d'état to become the emperor in 1851. As minister of foreign affairs, he was instrumental in organising the two state visits of 1855 between his cousin and Queen Victoria. He also chaired the 1856 Treaty of Paris, which ended the Crimean War, presiding over British statesmen such as the Earl of Clarendon and Lord Cowley. It was a proud moment for Alexandre, though one wonders what his father might have thought of his son bringing together France and Britain on joint imperial projects. All was not rosy, however. Anna-Maria, by 1857 had become the emperor's new mistress. What goes around invariably comes around.

After all, the two men had already shared Rachel Felix's affections. The two men coincidently began to disagree on political matters, but the second empire soldiered onwards.

In 1862, having chaired the design competition panel, Alexandre laid the foundation stone of the Opera Garnier (the Paris Opera House), the building which inspired the Leroux novel *The Phantom of the Opera*. A few years later in 1866, Count Alexandre was created a duke of the empire – perhaps as an apology from the emperor for various adulteries. With several awards, titles, offices and conquests under his belt, the often-overweight Alexandre, spitting image of his father, Napoleon, died in September 1868, survived by four children, and has many descendants living to this day. It is perhaps fortunate that he did not live to see the fall of the second empire and the ravages of the Franco-Prussian War. His son Charles, the 2nd Count Colonna-Walewski, served in and survived said conflict; however, as a veteran at the age of 66, he bravely volunteered for service on the Western Front in the First World War serving alongside the British forces. He contracted a respiratory complication while at the front, and died in 1916.

In many ways, the Bonaparte-Walewski family neatly illustrates the turnaround in European alliances between Waterloo in 1815 and the Western Front in 1914–18. In just three generations of one family, French foreign policy can be observed. From Napoleon (seeking to invade Britain), through Alexandre (bringing France and Britain together in the Crimea and double state visit), to Charles (fighting together with the British as part of the *entente cordiale*).

Published in 2013, research into DNA evidence between Count Antoine Colonna-Walewski (descendant of Alexandre) and Prince Charles Napoleon (descendant of Napoleon's brother Jerome) found a link between the modern-day Walewskis and Bonapartes. Bonapartes have a particularly rare haplogroup for Europeans. In short, the research confirmed that they were both of the male Bonaparte line, thus proving categorically that Alexandre was Napoleon's son. One would hope that this line of enquiry would be more widely picked up throughout Europe's royalty or aristocracy; it would answer many other unsolved questions – although, a considerable number of these families would rather it was not, lest they find something they did not wish to be known.

Alexandre Walewski, Napoleon's second son, was very different from his elder half-brother, Léon. Though he had many blunders to his name, he was comparatively successful, though this may be mostly down to the fact that he was easier to get on with than Léon and far wealthier thanks to his Polish relatives. Walewski had been successful in society on both sides of the Channel, as well as being decorated by his homeland, and had even married into the cream of English aristocracy. Perhaps strangest of all of this semi-Bonaparte's accomplishments, Alexandre had been an important contributor to Napoleon III's plan for France – a closer alliance with Britain. A surprising achievement for a son of Napoleon.

Napoleon Bonaparte may well have had other children aside from Charles, Alexandre and Napoleon II; however, no others are universally recognised as such. Napoleon died and was buried on British-held ground. His legitimate son died young and as a noble captive of Austria. His eldest son, Charles, fought a duel on Wimbledon Common and was a briefly a down-and-out in Bloomsbury. His other son, Alexandre, was ambassador to Britain and married to English aristocracy. No one would have predicted such a turn of events during Napoleon's earlier career.

Chapter 4

Joseph: Uncle Joe on Both Sides of the Pond

One might well sympathise a little with younger brothers who look up to, or are overshadowed by, their elder brother(s), but to have one's life and career hugely overshadowed by a younger brother, that must be especially difficult. Such was the lot of Joseph Bonaparte, elder brother of Napoleon and the eldest (surviving) child of their parents. Though Joseph was an able politician and lawyer himself, much of his career was spent effectively following the orders or directives of his brother. That said, this led him to obtain great wealth and to become king of two kingdoms, Naples and Spain, albeit briefly.

Despite having been at one time or another an influential European monarch, after the downfall of his brother the emperor, Joseph spent much of the rest of his life in other parts of the world. Not only was some of this in merry England but also in the United States of America – the land that arguably inspired the very revolution which led to the Bonapartes' eventual rise. With a country estate in New Jersey, a house in London, and even some family connections to the British Isles, Joseph had an altogether surprising second life after the fall of the First French Empire.

Born in Corsica in 1768 to Carlo and Letizia Bonaparte, Joseph was inseparable in childhood from his brother Napoleon, who had been born a year later. Both boys (and their six-years-older uncle, Joseph Fesch) received their initial education from their great-uncle Lucien Bonaparte, who was archdeacon of Ajaccio Cathedral at that time. Contrary to tradition, it seems Carlo intended for his eldest son to enter into the priesthood. After studying a while in the Lycée Autun, Joseph abandoned this career path and returned to the Bonaparte home in Corsica in 1784. He wanted, like his younger brother, to begin a military career at the same school, whereas his father hoped he would take up law. In fact,

Family Tree

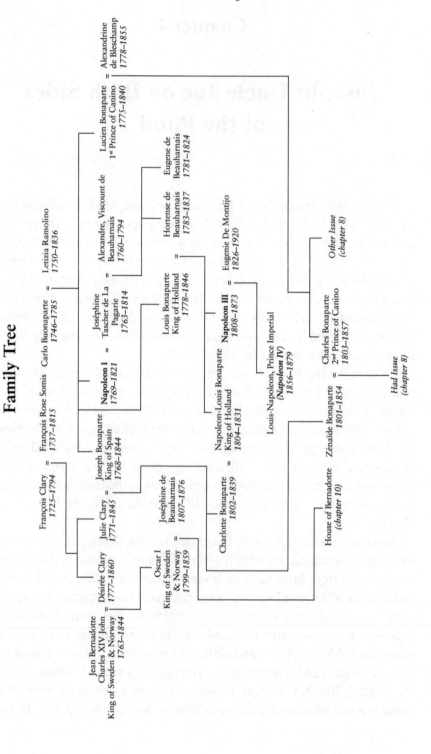

Carlo, on his deathbed, made Joseph swear to give up the military and take care of the family – which was a considerable brood consisting of a wife, eight children and an ageing uncle.

Carlo died in 1786. Aged 22, Joseph took up the mantle of the family finances – which were dire at that time. Perhaps by being thrown in at the deep end, Joseph developed skill in investments and became adept at turning a profit. True to his promise, he also went to study law at Pisa. During the Revolution, Joseph was able to take advantage of the fluid political situation to increase the family's standing. He obtained an influential civic office, and accrued wealth and contacts.

Continuing his closeness with Napoleon, both young men became infatuated and eventually engaged to two sisters, Julie and Désirée Clary. This was a circle of love that would span the majority of the Napoleonic world, influence it, and ultimately leave Napoleon (arguably) the worse for it. They were the daughters of François Clary, a wealthy ship-owner and silk merchant from Marseilles. It is possible that, based on surname alone, that the Clarys had Irish ancestry, though it would have to be centuries prior to this generation. Joseph and Julie were married in 1794. Theirs was a love match. Napoleon too was, in his fashion, ardently passionate about Désirée – they were engaged the following year – but one cannot help but wonder if it was the tidiness of two pairs of siblings marrying each other that was also a driver.

Within a year, Napoleon cast Désirée aside in favour of Joséphine de Beauharnais and broke off the engagement – which doubtless must have made life awkward for Joseph and Julie. The Bonaparte family at large were embarrassed and disappointed. Napoleon had chosen a noble widow older than him and of questionable virtue over a younger, virtuous girl. Napoleon and Joséphine married in 1796; it was thought to be a bad match by most of his family. Tension between the Bonapartes and Beauharnais began from here, and Désirée remained close to the Bonapartes. A year later, Désirée went on to marry Jean-Baptiste Bernadotte, another soldier. Napoleon approved the match and was regretful of any hurt he may have caused; however, he did not realise what fate had in store for Désirée.

Bernadotte, who had entered the French army as mere private, proved a good military commander under Napoleon's rule, and was eventually promoted to marshal. Such was Bernadotte's fame as a military leader he was invited to become the king of Sweden and elected Crown Prince in 1810 – meaning Napoleon's ex-fiancée would one day be the queen of Sweden. To add insult to injury, Bernadotte, as ruler of Sweden, allied with France's enemies, including Britain, to form the sixth coalition against Napoleon, which ultimately led to his fall and exile on Elba. Had Napoleon been true to his first fiancée, then perhaps he may have had more children of his own, and avoided unnecessary wars or alliances.

Alternative histories aside, through Joseph's sister-in-law becoming the queen of Sweden, he and his legitimate children would eventually become the uncle and cousins of the kings of Norway, Sweden and Denmark (and Iceland). In 1801 and 1802, Julie gave birth to Joseph's only legitimate children, Zénaïde and Charlotte, in Paris.

Joseph's career rose alongside his brother's. In 1797, he was elected to the Council of Five Hundred and also served as French ambassador to Rome. After his brother became the first consul of France, Joseph was appointed to the Council of State and became a notable diplomat through being a chief negotiator at the Treaty of Amiens – which marked the end of the Revolutionary Wars. After long discussions, the treaty was signed in 1802 and a short-lived year-long peace followed between Britain and France. Joseph's opposite number at the negotiating table was Lord Cornwallis, the British general who had had the misfortune of being defeated by George Washington and French forces at Yorktown in 1781. Although he was not happy with the concluding treaty and did not trust Joseph, the British government had only given Cornwallis a few days to either get an agreement signed or to walk away and continue the war. Cornwallis, however, had had enough of the conflict.

By the time Napoleon declared himself emperor in 1804, the wars had begun again. Joseph was now the Grand Elector, an Imperial Highness, and presided over the Senate. Following Napoleon's wars in Austria and Italy and the subsequent occupation of Naples, King Ferdinand IV of Naples was dethroned by the occupying force and he fled to his other kingdom of Sicily. Ferdinand was not popular with Napoleon as he was a Bourbon, a brother-in-law of Marie Antoinette and a friend of Lord Nelson and his mistress Lady Hamilton. The emperor, with ambitions of setting up a powerful dynasty, appointed his brother Joseph to be the new king of Naples in 1806 and to rule as a client kingdom of the French Empire. He was a reasonably popular monarch, ruling in the tradition of enlightened absolutism. Joseph enjoyed being the monarch of an Italian state; after all, the Bonapartes were themselves of Italian descent more that they were French.

Joseph's reign over Naples was short-lived, however. Just two years. By 1808, Napoleon had dethroned yet another Bourbon monarchy, this time it was the turn of Spain. Charles IV of Spain was forced to abdicate and was held prisoner in France. In order to govern the population, some of whom were hostile to French occupation, Napoleon needed a proven politician and leader to head an imposed government who would be loyal. However, he was running low on brothers at this point. Louis he had made king of Holland in 1806; Jerome he had made king of Westphalia in 1807; and Lucien was unreliable at best. In the most excellent example of nepotism, Napoleon decided to switch Joseph as king of Naples for his brother-in-law, Marshal Joachim Murat who was married to Caroline Bonaparte. Napoleon's sister and her husband became the new rulers of Naples, whereas Joseph was reluctantly transferred to the Iberian peninsula to be proclaimed José I Bonaparte, king of Spain and the Indies.

Spain was not like Naples. It was vast country on the edge of Napoleon's empire and a constant war zone beset by Spanish rebels and freedom fighters as well as the Portuguese and British armies, not to mention the Royal Navy. French rule was generally unpopular and atrocities were committed on both sides. More than once, Joseph was forced to flee Madrid, at one time because a British and Portuguese army occupied the city. The final humiliating retreat happened in 1813 and was followed by the allied victory at the Battle of Vitoria in June that year commanded by the Marquess of Wellington (the future duke). Joseph barely escaped with his life during the aftermath of the battle and abdicated the throne later the same year. The Bourbons were returned as Spain's monarchs. Ever a good eye for money, in his speedy departure from Spain Joseph managed to 'acquire' a number of valuable jewels and artworks from the royal treasury. He attempted to take them back to France with him. No doubt he saw these as his golden handshake or pension fund! However, over 200 paintings were captured by Wellington's forces. Eventually, he offered to return these to the newly restored king of Spain, Ferdinand VII (Charles IV's son). The king was touched but did not wish deprive the man who had won him his crown back of the spoils of war. Eighty-two paintings from the royal Spanish collection remain on display to this day at the duke's Apsley House in London. Perhaps to add insult to injury, there is also a portrait of Joseph in what is now the ticket hall. Wellington's army also came upon Joseph's treasure wagons and over

5 million francs in gold. When army officials caught up and inspected the money carts, somehow, only around 250,000 were left!

Joseph looked back on his reign over Spain with a certain amount of delusion, believing that were it not for his meddlesome younger brother and France's grand armies, he would have been able to successfully govern Spain. Such an idea was nonsense. In all likelihood, no invading force would have held on to Spain for long. However, it sowed the seed of resentment between the previously close brothers.

By now the empire was on the back foot. The combined disastrous campaigns at either end of Napoleon's empire in Russia and Spain set the tide against France in the War of the Sixth Coalition. Wellington had continued his advance from Vitoria far into the south of France towards Toulouse. By March 1814, the other allied powers were almost at the gates of Paris, having separated Napoleon's defending forces. Joseph was given one last honour in these last days of the empire and her hour of need, that of lieutenant general and nominal command of the defence of Paris. Rather like being made captain of a sinking ship. Joseph was chief adviser to the regent, Empress Marie-Louise, but the situation was hopeless. He gave his consent for the marshals to negotiate a capitulation to the coalition powers, who eventually persuaded Napoleon to accept the terms of surrender offered by the allies and to abdicate. Napoleon partly blamed Joseph for allowing Marie-Louise to flee to her father's forces, the Austrians, along with the heir to the empire, the king of Rome – although Joseph had attempted to persuade her to carry on the fight for France in the south.

Like the rest of the Bonaparte family, Joseph was exiled from France after the Bourbon monarchy was re-established. Britain and her allies were highly suspicious of Joseph during this time and were especially worried about attempts to rescue the emperor. Similarly, Joseph was concerned about Bourbon reprisals or attempts to murder or assassinate his brother. Instead, however, he settled in Switzerland, purchased Chateau de Pragins and busied himself with decorating it.

Despite the mighty Royal Navy patrolling the waters of Elba, Napoleon escaped and made it to mainland France with a small force in February 1815. The fateful Hundred Days Campaign began. Joseph was reinstated as Grand Elector and hurried with domestic politics and plans of persuading his brother to liberalise the empire. It was short-lived, however. All the courts of Europe united against Napoleon.

The French Empire was to have its last stand at Waterloo on 18 June 1815, a cataclysmic and historic defeat.

As we have seen, Napoleon and Joseph effectively went on the run from the coalition forces and Bourbon royalists. Ultimately, their original objective was to flee to the United States, but Napoleon's dithering and pondering of his limited options closed the opportunity. While hemmed in at Rochefort by the Royal Navy, and waiting for an escape route to be possible, Joseph offered to switch identities with his brother in order that he might get passage to the New World. This was, of course, impossible for the proud younger brother who, among other reasons, probably did not want to spent the next chapter of his life entirely in debt to his older brother. Joseph was unable to dissuade Napoleon from the last decision he would ultimately make about his life – the decision to surrender to the British. A few days after Napoleon handed himself over to Captain Maitland on HMS *Bellerophon*, Joseph boarded a brig, the *La Margaretha*, accompanied by a handful of retainers, including his cook. His destination was not the Devonshire coast, however; he set sail for the New World and the US.

Joseph knew he was entering a republic, a land that had, through great feats of arms, severed its links with monarchy and monarchs a few decades earlier. For that reason, perhaps, he decided to be known not as the ex-king of Spain, or an imperial prince of the French, but as the Comte de Survilliers – to draw less attention. Survilliers was the name of a chateau he owned in northern France; soon after his flight to America, he sold the castle to his wife's brother, Count Nicholas Clary. Joseph arrived at New York in August 1815. It did not take long before someone recognised him at his hotel and word spread throughout the city. He was summoned to meet with Mayor Jacob Radcliffe to explain his presence in New York. Being aware that this was a diplomatically sensitive situation, Radcliffe advised that because of Joseph's high profile he should formally seek asylum from the president directly. Joseph was therefore required to travel to Washington to seek an audience with the president – at that time, James Madison.

Though Madison was only America's fourth president, he was a Founding Father and an author of the Constitution and the Bill of Rights. He had walked the difficult path of treason, revolution and republicanism. Joseph, in his earlier days, had also walked a similar path but with an entirely different outcome – becoming a king by dint of nepotism, and supporting absolutism. On his journey to the White House, Napoleon's brother must have pondered what his chances were and if he was be allowed to stay in America. Only three years earlier, the British had burned the White House, so at least they had a mutual dislike of the British. Joseph did not make it to Washington, however. By the time he had reached Philadelphia, Joseph was informed he would not be received, partly so as to make his stay unofficial and partly so the president could distance himself from a failed monarch. The ex-king could remain in the US on the condition he kept himself to himself and did not meddle in American political affairs. He duly accepted this condition.

The Comte de Survilliers remained in Philadelphia a while, moving first into a hotel, then a town house and before long, a mansion called Lansdowne. (Coincidentally, the same name would form the title of his sister-in-law's lover's child, Emily, Marchioness of Lansdowne.) Joseph was correctly rumoured to be rich – he had brought considerable sums with him into exile and continued to have an eye for a good investment. He was a curiosity to the local American citizens and there were many who desired to meet the ex-king, although the interest was not as hyped as it had been for his brothers Napoleon and Lucien when they were in Britain (or its waters). Joseph liked America and looked forward to his wife and daughters joining him from Europe. He was reportedly generous to his neighbours and guests and was well liked by Philadelphian society. The ex-king was able to welcome fellow comrades exiled from France, from poor soldiers to deflated generals such as Marshal Grouchy (the man who unfortunately shouldered some of the blame for the defeat at Waterloo). Famous Americans were also in his new circle of friends, including Dr Philip Physick and Thomas Jefferson's own private secretary, William Short. The ex-king Joseph's attorney was even a son of one of the signatories of the Declaration of Independence.

Having settled amicably into society and become an accepted guest of the United States, Joseph decided he would purchase a property of his own. Almost exactly one year after the total disaster of Waterloo, Joseph Bonaparte moved to a site near Bordentown in New Jersey. Having acquired the land from American diplomat Stephen Sayre, Joseph set about creating the Point Breeze Estate which eventually totalled around 1,800 acres with views over Crosswicks Creek and the Delaware

River. It is strange to think that the river that was made famous by George Washington's victorious night crossing in 1776 was now host to a Bonaparte. Joseph poured hundreds of thousands of dollars into the estate, improving the house, giving it a rich empire-style interior, purchasing more land and developing the landscaped gardens. Joseph liked nothing better than to get involved in the improvements, be it decorating or gardening.

Joseph's objective was to make Point Breeze a centre for society and a beautiful place to live out his exile and possibly retire. American society affectionately called it the Good Mr Bonaparte's place (as opposed to the *Bad* Mr (Napoleon) Bonaparte)), and it became well known for its sumptuous art collection, impressive interiors and beautiful gardens. After a large fire at the house in 1820, Joseph rebuilt Point Breeze to an even grander scale and its reincarnation was generally regarded as the second finest house in America after the White House – which was also a reincarnation from the flames set by the British back in 1812. The original painting by Jacques-Louis David of Napoleon crossing the Alps hung on the wall at Point Breeze with other stunning works of art; meanwhile, the real Napoleon lived out his days in the tropical hell-hole of St Helena. Joseph lent certain items of his collection to the Pennsylvania Academy of Fine Arts and, probably in thanks, he was admitted into the American Society of Philosophy, a group founded by none other than Benjamin Franklin. During his seventeen-year stay at Point Breeze, Joseph entertained some of the cream of American society as he had hoped, including future US President John Quincy Adams (son of founding father John Adams, the second president after Washington). It was during the early years at Point Breeze that Mexican revolutionaries are rumoured to have offered Joseph the title of emperor of Mexico, after all, he had been king of Spain *and* the Indies. This offer does not seem likely, however, and certainly not something the cautious Joseph would contemplate accepting. Mexico later gained its independence from Spain in 1821.

Though Joseph's wife Julie never made the journey to join him in America, preferring the sophistication of Europe, where her sister at least was still a queen, his daughters, princesses Charlotte and Zénaïde, did visit and stayed with him in New Jersey for several years. However, in the midst of his family being partially reunited, Joseph, a Bonaparte to the core, did indulge in the occasional extra-marital affair. One such relationship was with Annette Savage of Philadelphia. The Savage family claimed descent from the famous Native American, Pocahontas. This claim stemmed from an earlier hostage-taking incident where members of the family were held by a Native American with a similar name to that of Pocahontas's tribe, the Powhatan. Although Pocahontas married an Englishman (John Rolfe) in 1614, moved to London, attended masked balls at Whitehall and has many descendants, it seems unlikely that the Savages (who are awkwardly named) are descended from her in the way that they claim. At best, they might be very slightly connected through other members of the wider tribe, or at worst the story is just a story. Two daughters, born in 1821 and 1822, were the products of Joseph and Annette's love and they were well provided for and looked after by their father and were even able to meet their older half-sisters at Point Breeze. These illegitimate children were born in America (Philadelphia) and therefore were US citizens, although they were not the first American-born Bonapartes. (That accolade went to the child of Joseph's youngest brother, Jerome, and his first wife, Betsy Patterson, in 1805.)

Much like the other men of his family, Joseph had a number of illegitimate children, two from his Neapolitan days, two from Miss Savage and a further two while in the US – a busy man indeed. The mother of these other suspected American children of Joseph's was Emilie Hémart. She was the wife of Felix Lacoste, a businessman and lawyer who had also left France for America. Mr Lacoste was often away on business trips and while he was away Emilie stayed at Point Breeze where an affair developed. The scandal was widely known. The famous Marquis de La Fayette attended a society dinner at Point Breeze in 1824 and was shocked to find Emilie acting as hostess. In 1827, Emilie's disgruntled and embarrassed husband moved himself and his wife back to France, only to find her starting off another affair. Coincidently, her next lover was Prosper Mérimée, the celebrated author of *Carmen,* and a 'close friend' of Maria Manuela Kirkpatrick – the mother of the future Empress Eugenie. Lacoste, outraged at being humiliated again, challenged Mérimée to a duel. Mérimée, being the artistic type, asked Lacoste if he would kindly aim for his left arm because he needed his right to write with. Lacoste duly obliged and shot him in the left arm winning the duel! Mérimée feebly took his revenge on Mr and Mrs Lacoste via his next lover, George Sand: together they wrote *La Vase Étrusque,* in which the character Mathilde is allegedly an unsavoury depiction of Emilie. Happily, Sand and Mérimée went on to discover the Lady and the Unicorn tapestries, now in the Museum of the Middle Ages in Paris.

After Napoleon's death in 1821, most people widely accepted Joseph as head of the Bonaparte dynasty, or at least assumed that he was. He was, after all, the elder brother. That said, Napoleon's will regarding the succession to his thrones had been clear. He favoured his own son, the king of Rome, and then, in previous renditions of the line of succession, the children of his younger brother and stepdaughter, Louis and Hortense. Nevertheless, the family was in exile and was presently spread from America to Eastern Europe, and the favoured young princelings either lacked experience or were noble captives in their lands of exile. Joseph seemingly became the *de facto* person at the helm of the Bonaparte clan. Joseph was a very careful man and did not make his intentions or political opinions widely known, probably so as to monitor the situation in France and Europe and be able to plan a possible return. After a further nine years in the blissful life of a wealthy American landowner, the former king of Naples and of Spain left his New Jersey home and headed for Europe. This was not, however, a triumphal return to France, but a trip to Napoleon's most generous of enemies, Britain. Liverpool to be exact – in August 1832. After being a prince of France, king of Naples and of Spain, and a wealthy landowner in America, one wonders how Liverpool must have stuck Joseph! He quickly moved to London and set up at a grand town house, 23 Park Crescent in London – an elegant series of stuccoed terraced villas by architect John Nash set between Portland Place and Regent's Park. The property belonged to Lieutenant General St George Ashe, an East India Company man and commander of the British Army of Bengal. Doubtless it amused him to have a bevy of Bonapartes in his house; regrettably, he was run over by a cab on Regent Street a year later. Joseph was now a London resident, living less than twenty-five minutes walking distance from the homes of King George IV, the Duke of Wellington and many other former enemies.

The Second French Revolution had taken place in July 1830. The people of France had, for a second time since 1789, toppled their Bourbon monarch. This time it was the turn of Charles X (younger brother of both Louis XVIII and the ill-fated Louis XVI, and uncle to Louis XVII). This was a momentous moment for the Bonaparte clan.

The last revolution had effectively created a platform for Napoleon to gain power; the people might now demand the return of the imperial family. Joseph's move to London was in order to decide if any action should or could be taken. When he arrived in England, he learnt of the death of his nephew, the king of Rome (Napoleon II) in Austria, making Joseph more than ever the effective clan leader.

In London, Joseph summoned a family conference of existing Bonaparte family members to discuss the future, if they were able. Lucien, Louis and his son (Napoleon III), Achille Murat, Charlotte and possibly Jerome were all present for meetings at one time or another at the house in Park Crescent from 1832 to 1833. There were disagreements about how to proceed. His nephew, the hot-headed Louis-Napoleon (the future Napoleon III), demanded action and popular uprisings. In the quiet surroundings near Regent's Park, Joseph preferred caution – which has often been interpreted as inaction. The young future emperor, in exile in England at that time, despaired of his odious, outdated uncle and planned to continue with his ill-advised plots and schemes (which eventually led to his arrest and imprisonment). By the end of the various family meetings in London, it was clear that the imperialist party was divided. It was the last roll of the dice for the senior Bonaparte generation and it had produced nothing, although Joseph and Lucien did propose that the people of France vote for an emperor out of the three pretender families: Bonaparte, Bourbon and Orleans.

In the end, there was little to be done. The July Revolution resulted in the Bourbons being replaced by a cadet branch, the House of Orleans, and Louis-Philippe became king of a more liberal French monarchy. King Charles X fled from riotous crowds to Britain. The then prime minister, the Duke of Wellington, insisted they arrive as private citizens. The royals had to adopt pseudonyms. As a sign of mockery, the English crowds waiting ashore to greet the new royal arrivals, waved the tricolour! These last of the ruling Bourbons were permitted to live at Lulworth Castle in Dorset for a time before being rehoused at Holyrood Palace in Edinburgh. Charles was not the first French monarch to live there; Mary Queen of Scots first arrived there around 1561 and was the widowed Queen of France. So, one hopes the Bourbons felt at home in Edinburgh!

It was around this time that Joseph was approached by, and became friends with, Doctor Barry O'Meara, the late Napoleon's old physician on St Helena. Since his time on St Helena, O'Meara had become something of a Bonapartist. The Irish surgeon, who had conducted Napoleon's first medical operation back in 1817 (removing a wisdom tooth), sought out the late emperor's elder brother in London in 1832 and Joseph gladly accepted his friendship and services. The following summer of 1833, there was an outbreak of cholera in the city; perhaps on O'Meara's advice, Joseph left London for the country. O'Meara was able to show Joseph around some country houses as possible retreats. They initially settled on Marden Park near Woldingham on the North Downs to the south of London. At one time, William Wilberforce had been a resident at the house. The doctor and the ex-king went on a tour of England visiting Brighton, Cambridge, Newmarket and Windsor where they stayed at White Hart Hotel (which they complained was both bad and expensive!). O'Meara even managed to introduce Joseph to the Irish reformer politician Daniel O'Connell. In 1834, Joseph settled upon the tenancy of a new country estate, Denham Place near Uxbridge, property of the Way family and famed for good fishing. The British press reported that Joseph was merely waiting in the aisles of the theatre of Europe, hoping to play a trump card in the power politics of France or indeed in Spain. However, Joseph was an intelligent man. He knew that a return to kingship or similar power was not likely for him. By October 1835 he had returned to his American estate at Point Breeze. Joseph believed that his long stay in England had only brought setbacks not breakthroughs.

While back in New Jersey, Joseph focused more on business than politics. The US was a land of opportunity and was developing very quickly. He managed to acquire a thousand shares of the Baltimore railway company. Yet despite the success and comforts of his American home, tragedy was not far behind. Joseph's mother, Madame Mere, the matriarch of the Bonaparte dynasty, died in Italy in 1836. That same year was his nephew, Louis-Napoleon's, ill-fated Strasbourg coup to overthrow the July Monarchy, which only led to many Bonapartists being arrested in France. Louis-Napoleon fled to the US and to New York where he attempted to visit his uncle but was refused. A few years later, Joseph's daughter Charlotte also died in Sardinia in 1839 probably in childbirth (from an affair) aged 36. That same year, his uncle Cardinal Fesch and his sister Caroline (Princess Murat) also died. Feeling alone and isolated in America, Joseph decided to return to Europe for the last time.

He boarded a liner, the *Philadelphia,* and docked in London in winter that year. Having returned to the British capital, the deflated Joseph rented a property in Cavendish Square a square which would later be associated with many famous British names such as the Dukes of Portland, Princess Amelia, Herbert Asquith, Quintin Hogg and even the fictional Jekyll and Hyde. Unfortunately, 1840 was not altogether an improvement on 1839 for Joseph. While still unable to return to France, King Louis-Philippe had negotiated with the British to have Napoleon's body returned to France, and he intended to lay on a lavish state funeral with much pomp and ceremony and a reburial in Paris. Despite offering to help fund the event, Joseph's request to be permitted to attend the reburial of his brother was denied. It was a political stunt for the king to acquire more support from Bonapartist and revolutionary factions; the presence of Joseph would cloud the message and be a potential political threat. That same year, Joseph's younger brother Lucien died, after which Joseph suffered a terrible stroke, partly paralysing the right side of his body. Now in ill health, he was permitted by the relevant authorities to travel first to a spa in Germany and then on to Florence where, after the long separation he was reunited with his wife Julie. He never fully recovered from the initial strokes and was beset by more. In 1844, he passed into a coma one evening and died the next morning surrounded by his wife and brothers Jerome and Louis. He was buried next to his daughter Charlotte in the basilica of Santa Croce in Florence. During the second empire, however, he too was brought back to Paris to be reburied in a state ceremony near to his brother Napoleon in Les Invalides. Joseph's nephew, Emperor Napoleon III, did not attend the ceremony – perhaps in repayment for not receiving him in New York and their various disagreements!

Though Joseph had been a king of Spain and of Naples, and was a Corsican Frenchman, he had spent the majority of his final years in both the US and the UK. He has often been looked on unfavourably by historians as inactive or ineffective, which may not be fair given the many situations he inherited. He was shrewd and clever but also quite unlucky. Had the timing of political changes been different he might well have been summoned from London to take a regnal position in Spain, Naples or even France. It was not to be.

Joseph, unlike his brothers, only had daughters. Both infantas of Spain and princesses of France. Each was to make a dynastic marriage that was to help the Bonaparte dynasty. These were not, however, with princes from other lands. Both daughters entered into arranged marriages with other Bonaparte princes – their first cousins. This was to strengthen future claims to the headship of the dynasty but also because Joseph was very rich and his daughters were due to receive a large inheritance. Why not keep that money in the family? Charlotte married Louis's son, Napoleon-Louis, in 1826. He had previously briefly been King Lodewijk II of Holland for nine days following his father's abdication in 1810. Napoleon-Louis died of measles in Italy aged 26. The couple had not yet had children. Charlotte, who spent several years at Point Breeze, painting and sketching the American countryside took lovers and died from complications related to pregnancy in Sardinia in 1839.

Charlotte's older sister, Zénaïde, married another first cousin, Charles, in Brussels earlier in 1822. This time it was the eldest son of her uncle Lucien. The couple soon joined Joseph in Philadelphia. Charles was an ornithologist and was well published on the subject in America. The couple briefly lived in London from 1826 where Charles became close to the zoologist John Edward Gray and the British Museum, before moving to Rome in 1828. Charles conducted research into bird species in Italy and Philadelphia and introduced a genus of American doves which he named Zenaida doves after his wife. Years later he was elected as a fellow of the American Antiquarian Society. Continuing his study of birds, Charles travelled to Britain to a meeting of the British Science Association, and travelled to Scotland to meet with the Scottish naturalist, Sir William Jardine 7th Baronet (an ancestor of the Olympian Sir Matthew Pinsent CBE). In 1840, after the death of his father, Charles succeeded to the papal titles of Prince of Canino and Musignano. Under the second empire and patronage of his cousin Napoleon III, Charles was made director of the Jardin des Plantes in Paris in 1854. In 1855, he became a foreign member of the Royal Swedish Academy of Sciences – although his wife being a cousin of the Swedish king may have been an advantage. Nevertheless, Charles's contribution to ornithology is internationally revered to this day.

The children of Charles and Zénaïde were simultaneously the heirs of both Joseph Bonaparte and Lucien Bonaparte. It was they who would inherit Joseph's estates, including Point Breeze, which they sold. The title of Prince of Canino and Musignano passed through three of their sons including the fourth prince who was a cardinal. The fifth prince's daughter, Princess Eugenie (1872–1949) married Léon Napoleon Ney 4th Prince of Moskowa – the great-grandson of one of Napoleon's most famous generals, Marshal Ney. Owing to a lack of sons, the title passed via male-preference primogeniture to a cousin, Prince Roland who was the sixth and last Prince of Canino (more on him later).

To this day, Joseph Bonaparte has many living descendants, both legitimate and illegitimate, on both sides of the Atlantic. Despite being the brother of 'Boney the Ogre' he was in his lifetime an honorary citizen of the US and welcome guest in Britain. Both countries were home to him at one point or another.

Chapter 5

Louis and Hortense: A Family Affair

There are rarely examples of a full or complete Bonaparte family tree simply because it is very difficult to draft one in a way that is not a little bit confusing. There are several reasons for this, but the chief among them is Louis and Hortense's marriage. (That said, we should not forget that the Bonapartes, though a relatively new dynasty, also fell prey to the royal habit of first cousins marrying each other.) Louis and Hortense were not made for each other. Their union was family politics; however, the couple and their offspring were, for a time, the future of the Bonaparte dynasty. It is their son, Napoleon III, who finally succeeded in restoring the family fortunes and the French Empire, although his remains rest in Hampshire to this day. Like many of the wider clan, Louis and Hortense spent some of their exile in England, albeit temporarily, but they have other more surprising connections to the isles of Britain.

Louis was the fourth surviving son of Carlo and Letizia Buonaparte and was born in Corsica in 1778. He, like others in the family, followed on the coat-tails of his elder brother's success or influence. With the help of Napoleon, he was able to gain an artillery commission and serve with Napoleon in both the Egyptian and Italian campaigns. Napoleon even managed to lobby to get Louis made a general at the grand age of 25 – a promotion that Louis felt he was most unworthy of, but his brother was doubtless pleased. There were now two Bonaparte brothers in politics (Joseph and Lucien), and two Bonaparte brothers who were generals. After the Italian campaign, Louis assisted his brothers in the coup d'état of 18 Brumaire in 1799, which brought Napoleon to power as first consul of France. Following the coup, the new first consul decided that it was time his younger brother Louis should marry. Napoleon selected as the bride, his own stepdaughter, Hortense de Beauharnais – Joséphine's daughter from her first marriage.

Neither was particularly interested in each other. Louis was pensive, prone to anger and rage, and sometimes depressive; Hortense on the

65

Family Tree

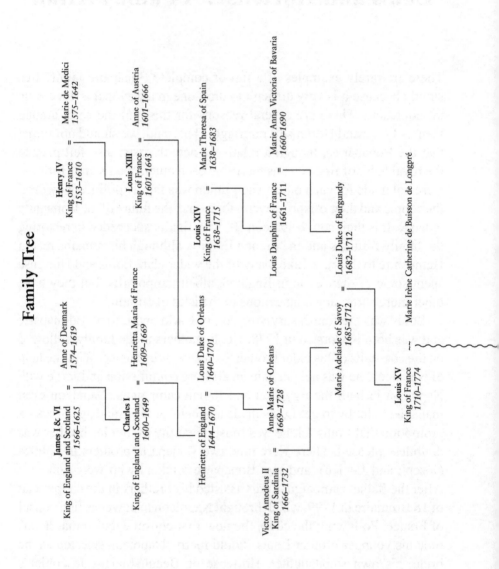

James I & VI
King of England and Scotland
1566–1625

=

Anne of Denmark
1574–1619

Henry IV
King of France
1553–1610

=

Marie de Medici
1575–1642

Charles I
King of England and Scotland
1600–1649

=

Henrietta Maria of France
1609–1669

Louis XIII
King of France
1601–1643

=

Anne of Austria
1601–1666

Henriette of England
1644–1670

=

Louis Duke of Orleans
1640–1701

Louis XIV
King of France
1638–1715

=

Marie Theresa of Spain
1638–1683

Victor Amedeus II
King of Sardinia
1666–1732

=

Anne Marie of Orleans
1669–1728

Louis Dauphin of France
1661–1711

=

Marie Anna Victoria of Bavaria
1660–1690

Marie Adelaide of Savoy
1685–1712

=

Louis Duke of Burgundy
1682–1712

Louis XV
King of France
1710–1774

~

Marie Irène Catherine de Buisson de Longpré

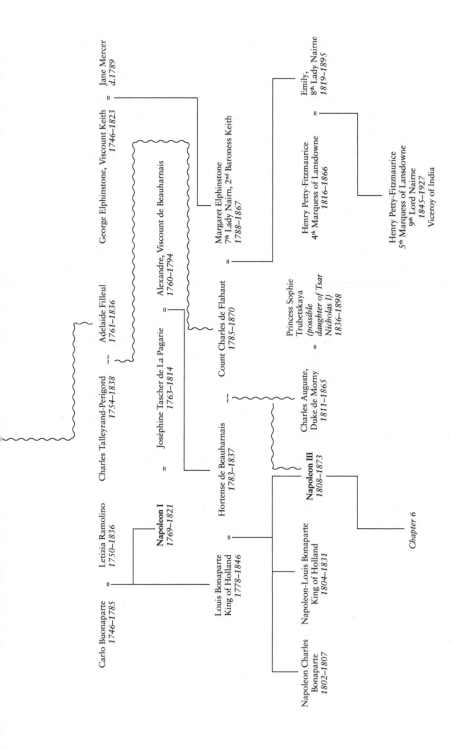

This family tree shows two possible fathers of Napoleon III, though it is still widely accepted/assumed that his father was Louis.

other hand was more vivacious, charming and outgoing. She strongly objected to the match and appealed to her mother but was persuaded by Joséphine that it was in the best interests of the family – though arguably her own. Napoleon had been (legally) married to Joséphine for six years and no issue had come from their union. Napoleon, at this time, falsely assumed that neither of them was capable of siring children – a problem if he wished to found a dynasty. The solution was to marry a Bonaparte to another de Beauharnais, or, better still, his own brother to the daughter of his wife. In reality, it was Joséphine who could not have children, mostly due to her age. The marriage would certainly help secure Joséphine's position as Napoleon's wife for the time being. Louis and Hortense were married in 1802. A few years later, after Napoleon had become the emperor in 1804, he named as his heirs and successors the sons of his brother and stepdaughter – who would have his blood and the blood of Joséphine.

Hortense was the daughter of General Alexandre, Vicomte de Beauharnais and Marie-Josèphe-Rose Tascher de La Pagerie (Joséphine). As we have seen, Joséphine was born in the Caribbean in Martinique, or possibly in St Lucia. By location of birth, she might narrowly have been British, though legally speaking, more likely French. Alexandre had come face to face with the British in America. He fought in the American Revolutionary War as part of the French army. He later became a general during the French Revolutionary Wars; however, he did not wholly support the Revolution. He was arrested during the Reign of Terror and guillotined in 1794 aged just 34 alongside his own cousin in the Place de La Concorde. They were buried in a mass grave. Joséphine was also imprisoned for a time but was released days after Alexandre's execution, mostly due to the fall of Maximilien Robespierre. The Viscount and Viscountess de Beauharnais had had a frosty marriage; it too had been arranged, though this time for financial reasons. Both eventually took lovers. During the Revolution, Alexandre had become the lover of a German princess resident in Paris, Amalie of Salm-Kyrburg, who was also unhappily married. Curiously, Amalie's great-grandfather was Thomas Bruce, 3rd Earl of Elgin. A Scottish aristocrat and descendant of King Robert the Bruce, he lived a life of exile in Brussels for forty years to avoid being arrested for treason in Britain for supporting the Jacobite cause. Amalie and Alexandre's affair was quite literally cut short by the Revolution. On the other hand, Joséphine continued to have a series of lovers right up to, and initially during, the time she met Napoleon – mostly as a way to survive through the perilous political times. Because of this, some of the other Bonapartes regarded the Beauharnais as scandalous, money grabbing and beneath them; hardly ideal foundations on which to build a marriage.

In time, however, Louis and Hortense were able to produce three sons: Napoleon Charles Bonaparte (1804–1807), Napoleon-Louis Bonaparte (1804–1831) and Charles Louis-Napoleon Bonaparte (1808–1873) – the future Napoleon III. Three heirs for the emperor – although they awkwardly became surplus to requirements once Napoleon had left Joséphine, married Marie-Louise and produced his own son in 1811. As part of his empire-building, Napoleon made his brother king of Holland in 1805. The emperor's plan was that the new kingdom would be a vassal state to France; a junior, subordinate partner, with a Bonaparte ceremonially at the head. In reality, Louis was able to assert his own independence once far enough away from his brother. He was generally liked in Holland and some of his reforms were popular; however, under his governance, the country looked to be growing in independence and he personally disagreed with the emperor on political matters. Louis began to choose his own ministers (instead of the ones provided by his brother) and insisted that Dutch should be the official language spoken not French. He announced that he himself was Dutch not French and adopted the name Lodewijk. This was not in Napoleon's plans for the Low Countries. The main purpose for having Louis as king was so that Napoleon did not have to annex the territory, and that King Louis would muster a large army to protect the northern coast from the British, who hoped to open a new northern front in the Netherlands. Conscription was unpopular and Louis refused to institute it, much to his brother's annoyance. It was difficult to enlarge the Dutch army due to a frequent shortage of recruits. Any rumours or suggestions of conscription being introduced led to rioting. The economy of Holland also suffered under France because of the ban on any trade with Britain – many merchants resorted to illegal smuggling, however.

In July 1809, the British, under General John Pitt, 2nd Earl of Chatham (son of Prime Minister William Pitt the Elder), launched a disastrous raid on Walcheren, a former island in the Dutch province of Zeeland, where they hoped to open another front against the French which would assist their Austrian allies to the east. The British hoped to clear the road to Antwerp and capture it. In the event, however, the Austrians had already been defeated at the battle of Wagram just weeks earlier, and were now seeking a peace with Napoleon. The French had reinforced their position in the Low Countries with a large garrison at Antwerp. Although the British captured Flushing, Antwerp, with its large French force commanded by Marshal Bernadotte, seemed a bridge too far. Despite spending millions on the expedition, and with thousands dead (many from disease), the British had to withdraw. It was a military and political embarrassment for many involved.

To add insult to injury, we also have the pluckiness of the French, Louis, and Bernadotte for the introduction of a weed into Britain. The retreating British, after Walcheren, packed mattresses for sick soldiers with local hay – as was usual at that time. However, this hay contained seeds of a local weed, *Lepidium draba*, Hoary Cress, and it was shipped, along with the soldiers, back to southern England. At some point the hay was recycled and ploughed by a farmer on the Isle of Thanet (also a former island) and within a few decades the plant and its little white flowers could be found in abundance in areas around port towns. Thanet cress as it is now known, is found throughout the UK today particularly in the South-East – a little reminder of how the British failed to topple King Louis Bonaparte's Holland.

There was no glory for Louis, however. After Walcheren, Napoleon lost confidence in his would-be independent brother. He began to annex Holland with an invading French army effectively deposing his own brother. In 1810, Louis abdicated as king in favour of his 5-year-old son Napoleon-Louis (Lodewijk II), who, like Lady Jane Grey, reigned for only nine days before he too had to abdicate – when his uncle Napoleon had seized control of the country. Louis's wife, Queen Hortense, very briefly reigned as regent of Holland. Later, after the Napoleonic Wars, Napoleon's creation of the short-lived kingdom of Holland was the pretext for the House of Orange, the premier family in the area, elevating themselves to the kings of the Netherlands rather than stadholders of the Dutch Republic and Princes of Orange. It is from this same family that England has had its only Dutch monarch, William III (of Orange) in 1689.

The now ex-king Louis retreated initially to his home in Saint-Leu. Though no longer a king, he had at least briefly been one. He still held the title of Constable of France, a far older title than the newly invented (and short-lived) king of Holland. Constable of France was an ancient medieval military position, the most important officer in the Valois and Bourbon monarchies, but briefly hijacked by Napoleon who bestowed it on Louis. In Britain, however, the title is more commonly associated with the victorious Battle of Agincourt 1415, where the Constable of France, Charles d'Albret was slain on the field – as depicted in Shakespeare's *Henry V*. For Louis, however, the position was purely ceremonial, though he decided to put some distance between himself and his overbearing brother.

He was permitted to move to Austria, ruled by Napoleon's now father-in-law, Emperor Francis. Louis took to writing and by now was estranged from Hortense as the two could not abide each other's company, and she, of course, had her lovers. During the steady collapse of the first empire following the Russian campaign, Louis did offer his brother his services as a mediator between France and Austria, but Napoleon was not interested. With French withdrawal and itself under threat from invasion, the Low Countries were once again independent. There were genuine proposals for Louis to be recalled as king – a testament to his popularity. The decision was made, however, to install Prince William of Orange as king of the Netherlands in December 1813. Louis retired to Rome where many other family members were. Perhaps wisely, he did not rejoin his brother for the sequel that was the Hundred Days from Elba to Waterloo. He was committed to his writing, eventually publishing a history of the kingdom of Holland. Years later he was even granted permission by the new ruling House of Orange to be allowed to revisit Holland. He was met with cheering crowds, and it was heartening to see that he was remembered with affection; to this day, among the lists of Dutch rulers, he is known as Louis the Good.

By now, of course, Louis and Hortense had been estranged for some years, and it is on that matter that historians, biographers, and general opinions have been concerned. The debate centres around dates. By 1807, despite having two sons, the king and queen of Holland were separated. Hortense very probably had gentlemen callers. The jealous and prone-to-rage Louis pressurised Hortense into a reunion in Toulouse. However, just over eight months later, she gave birth to a third son. Eight months, not nine, and little report of a premature birth. If (for it is still just an if), the child was not Louis's, then whose? Of this list of Hortense's 'friends', one name stands far taller than the rest: Charles de Flahaut.

Born in Paris in 1785, Charles was a tall, handsome and rather dashing ADC in Napoleon's forces. During his career he was ADC to Marshal Bertier, Murat and Napoleon himself. It is difficult to say exactly when and where his affair with Hortense began. Even though his regiment was at the key time (of conception) in Germany, they had certainly been secretly communicating by letter that year, and he may well have obtained some leave to visit France. However, the boy was recognised by Louis and named Charles Louis-Napoleon Bonaparte. That said, the Flahaut affair continued and indeed blossomed after this birth. In 1811, Hortense gave birth to another son, Auguste de Morny, in relative secrecy. The child was registered as the son of a couple who were friends of the Beauharnais family; however, in later years the truth was known by all and Auguste was accepted as the natural born son of Hortense and Flahaut. These two surviving sons of Hortense, grew to look rather similar, indeed near to identical in some portraits and photographs, which does fuel the fires of debate over true paternity – especially because the elder (Charles Louis-Napoleon) became Napoleon III and emperor of the French. Auguste later served his half (or full) brother during the second empire.

What has this to do with Britain? One might well ask. It is Flahaut. Flahaut's fascinating background, career and private life seem entangled with Britain, and make for a fascinating yet surprising story – especially as he may (or may not) be the real father of the future French emperor. There are a lot of 'ifs' to this tale.

Flahaut was born to Marie-Adelaide de Filleul and Field Marshal Charles-François, Comte de Flahaut de Billaderie. The couple were 18 and 53 respectively when they met. They were married in 1779; their son, however, was widely known and accepted to be the illegitimate son of Talleyrand, one of Napoleon's chief ministers. To this day, most accept that Talleyrand was the father of Charles; he took a special interest in his son's career. That said, Marie-Adelaide also is rumoured to have had an affair with British politician William Windham, Secretary of War, an early supporter of the French Revolution, and a kinsman of the Wyndham Earls of Egremont (of Petworth). He does remain, however, a most unlikely candidate. Nevertheless, IF he was the father of Charles, and IF Charles was the true father of Napoleon III, it would mean that the last emperor of the French was in fact English (or at least a quarter!).

Wild theories aside, Talleyrand and Adelaide's affair continued from around 1783 to 1792, so it is safe to assume he is the father of Charles. Marie's own background was even more salacious. A successful novelist in her own time, her family history might be worthy of a novel or two. After her affair with Talleyrand and the death of her elderly husband, she married in 1802, the Portuguese ambassador to France, José de Souza. Marie's mother was Irène du Buisson de Longpré, a minor noblewoman who was a one-time member of the harem or private brothel of King Louis XV, a house which he kept in the grounds of Versailles, Parc-aux-Cerfs. Many of Louis XV's famous mistresses, such as Madame du Barry, were regulars there. Like many royal mistresses at that time, Irène was hastily married off, for appearance's sake – in her case to a middle-class Norman wine merchant, Charles Filleul. She had two daughters, including Adelaide. They are unlikely to be the daughters of her husband, and therefore there is a strong case to say that they are royal bastards, particularly as it is thought that the king continued the dalliance long after the marriage and Adelaide's sister, Françoise, laid claim to that fact.

So, perhaps the Bourbons got their revenge on Napoleon after all, for if Napoleon III's real father was Flahaut, and he in turn was the grandson of Louis XV, it would mean that the last emperor of the French was not a Bonaparte, but far more a Bourbon! Again, though, those are some large assumptions – but not altogether without evidence.

Continuing on the royal theme, Louis XV was, of course, the great-grandson of his predecessor, Louis XIV. His father and grandfather all died before they could succeed to the throne. The Bourbons had been the ruling family of France since they had taken over from their Valois cousins in 1589, who in turn had picked up from the main Capetian line in 1328 – an event which helped trigger the Hundred Years War with England. They were the cadet branches of the House of Capet which traces its royal origins back to Hugh Capet, king of the Franks from 987. Royal dynasties often marry other royal dynasties. Such was the case with the houses of Bourbon and Stuart in the seventeenth century. The fateful King Charles I of England (and Scotland) arranged for a marriage between his daughter Princess Henrietta and the younger brother of Louis XIV, Philippe Duke of Orleans. Through her mother, they were cousins. Thanks to further good old-fashioned cousin-marrying over the next few generations, Princess Henrietta's great-grandson was also

King Louis XV – making him and subsequent Bourbon kings of France descendants of the English royal dynasties of Stuart, Tudor, Plantagenet et al. So, as Shakespeare would say of French and English royal lines, ''tis clear as the summer sun'!

On an unrelated note, albeit an interesting one: perhaps the unfortunate King Louis XVI, while on the guillotine scaffold in Paris in 1792, waiting for the final chop, spared a few thoughts for his great-great-great-great-grandfather, King Charles I of England. He too lost his head in in a similar manner in London in 1649.

With all this in mind, there is potential irony and an inevitable sentence involving the of the word 'if'. IF Napoleon III was not the son of Louis Bonaparte but the son of Flahaut, and IF Flahaut's mother, the mistress of Talleyrand, was a product of a royal affair with Louis XV, then the last emperor of the French was not only descended from one of Napoleon's most treacherous advisers, but French Bourbon royalty and British royalty as well.

Admittedly, these grand theories have been conjecture based on light evidence such as dates around conception, and the fact that Napoleon III looked so much like his illegitimate half-brother. The question of Napoleon III's paternity was used as a weapon against him during his lifetime, though often coming from family rivals in the Bonaparte clan and political enemies. As his whole claim to the headship of the dynasty rested on him being a Bonaparte, he obviously avoided or suppressed such rumour, although once president and then emperor, the gossip became fairly superfluous. It is true that the young would-be emperor had a difficult and initially distant relationship with his father, always seeking approval from a usually over-dismissive Louis. On the other hand, this was merely in Louis's nature and he took an interest in the boy's education as well as continuing to acknowledge him as his heir (without any fuss) after his second son, Louis-Napoleon (Lodewijk II), predeceased him, dying from measles in 1831 aged just 26.

Meanwhile, Hortense's other son, Auguste de Morny, grew into a handsome chap, greatly resembling his half-brother, the future Emperor Napoleon III. Having briefly served as a young man in the French army in Algeria, Auguste returned to Paris to become a successful businessman. As a wealthy and influential businessman, he was particularly useful in the coup of 1851, in which his brother the prince-president became the emperor. Auguste was duly created the Duke de Morny, which recognised his close relation to the emperor, albeit on the wrong side of the blanket. He had a curious social position. He was wealthy, but the illegitimate son of a queen, the illegitimate half-brother of the emperor, an illegitimate descendant of Louis XV and a half-brother and uncle to British aristocracy. Quite a collection of connections. Not your average aristocrat or royal, and, arguably, he was neither. Like the Bonapartes, the Beauharnais', and the Flahauts, Auguste had mistresses, but, while serving as French special envoy to St Petersburg in 1857, he married Princess Sophie Trubetskoy (Trubetskaya). Sophie might well have been made for Auguste. Although she was daughter of an ancient, noble Russian Lithuanian family, her mother (a member of the Pushkin family) was a known lover of Tsar Nicholas I. Rumours persisted throughout her life that Sophie was his child. Her legal parents had no other children and were often apart. Completing this royal circle, Auguste's cousin, Maximilian de Beauharnais, was married to the Tsar's daughter, Maria. The newlywed Auguste and Sophie were children of passion and scandal, therefore arguably well suited. Simultaneously, they were royal and non-royal.

During the second empire, Auguste became a strong advocate of thoroughbred horseracing, both in England and in France. Inspired by such racecourses as Newmarket, Ascot, Goodwood and others, Auguste founded the racecourse at Deauville in Normandy in the 1860s, where the Prix Morny (a flat race named after him) is still held. He even purchased the English Triple Crown winner, West Australian, for breeding, and many subsequent famous thoroughbred British, French and US racehorses are from his bloodline. The Duke de Morny died soon after the founding of Deauville. Though he was understood to be the emperor's half-brother, their more-than-passing similarity in appearance sometimes led to onlookers wondering if the two were somehow related more closely – perhaps even full brothers.

In recent years, French scientists (Lucotte, Macéand and Hrechdakian) were able to study Y-DNA from the Bonaparte family. They published their findings in 2013. As we have seen in this study, using known living descendants' DNA, they were able to prove that Alexandre Walewski was indeed Napoleon I's illegitimate son. However, when it came to testing Napoleon III's DNA, the challenge was more complex. Allegedly, a hair belonging to the last emperor was compared with that of one of his presumed illegitimate descendants (in the male line) by a mistress (Eleanor Vereot), Jean-Marc Banquet d'Orx (the Count d'Orx). This DNA comparison confirmed that the d'Orx counts were patrilineally descended from Napoleon III, but the test also confirmed that Napoleon III belonged to a different DNA haplogroup from Napoleon I – suggesting that he was not descended from the Bonapartes in the male line. If this is true, then it is ground breaking and certainly would shake up many accepted truths in European royal history. A more official investigation is certainly warranted, although the French government might have objections and the Catholic monks who guard the tomb of Napoleon III in Hampshire might oppose any desecration. Whatever one's opinion, one can certainly say that there is reasonable doubt concerning the paternity of the last emperor of the French.

Hortense's affair with Flahaut continued for a time. Charles did have other liaisons, most notably with Caroline Murat (possibly) and with Anna Potocka, another member of the Poniatowski family, but he was ever dutifully in attendance on the ex-queen of Holland where possible. Flahaut served in the Russian campaign; he was later promoted to general and became ADC to Napoleon. Upon Napoleon's return for the Hundred Days Campaign, Flahaut was again appointed ADC to the emperor and was present at the Battle of Waterloo. In the aftermath of that disaster, he was only spared arrest and exile thanks to the interventions of his father Talleyrand, who by now had turned his loyalties to the Bourbon Louis XVIII. Regardless, Flahaut decided to travel to Britain, perhaps wisely some distance between him and any possible Bourbon reprisals. The dashing young officer and count must have been an exotic proposition to the ladies. While in Scotland in July 1817, he married into British aristocracy. He wed Margaret Mercer Elphinstone, daughter of Admiral Lord Keith – the same man who had informed Napoleon of his grizzly fate on the *Bellerophon* in Plymouth after the emperor's capture in 1815.

George Keith Elphinstone, later Viscount Keith, was a celebrated senior British admiral who, years before confronting Napoleon on *Bellerophon* in 1815, had served in the British fleet for many years and in many actions, including during the brief occupation of Toulon in 1793. He may well have even fired a shot at Napoleon there too, albeit at great distance. Keith belonged to an ancient Scottish family. Having had no sons, his daughter Margaret inherited his lesser titles of Baron Keith (in both the British and Irish peerages) on his death in 1823. The wedding between Margaret and Charles must have had a share of awkwardness – the groom having been at Napoleon's side at Waterloo, and the father of the bride being the man who sent Napoleon into captivity and exile. One can imagine the wedding breakfast speeches!

Not long after Keith's death, the Flahauts were able to return to Paris. Charles, with the support of his father, Talleyrand, was able to join the diplomatic service of King Louis-Philippe, holding a short appointment as ambassador to Berlin. However, following the coup of 1851, Napoleon III was keen to draw all the old Bonaparte supporters and retainers to him. When the emperor looked for a new ambassador to London, Charles, with his British connections and family, seemed an excellent fit. (The fact that Flahaut was the emperor's mother's ex-lover was obviously no obstacle.) He was appointed French ambassador to the Court of St James in 1860 – a role which his father had filled for Louis-Philippe. One wonders if he visited the Travellers Club in Pall Mall to inspect the handrail they had had specially installed for his father's famous limp.

Charles and Margaret had five daughters, meaning Margaret's title of Baroness Keith in her own right would die with her. Their girls, all half-French and half-Scottish, and from two famous (or infamous) families, had great potential on the marriage markets. The Flahaut family were noted society members on both sides of the Channel. The eldest, Emily, married in 1843 at the British Embassy in Vienna, Henry Petty-FitzMaurice, soon to become the 4th Marquess of Lansdowne. Years later, Emily de Flahaut, now Marchioness of Lansdowne, was recognised by the House of Lords as Lady Nairne – a Scottish peerage which she had inherited from a cousin of her mother. More worthy of note is the fact that Emily's son, Henry, the 5th Marquess, Charles's grandson, had a particularly successful career and was appointed Governor General of Canada in 1883 and Viceroy of India in 1888. Henry was particularly wealthy. His former London house, Lansdowne House, now partly occupied by the Lansdowne Club, still has some of the decorative railings ornamented by crowned letter Ls. Though this is, of course, a reference to Lansdowne, it may as well be a stronger reference to his possible ancestor (through Flahaut), Louis XIV, who adorned Versailles with similar motifs.

Depending on one's opinion of Napoleon III's paternity, and the DNA investigations, it is intriguing to think that a possible great-nephew of the emperor of the French briefly became the ruler of India and indeed Canada, a former French territory. Indeed, photographs of the young 5th Marquess certainly show remarkable similarity both to his uncle, the Duke de Morny, and to Napoleon III – or perhaps it's just the moustache! The descendants of Flahaut to this day include English, Irish and Scottish nobility.

But what of poor old Louis Bonaparte? By now, given the Bonapartes' propensity for extra-marital dalliances, it will no doubt be unsurprising to learn that Louis reportedly had his own illegitimate issue, some of the descendants of whom are British. Louis did indeed visit Britain in his lifetime. On one occasion this was to attend a family meeting of the remaining Bonaparte brothers following the death of Napoleon's own legitimate son, Napoleon II, in Vienna in 1832.

Louis is credited with a brief affair during his exile years. The ex-king of Holland sired a son with Jeanne-Félicité Roland in 1826 in Rome. Their son Louis-Gaspard François Castel, known as the Count de Castelvecchio, like many Bonapartes made a life for himself in Italy – Florence. He had three daughters, the youngest of whom he named Joséphine – probably in honour of his famous aunt, the Empress Joséphine. Joséphine de Castelvecchio (1857–1932), Louis's granddaughter, married several times and lived in London, eventually moving to New York. Her daughter, Elisina, married famous publisher Grant Richards in London in 1898. As a young man, Richards had set up The World's Classics Series, and published such authors as George Bernard Shaw and James Joyce. Elisina had four children with Grant before their divorce in 1914. They have descendants alive today. Her second marriage was later that year in London but this time to a curiously named American, Royall Tyler. Their son William R. Tyler had a successful career as a US diplomat. Having served as Under Secretary of State for European Affairs under John F. Kennedy, in a rather pleasant twist of fate, Lindon B. Johnson appointed Tyler as US ambassador to the Netherlands in 1965. As descendant of the first king of Holland, this must have been very pleasing to all. Tyler married a British woman and their descendants continue to live in the US.

Allegedly, Louis had a final adventure. In 1838, he may have married an Italian girl, Julia Livia di Strozzi. By this time, he was a man of 60, she was merely 16! It is not clear if the wedding actually took place or not, and Julia in fact died only a year later aged 17. There was to be no long-term romance or young wife to nurse him through old age. Once again, given the promiscuity and reputation of the Bonaparte family back then, it difficult to doubt this story.

After the death of his eldest brother Joseph in 1844, Louis was for a time the official heir to the empire in the eyes of most Bonapartists. However, unlike his son, Louis did not really do much to act on this circumstance. His son and heir, Prince Louis-Napoleon, was at that time being held prisoner in Ham Prison by the Somme, for attempting to seize power in France. The future emperor escaped from prison, making his way to England in May 1846. Just a month later, Louis Bonaparte died at home in Tuscany. Just over two years later his son would return to France having been elected France's first president – mostly thanks to having the name Bonaparte.

Of the five Bonaparte brothers, Louis was not the most successful nor the happiest during his life. He had an unwanted bride thrust upon him, and the moment he was given some autonomy by his brother, the emperor, it was effectively taken away because he was becoming too independent. That said, Louis had been a king, was the father of the future Napoleon III, and, like so many of his relatives, has British descendants.

Chapter 6

Napoleon III: A French Emperor. An English Gentleman

The first president of France and last emperor of the French, Napoleon III was a politician, innovator, moderniser, and, chiefly, a charmer. He was also perhaps the most pro-British French monarch there has ever been. He and his immediate family led roller coaster lives, marked with splendour and tragedy, but perhaps most surprising is their connection to France's oldest adversary – Great Britain. Napoleon III stayed in the UK on several occasions. He lived there, plotted there, fell in love there, fought a duel there, represented his empire there, died there, and is buried there. He is one of the most fascinating French rulers most of us know very little about.

Napoleon III's rise to the throne was by no means assured. In fact, for decades that seemed rather unlikely. Born Charles Louis-Napoleon Bonaparte in 1808, the third (and eventually only surviving) son of Louis Bonaparte, the younger brother of Napoleon I, and Hortense, the stepdaughter of Napoleon I and daughter of the Empress Joséphine by her first marriage. Louis Bonaparte and Hortense had been made king and queen of Holland in 1806 (to 1810). Their marriage had been proposed by Joséphine in order to produce an heir for the emperor – as Joséphine was by this time unable to bear children. Louis and Hortense's children were considered Napoleon's heirs until Napoleon, having divorced Joséphine, married Marie-Louise of Austria and sired a son, Napoleon François Joseph Charles Bonaparte Duke of Reichstadt (1811–1832) – who briefly became Napoleon II. Louis and Hortense's marriage had been arranged and was rather loveless. They were estranged for much of their marriage. Hortense took lovers, and there were rumours of Louis's homosexuality. Political opposition to Napoleon III's rule used these facts and rumours against him later, calling into question his paternity.

After the Battle of Waterloo and the Bourbon restoration, all members of the Bonaparte family were forced into exile all over Europe, and even to the US. Napoleon III (by now known as Louis-Napoleon) and his mother eventually moved to Arnenberg in Switzerland. He grew up speaking French with a noticeable German accent. Later moving to Rome, and now a young man, *Louis-Napoleon* with his older brother *Napoleon-Louis*, became involved in revolutionary Italian politics. While on the run from both the police and the Austrian army, the elder brother died of measles in 1831. Louis-Napoleon now became the third most senior heir to Bonaparte dynasty behind his uncle Joseph Bonaparte (eldest brother of Napoleon I and former king of Spain, living in exile in the US) and his cousin, Napoleon II (son of Napoleon I and former king of Rome, now the Duke of Reichstadt, who was living in noble captivity in Austria – closely watched by his suspicious Habsburg relatives).

Hortense and the now unwell Louis-Napoleon fled to Britain. This would take them through France, putting them in defiance of the edict of 1816 forbidding the Bonaparte family from re-entering the country. They did so, however, on a British passport Hortense had charmed out of the British minister in Florence, and sought permission to stay in Paris from the new Bourbon king, Louis-Philippe – a friend of Queen Victoria's father. He initially granted them permission provided they remained incognito. However, word spread of a Bonaparte being in Paris, and eager crowds formed outside their hotel in the Place Vendôme. Despite young Louis-Napoleon's ill health, and, seeing the crowd as a threat to the stability of his regime, the king ordered mother and son out of France. Their departure was delayed long enough for the future Napoleon III to hear the crowds cry 'Vive Napoleon'. They then travelled hastily to England.

After a stormy crossing and arriving in London in the summer of 1831, the relatives of old 'Boney' went relatively unnoticed by the people. The population was in the midst of a general election and a new king – William IV. Hortense was disappointed at their reception and blamed the now-tattered coach which had come thousands of miles since Arnenberg. Initially, their acquaintances were few and they made do in hotels in Regent's Park and St James (such as Fenton's); however, Hortense soon became a social sensation amongst leading London families. Meanwhile, Louis-Napoleon occupied himself in education and seeing the sights, such as the Tower of London and even being given

Family Tree

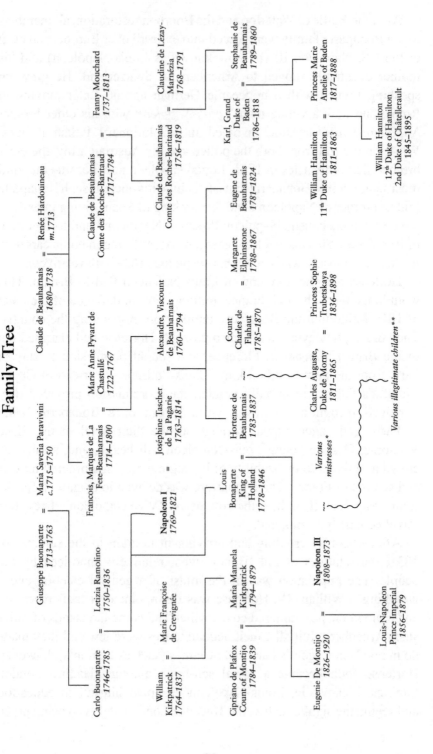

**Incomplete list of illegitimate children of Napoleon III, known, likely and supposed:

1839 – Bonaventur Karrer – by Maria Anna Schiess
c.1840s – John Henry Edward Joseph Harris
1842 – Martin Hariet (Bonaparte)– by Elizabeth Ann Haryett
1843 – Alexandre Louis Eugene Bure, Count d'Orx – by Eleanore Vergeot
1843 – Charles Jean Tristan de Montholon – by Caroline O'Hara
1845 – Louis Ernest Alexandre Bure, Count de Labenne – by Eleanore Vergeot
c.1860s – Benoni Depuille – by Armance Depuille
1862 – Georges Feydeau – by Léocadia Bogaslawa Zelewska, Madame Feydeau
1862 – Arthur Hugenschmidt – by Elizabeth Hugenschmidt
1864 – Charles Leboeuf – by Marguerite Bellanger
1865 – Jules Hadot – possibly by Valentine Haussmann

*Incomplete list of known and supposed mistresses and 'acquaintances' of Napoleon III:

Marguerite Bellanger 1838–1888
Princess Mathilde Bonaparte 1820–1904 – probably platonic
Eleanore Marie Brault, Lady Archer 1808–1849
Augustine Brohan 1824–1893
Marie Countess De Guyon b.c.1820
Valtess de la Bigne 1848–1910
Clothilde de la Rochelambert, Countess de La Bedoyere, later Princess de la Moskowa 1829–1884
Marie-Clotilde-Elisabeth Louise de Riquet Countess de Marcy-Argenteau 1837–1890 – probably platonic
Armance Depuille 1830–1913
Mathilde-Pauline-Gabrielle Elluin b.1849
Elizabeth Rachel Felix 1821–1858
Caroline Frédérique Bernardine Hamaekers 1836–1912
Elizabeth Ann Haryett aka Harriet Howard, Countess de Beauregard 1823–1865
Valentine Haussmann 1843–1901
Elizabeth Hugenschmidt 1825–1915
Maria Kalergis 1822–1874
Egle Ney de la Moskowa, Duchess de Persigny 1832–1890
Caroline Jane O'Hara 1801–1886
Virginia Oldoïni, Countess of Castiglione 1837–1899
Alice Ozy 1820–1893
Marie-Ann Poniatowska, Duchess Colonna-Walewski 1823–1912
Barbara Rimsky-Korsakova 1833–1878
Emily Rowles Marchioness di Cavelli
Maria Anna Schiess 1812–1880
Eleanor Alexandrine Vergeot 1820–1886
Léocadia Bogaslawa Zelewska, Madame Feydeau 1838–1924

a tour of the tunnels being constructed under the Thames by Isambard Kingdom Brunel himself.

Despite being the other side of the Channel, Louis-Napoleon was a continual worry to the French administration, and he dabbled in conspiratorial politics. This was not helped by the fact that the French ambassador to England, Talleyrand, was the natural father of the Comte de Flahaut, who was known to have been Hortense's lover and by whom she had a child. (Talleyrand's son, Flahaut, however, went on to marry the daughter of a British admiral and his grandson succeeded as the 5th Marquess of Lansdowne.) There was speculation that the Bonapartes had designs on the throne of Belgium, but though a family of plotters they were no match for the Coburg family. When Queen Victoria's uncle, Leopold, prepared to leave London to take up his role as the newly elected king of the Belgians, he is rumoured to have remarked that Hortense could travel back to Switzerland through Belgium if she wished, so long as she did not take his kingdom with her. With the stress of rumours and conspiracies surrounding her son, Hortense sought to move them away from the politics of London to the restorative waters of Tunbridge Wells in Kent. The future emperor socialised with the English gentry, and, while in Kent, he began to discover other evening activities – and may have fallen in love too – once or twice. A certain Miss Geffrey is recorded, as well as the Rowles family of Camden Place, Chislehurst – where he would one day return.

Mother and son journeyed back to Arnenberg via Boulogne where Hortense had witnessed the French forces preparing for the unsuccessful invasion of England in back 1805. They also visited the tomb of her mother, Empress Joséphine. After returning to Arnenberg, news came of the death of Napoleon II (alias the king of Rome, or the Duke of Reichstadt) aged just 22. As the three young boys ahead of him in the succession were now dead, Louis-Napoleon might well have felt the hand of destiny reaching for him. However, for now, the head of the Bonapartes was his uncle Joseph who decided to travel from his home, Bordentown, New Jersey, to London to hold a conference of the senior Bonapartes (brothers and nephews of Napoleon I). It is strange to think that less than twenty years after Waterloo, London was the backdrop to such a meeting. The young Louis-Napoleon, frustrated at his uncles' compromising and lack of planning or flair, eventually left and returned to Switzerland.

He enrolled in the Swiss army and trained to become an officer. During that time, he published works on political philosophy as well as artillery, despite being only in his mid-twenties. Inspired by his uncle's popular return to France from exile decades earlier, Louis-Napoleon planned a similar re-entry into France that would inspire the common people to rise up in support and hopefully topple the regime: the July Monarchy, headed by King Louis-Philippe. This was, however, a young man's fantasy. While staging the coup in Strasbourg in 1836, he managed to win over the loyalty of a small regiment but did not have the mass of growing popular support his uncle had had on his return in 1815. The Bonapartist forces were quickly surrounded by regiments loyal to the July Monarchy. Louis-Napoleon's grand adventure failed at its very first hurdle and once again his mother pleaded for generosity from King Louis-Philippe, who, not wanting to cause a national or international scene, forgave the conspirators and the young Bonaparte – provided he go to America. The king even gifted him money to go.

Prince Napoleon's time in New York was marked by social rounds, theatre, visiting other Bonaparte exiles and a visit to Niagara Falls. This pleasant exile was cut short by news of his mother Hortense's failing health. Having caught the earliest ship back to London, he desperately needed funds and help in obtaining a passport that would allow him to cross to France and then on to Switzerland. The French government leant on the British to make sure no help was given to Napoleon. Uncle Joseph ignored his nephew and retreated to his home of Brettenham Hall, near Lavenham in Suffolk. Napoleon decided to take action. From his hotel in St James, he took a train to Richmond, openly and with all his luggage. However, with a US passport on his person, he about-turned in the direction of London and caught an omnibus, incognito, to the Thames and boarded a Dutch steamer. The police informed the French embassy that they had 'lost touch' with the prince. Napoleon made it back to Arnenberg and was with his mother at the end.

By 1838, his presence in Switzerland became politically flammable. Napoleon, now a rich man thanks to his inheritance, travelled again to London, renting houses at 17 Carlton House Terrace and 1 Carlton Gardens, and populated them with friends who had attended on the late emperor in St Helena years before. He wore clothes from Savile Row, hired top chefs and adorned carriages and other items with imperial eagles. He was now something of a glamourous celebrity, and a living link to the recent past for British high society – who had always been fascinated by the glamour of old 'Boney'. Napoleon observed the 'British season', even wintering in Leamington Spa. He was associating with the cream of society – he even took Mr and Mrs Disraeli for a boat row, ran it aground, and nearly capsized it! The Duke of Wellington, the nemesis of Napoleon III's uncle, who was still a huge figure British life remarked: 'would you believe it, this young man will not have it said that he is not going to be emperor of the French.'

On his travels through England, this young Bonaparte is reported to have stayed for a time at Southport in Merseyside, in lodgings near Lord Street. To this day, the town claims that it was his admiration of the beautifully laid out shopping promenade, Lord Street, that inspired Napoleon III to instruct Haussmann to create the beautiful tree-lined boulevards of Paris we recognise today. A fairly large claim, and one which the town's civic society has put in writing on a plaque on Lord Street 'Boulevard'.

Soon Prince Napoleon visited Scotland. He stayed at Brodick Castle on the Isle of Arran, a home of the Dukes of Hamilton. (Napoleon's cousin on his mother's side, Mary, had married the 11th Duke.) Napoleon joined in hunts and shoots, though he preferred good conversation. While in Ayrshire, he took part in the famous Eglington Tournament of 1839 – a medieval re-enactment spectacle organised by the Earl of Eglington. Back in London, Napoleon was seen with fashionable and disreputable characters of society – such as Lady Blessington and Count d'Orsay. He was a curiosity to many ladies but by no means a safe prospect. He gave his heart for the first time, however, to Emily Rowles, daughter of Henry, a wealthy Kentish builder. Prince Napoleon stayed at their pretty home Camden Place in Chislehurst. He never forgot this place. But he could not have known it was where he would return and meet his end.

While the prince partied, the French government worried. They suspected that his lavish social life was merely a cover for him and his conspirators to plot a return to France. It did not help that he published books on Napoleonic Idealism. Yet family drama, even in London, nearly brought the dynasty to disaster. Prince Napoleon's cousin, Count Léon, an acknowledged illegitimate son of Napoleon I by Eléonore Denuelle, was also in London – Fenton's Hotel in fact. He had had a less glamorous story and constantly suffered from a lack of funds. His presence in London at this time was either to ask exiled relatives for money, or possibly to spy on his cousin Prince Napoleon in return for payment from the French authorities. Uncle Joseph, living in Cavendish Square, wrote openly that he would have nothing to do with Léon. When Léon received similar treatment from his 'little cousin', Prince Napoleon, he sent a second to challenge him to a duel in return for the perceived insult. Though duelling was by now a crime, the only honourable option as a gentleman was to accept. The duellers and their seconds met on Wimbledon Common on 3 May 1840. However, a new argument broke out. Napoleon, as the challenged party, chose swords. Léon insisted upon pistols – far more dangerous but also wise as Napoleon was likely the better trained swordsman. The dispute was decided in favour of Léon, but before firing commenced, a police inspector and several constables emerged from behind the bushes and arrested the lot. They were taken to Bow Street Magistrates Court and released on bail. Barings Bank paid for Prince Napoleon, Fenton's for Count Léon. He could neither repay the bail nor pay his bills, and retreated to Bloomsbury lodgings. Napoleon, meanwhile, appeared that evening in a box at Her Majesty's Theatre. Though the duel may have been designed to discredit Prince Napoleon, it served only to further romanticise him in the eyes of the British public.

Tired of the comforts of London, Prince Napoleon attempted yet another ill-fated and foolhardy coup in France. He may have made many of his plans and preparations from a country house in Kent in which he was residing for a while during 1840. Brasted Place, near Sevenoaks, was close enough to London for social purposes and far away enough for plotting purposes. A Palladian Robert Adams villa, Brasted had been the home of George III's doctor, John Turton, who treated the king's madness. Perhaps while at Brasted, Prince Napoleon plotted some madness of his own – another coup. Assembling a small group of about sixty loyal supporters, he hired a pleasure steamer, loaded it up at London Bridge docks and 'secretly' set out to retake his throne in France, hoping for popular support from the French people. In short, the attempt was a complete disaster and led to Napoleon's imprisonment at the fortress of Ham near the river Somme. A future of dark, damp imprisonment looked bleak, though he was able to study and write under confinement, as well as managing to father two illegitimate sons with the washer-woman. Although his eventual escape from jail is reminiscent of

Grahame's Toad (of *The Wind in the Willows*) leaving disguised as the washer-woman, the truth is not far off. In 1846, after complaining to the governor about the state of his rooms, workmen began to start renovating the apartments, and Napoleon, disguised as a humble labourer-cum-decorator, strolled out past the sentries – complete with clay pipe and a plank across the shoulder. Meanwhile, a dummy had been left behind in his bed, and faithful retainers remained behind explaining to the guards that he was unwell and resting – in order to buy time. A day later, he was back at Gore House in London, his victory being celebrated by Lady Blessington and friends. Only then did the French realise what had happened.

Prison had taken six years of his life, given him a limp (rheumatism), and damaged his eyesight. He had lost his youth and much of his optimism. He gave up plans of invasion and settled on rehabilitating himself in England, ordering new suits from Savile Row (Henry Poole & Co.), taking the waters at Bath, the sea air at Brighton, and becoming a guest at many of the finest houses and families in Britain. His health back in order, Napoleon famously had many romances and liaisons, the most formidable and lasting of these being with Elizabeth Anne Howard (alias Haryett, known to posterity as Harriet Howard). Harriet was the offspring of a bootmaker and the granddaughter of a hotel owner from Brighton. Like Napoleon's future wife, Harriet was vibrant and red-headed. She was upwardly mobile with designs on being a great actress or courtesan. At 15, she ran away with a famous jockey, only to switch her affections later to a major in the Life Guards, with whom she had a child. Both men bestowed fortunes on Harriet. She became able to mix with some of the upper crust of London society. Those thought to be her lovers were: George Stanhope 6th Earl of Chesterfield; Count d'Orsay; Major Francis Mountjoy Martyn; Henry Somerset 2nd Duke of Beaufort; and James Harris 3rd Earl of Malmesbury. Earlier, in 1846, at one of Lady Blessington's London parties, she was introduced to Prince Napoleon and the two began an affair. Her home, 9 Berkeley Square, was only a short stroll from his new residence on King Street, which he practically turned into a museum of the first empire, and where he enjoyed entertaining. (It was not clear which one of them had moved into the other's home.) A few years later (in 1867), while Napoleon was emperor, the Society of Arts decided to put a plaque on the side of the house: *Emperor Napoleon III lived here 1848*. An imperial eagle is

Above left: The Duke de Morny *c*.1860 Atelier Nadar. Gallica Digital Library

Above right: Carlo Buonaparte, Napoleon's father. Attributed to Anton Raphael Mengs. National Museum de Malmaison

Right: Napoleon on *Bellerophon* in Plymouth Sound 1815 by Sir Charles Lock Eastlake. National Maritime Museum

Fouth-century urn containing Freud's ashes, originally a gift from Marie Bonaparte, at Golders Green Crematorium, London. Photo by Stephen C. Dickson, 2013.

Coat of Arms of the current king of Sweden, Carl XVI Gustav. It retains the Bernadotte arms and the Bonaparte Imperial Eagle.

Above left: Prince Roland
Bonaparte *c.* 1914. George
Grantham Bain Collection
(Library of Congress).

Above right: Princess Marie
Bonaparte 1921 by Philip de
Laszlo MVO. The De Laszlo
Archive Trust

Right: Lord Dudley Coutts
Stuart, 1839, after Count
d'Orsay. British Museum
Collection.

Left: *The Surrender of Buonaparte on Board Bellerophon*. A stylised print of 1816 by G. M. Brighty. National Maritime Museum

Below: Wedding of Princess Marie and Prince George of Greece and Denmark in Athens, 1907. Bibliotéque National de France.

Point Breeze Estate *c*.1817–1820. Attributed to Charles B. Lawrence. Art Institute of Chicago

Napoleon on HMS *Bellerophon* on 23 July 1815 watching the last visible parts of France disappear from sight, by Sir William Quiller Orchardson, 1880. Tate Britain.

Prince Pierre Bonaparte shooting Victor Noir. *Illustrated World Journal* (Russian), 17 January 1870, No.55, p. 49.

The 'first' Blue Plaque on King Street, London.

Right: Admiral George Keith Elphinstone, Viscount Keith, GCB, Napoleon's bringer of bad news. By George Saunders after 1815. National Maritime Museum.

Below: Prince Roland Bonaparte's 1884 expedition (Roland in the centre measuring a Sami woman's head), by François Escard.

Above left: Charles Joseph Bonaparte *c.*1903. Library of Congress.

Above right: Coat of Arms of the short-lived Anglo-Corsican kingdom 1794–1796, by Samhanin 2017

Left: Edward Hilary Davis and Prince Jean-Christophe Napoleon in 2015 at the Waterloo Bicentenary Banquet, London.

Betsy Elizabeth Patterson, 1804, by Gilbert Stuart. Metropolitan Museum of Art, New York.

Empress Eugenie, 1853, by Franz Winterhalter. Chateau de Compiegne.

Left: Eugene de Beauharnais, 1815, by Karl Stieler. Pushkin Museum of Fine Arts.

Below left: The Count de Flahaut, 15 December 1860. *Illustrated London News.*

Below right: Lucien Bonaparte, Prince of Canino, by Robert Lefevre. Chateau de Versailles.

HIS EXCELLENCY COUNT FLAHAULT DE LA BILLARDERIE, AMBASSADOR FROM THE EMPEROR OF THE FRENCH TO THE COURT OF ST. JAMES'S.

Above left: Napoleon III coat of arms as a member of the Order of the Garter from 15 April 1855.

Above right: Napoleon III *c*.1852, by Gustave Le Gray. Metropolitan Art Museum.

Scene in Plymouth Sound in August 1815. The *Bellerophon* surrounded by crowds on small boats all hoping to catch a glimpse of the fallen emperor. 1817, by John James Chalon. National Maritime Museum.

Jerome Bonaparte *c*.1850s by
A. A. E. Disderi. Musée Carnavalet.

King Joseph at Point Breeze,
2 February 1832, by Innocent-
Louis Gouband. Museum
National du Chateau de
Fontainebleau

Above: Longwood House, Napoleon's final home of St Helena, by David Stanley, 2014.

Right: Louis Bonaparte shortly after abdicating as king of Holland, wearing Dutch uniform, 1813–1815. Chateau de Versailles.

Left: Henry Petty-Fitzmaurice 5th Marquess of Lansdowne, KG, GCSI, GCMG, GCIE, PC, descendant of Empress Josephine. By William James Topley. Collections Canada.

Below: Napoleon III's death in Chislehurst, Kent, 1873. *Illustrated London News*, 25 January 1873 from a photo by Mssrs Downy.

NAPOLEON III. AFTER HIS DEATH.
ENGRAVED, BY SPECIAL PERMISSION, FROM THE PHOTOGRAPH BY MESSRS. DOWNEY.

Prince Imperial in British Uniform *c*.1875, by Stereoscopic Company. Mitchell Library, State Library of New South Wales.

Queen Hortense (de Beauharnais) of Holland and her son Louis II of Holland, 1807, by Francois Gerard. Royal Collections of the Netherlands.

Photo of memorial to Paul Amadeus Coutts Stuart, great-nephew of Napoleon.
Died in 1889. Photo by Edward Hands.

depicted, and English Heritage describe it as the earliest surviving blue plaque. In fact, the chosen colour of many subsequent plaques is likely due to the first being made in imperial French blue.

The prince had not returned to London alone. He brought with him the two boys he had fathered while in the prison of Ham. Harriet looked after them and they were educated with her own son.

Napoleon continued to be a magnificent socialite, entertainer and learned gentleman. He gambled, attended Newmarket and hosted bachelor dinners; he attended lectures at Oxford, enjoyed matters of science and was a companion of Florence Nightingale. However, 1848 was a year of revolution in many European kingdoms, empires and grand-duchies. A revolution ousted Napoleon's old captor, King Louis-Philippe, who travelled into exile in England too. The ex-king of the French set up his home in Claremont, Surrey and died there two years later. In Britain things were far from harmonious. Rioters set upon Buckingham Palace causing much damage. Napoleon enrolled as a volunteer special constable at Marlborough Street Police Station. He went on duty, walking his beat, on London Bridge on 10 April 1848. However, when a mob of Chartists made in the direction of the Houses of Parliament, his only contribution was reportedly to assist in the arrest of a drunken elderly lady.

During the initial months of rioting and uncertainty in Paris, Napoleon bided his time and waited for the safest moment to re-enter French politics. The new republic held many elections to the National Assembly. Having been absent from France, his reputation was clean from the recent troubles. Citizen Louis-Napoleon Bonaparte, financially backed by London bankers and his wealthy English mistress (Harriet Howard), entered his name on the ballot and was elected a member of the National Assembly. He travelled swiftly from London to Paris. The new government quickly prepared for a presidential election – the first ever in France. Representing the Bonapartist party, Louis-Napoleon was elected the first president of the Second French Republic with a majority of 74.3 per cent on 20 December 1848. A huge vote of confidence from a country he had been expelled from, and hunted and imprisoned by.

As Napoleon moved to Paris as president, Harriet followed as the official mistress and was housed close to the Elysée Palace. She had the tact to keep herself in the background, knowing full well that, no matter how rich she was, as an English bootmaker's daughter she was never going to be married to the premier of France. She did, however, have the occasional confrontation with Princess Mathilde, Napoleon's ex-fiancée and cousin.

His years of hardship had paid off. Napoleon became known as the 'prince-president' and received support from peasants and intellectuals alike, such as Victor Hugo (initially). However, like his uncle, the allure of the throne was too tempting. The constitution permitted a president to serve only one term. Determined not to leave office, in 1851, the president staged his own coup d'état, which was largely funded by Harriet. This eventually led to the dissolving of the National Assembly and the founding of the Second French Empire. Having been ratified by a referendum, Louis-Napoleon Bonaparte became Napoleon III, emperor of the French on 2 December 1852, on the anniversary of his uncle's coronation in Notre Dame (1804) and greatest victory at the Battle of Austerlitz (1805). It is amusing to think that much of this was made possible by the generosity of an English bootmaker's daughter who had acquired her cash from a jockey and a Life Guards officer! Less than a month later, the new emperor announced his engagement to his future wife, Eugenie.

The new emperor had always been in awe of Queen Victoria and had seen her, from his days in London, progress from girl-queen, to wife, mother and strong woman. For both political and personal reasons, he had hoped to align himself with Britain by marrying Victoria's niece, Princess Adelaide, and Victoria was not opposed. However, family and politics were a problem. Victoria was controlled by her husband Albert, he in turn by his uncle, Leopold, king of the Belgians. The Saxe-Coburg family did not see eye to eye with the Bonapartes. Also, in Britain, the French were still perceived as the old enemy, the only threat to their own mastery of the world. In addition, there was doubt in London as to how secure Napoleon's position was in France, long term. Children were told to behave 'or else Boney the Ogre will come and get you'. A British match was therefore not to be. But Napoleon had an admirer closer to home.

Eugenie too had connections to England, but particularly roots in Scotland. Born in Granada, María Eugenia Ignacia Agustina de Palafox-Portocarrero de Guzmán y Kirkpatrick was a Spanish aristocrat. Her mother's ancestors were Scottish. One or two were executed for supporting the Stuarts and Bonnie Prince Charlie. Eugenie's grandfather

William Kirkpatrick of Cowheath was a wine merchant and emigrated to Spain and became US Consul at Malaga. Eugene was educated at a boarding school in Clifton, Bristol, which she despised. Bullied for her red hair and called 'Carrots', she reportedly tried to run away to India and even made it as far as boarding a ship in the Bristol dockyard before being dragged back. The couple had met before at large functions, but it was on a hunt at Fontainebleau that their romance began. Both of them were excellent horsemen, and Eugenie was the star of the day: first in at the kill and showing superb Spanish and English riding style. Napoleon presented her with the horse she rode that day, and fell in love. She was also clever. When the lecherous emperor asked: 'Madame, what is the way to your heart?' Eugenie replied: 'through the chapel.' While this seems like a conservative put-down, it should be noted that at this point in time, the way to her bedroom was also physically through the church next door! Nevertheless, the couple were married in a civil ceremony at the Tuileries on 29 January 1853 and in a religious ceremony at Notre Dame the following day.

As soon as the engagement had been announced, Harriet Howard had been given her marching orders, and compromising letters were destroyed. A true (English) gentleman, the emperor paid back much of the money he owed her for sponsoring his plots. She acquired the Chateau de Beauregard about 3 miles north of Versailles, and he made her the Countess de Beauregard. Her son by the Life Guard was also given the title of Count de Béchevêt. Within months of the imperial marriage, Napoleon went back to seeing his English mistress, until his wife reminded him of his obligation to create a legitimate heir. After a failed marriage to a gentleman named Trelawny, Harriet died at the chateau the same year as her divorce in 1865. A few years later, the castle was utilised as the headquarters of the Prussian army during the Franco-Prussian War.

Having had a swift rise to power, from convict, to exile, to president, to emperor and husband in just seven years, Napoleon turned his attention to international politics. He had learnt not to make the same mistake as his predecessor: to ignore or underestimate British strength and influence in Europe. Therefore, the key to his policy was a reconciliation and bond with the old adversary and new industrial world super power, Great Britain. He needed to be admitted to the 'sovereigns club of Europe'; recognition from Britain would provide that. Plans were drawn up for a potential state visit to England. Empress Eugenie was keen on the visit too. She had already made several incognito visits to Britain, staying at Watford near the country house of the then foreign secretary – perhaps to make the arrangements. Old military officers and Queen Victoria, however, were less than enthusiastic about the plans, so Napoleon launched a counter-attack by proposing marriage between his cousin (Prince 'Plon-Plon' Napoleon) and her cousin (Princess Mary of Cambridge). The royal court at Windsor quickly shrugged this off.

However, events in the Crimea in 1853 led to closer ties. France joined forces with Britain against Russian expansionism in the Black Sea. It was somewhat of a difficult thing to get used to, being on the same side. The commander of British troops in Crimea, Lord Raglan, who had been on Wellington's staff at Waterloo, persisted in calling the enemy 'the French' when discussing battle plans throughout the war's duration, even when the French were at his side. Nevertheless, because of the joint venture the two countries had embarked upon, relations between Windsor Castle and the Tuileries Palace improved. The slightly prudish Prince Albert was still to be convinced a meeting was a good thing. Napoleon was lecherous, had fathered illegitimate children, and lived openly with an English publican's daughter. Albert feared the royal family's reputation might become scandalised if they associated with such naughtiness. So, as a test of Napoleon's character, Albert sent his already scandalous and syphilitic brother, Ernest Duke of Coburg, to visit the emperor at the Tuileries. The queen's cousin, George, the Duke of Cambridge, was also sent to test the waters; (he also had illegitimate offspring and was living with an actress). Ernest and George gave positive reports back to Windsor, and Albert organised a 'final check'. From Osborne House, he left the Solent on his own royal yacht and made for Boulogne. Waiting on the dockside to receive him were Napoleon and the British ambassador. Albert and Napoleon spent a few days together discussing politics and carrying out military inspections. Albert was delighted by Napoleon's strong German accent but also by his intellect. A state visit was eventually agreed upon (if only to prevent Napoleon from commanding troops in person in the Crimea as he had threatened). Eugenie and Napoleon would visit England in April; Albert and Victoria would visit France in August 1855.

As Napoleon had previously waited at the dock in Boulogne, Albert waited to receive the emperor and empress at Dover on the morning of

16 April 1855. A private train took the trio on to London and then to Windsor where Victoria waited to receive them. Crowds gathered near the railway terminus in London, hoping to catch a glimpse of their old local dashing celeb-now-turned-emperor and his beautiful wife. Even the less easily impressed were fascinated by the state visit of an Emperor Napoleon – whose predecessors would never have been afforded the privilege. It is perhaps a shame that the grand old Duke of Wellington did not live to see it – having died three years earlier. He would have had to eat his words from decades earlier.

The emperor wore military uniform, as was his style by now, while the empress, wishing to show her British roots, and aware of Victoria and Albert's love for Scotland, wore the Kirkpatrick tartan.

Their visit to Windsor lasted only a few days. However, in that time Napoleon III did things no one thought imaginable a few years earlier: he reviewed the British Guards and attended a ball and dinner in the Waterloo Chamber (a room dedicated to the victors of that battle, complete with portraits of the main commanders: Wellington, Blücher, Orange et al.). Most propitious of all, in a small ceremony, Napoleon was personally invested with the Order of the Garter by Victoria herself. Napoleon beamed triumph; the order was not only the oldest highest honour in the land, but had been founded amidst the Hundred Years War against the French. He reportedly whispered to Victoria: 'Finally, I am a gentleman.' In London, the state visit continued to the Guildhall and lunch with the lord mayor, sheriffs and officers of the city, as well as a tour of the now four years old Crystal Palace and visits to the opera – not far from the Magistrates Court Napoleon 'visited' his youth. Crowds gathered and cheered wherever they went. There exists a black and white photograph of the two couples sitting together at the Crystal Palace.

With the backdrop of the Crimea and this imperial visit, a feeling of comradeship and common bonds with the 'old enemy' began to emerge and grow. These have stood the test of time and doubtless started a relationship which led to the *entente cordiale*. Britain and France, previously the worst of enemies, were now practically the best of friends.

Arguably, for the quartet at the centre of this, it was probably among the most important few days of their lives. But Napoleon, as the most senior in years, was the star. His time spent in London as a younger man, and learning from his previous mistakes, made him a consummate performer in what today we call networking. He had learnt English charm, or how to charm the English at any rate. He said the right things to the right people – especially Victoria, who by some reports was completely enamoured of him. Napoleon was one of the few actual men of the world who could converse with her as an equal. Albert too, lacking an older, wiser male friend, enjoyed his time with Napoleon – who pushed himself to keep up with the energetic, outdoors-loving prince. Yet the bonds of friendship between Albert and Eugenie formed a further closeness. He had never shown his affections elsewhere, yet he found her enchanting. It is perhaps safe to assume there may have been a slight crush on his side – not that the monogamist Coburg would have acted on this. Eugenie was on an equal footing with Albert, and, unlike Victoria, had received a formal education and seen some of the world. It would not be surprising if that was the case. Victoria was pleased the two got on so well too. She, meanwhile, always happy to be guided or steered by older men, benefited from the wisdom of Napoleon, who knew much more of the world than her husband.

The most telling sign of success was that when the imperial pair left, Victoria felt withdrawal and sadness at the passing of the happy times they had all had together. Napoleon and Eugenie knew they had made a friend for life, and if they ever needed her help in the future – help would come.

On 18 August the same year, Napoleon again waited at Boulogne to receive his British guests. The port that witnessed his uncle's planned invasion of England, was now to welcome the queen of England. The significance of this day could not be ignored. The last English monarch to formally make the journey to Paris was Henry VI who was crowned king of France in 1432 in the Notre Dame (coincidently, the same place as Napoleon I). By now, however, the British monarchs had given up their claim to the French throne – after George III dropped it in 1800 – so there was no awkwardness on that score.

Eugenie did not go to meet them, having recently become pregnant with her first (and only child). Queen Victoria, the older of the two, in her usual way, had given plenty of advice (when none was asked for) in her letters to the young empress – recommending spending as much time as possible outdoors but not to overdo it, and no hot baths! That said, Victoria could claim a little authority on the subject of giving birth, having by now had eight children. The ninth child, Beatrice, would follow in two years – but more on her later. Doubtless, the maternal planning and conversations between queen and empress brought the two closer.

Napoleon wanted to impress and possibly outdo his royal guests. This is certainly one of the reasons for his appointing the architect Baron Haussmann to remodel Paris in imperial splendour. Much of what one sees in Paris today – from the Opera, railway stations and wide boulevards – owes its splendour to Napoleon and Haussmann. The fine public parks, such as the Bois de Boulogne, were directly inspired by Napoleon's years strolling through Hyde Park.

In typical Anglo-Frankish style, the train bringing the guests and their host to Paris was slightly delayed. They made it to Paris not during the day as planned but when it was almost dark. Delays had occurred because at every stop on the journey, crowds of townsfolk and officials had gathered for their own glimpse of the historic visit, complete with bands and speeches. It was also 1855 and there were no lavatories on board! When it arrived at Paris, the party was greeted with great cheers from thousands of French and foreigners alike The city sparkled in the night light. Victoria wrote to her uncle Leopold that 'I am amused.' The queen must have seemed an odd fish to the oh-so-fashionable Parisians, in her straw hat and other accessories made by her children. After impressive tours of the Tuileries, Chateau Sainte-Cloud, the Louvre and attending various balls, Napoleon led the queen and prince consort to the climax of the tour – a ball at Versailles.

Versailles was by then famed as the creation of Louis XIV, as the home of Marie Antoinette, and its historical significance in shaping France. It was known throughout Europe as one of the most spectacular palaces created, though some of the gilt had worn off since the Revolution had plundered through it and items had been stolen – many of which would find their way into grand English houses. Versailles was the site where so many wars against Britain had been planned: The Seven Years War, the Wars of Spanish and Austrian Succession, and the American War of Independence. It had been a Bourbon palace, but now it 'belonged' to the Bonapartes – who *invited* the British.

Great preparations had been made for this historic moment. Gas lighting was installed in the Hall of Mirrors, the marble courtyard and opera. Four orchestras were brought in along with the celebrated conductor Isaac Strauss. The sovereigns danced with each other's partners among the 1,200 other guests. They adjourned for dinner in the opera house, and continued dancing until the following morning. The Versailles expedition, inspired by the past, also included a further party at the Hotel de Ville, a hunt through the forest of St Germain, and a lunch at the Trianon – a house formerly lived in by Marie Antoinette and later Pauline Bonaparte (Napoleon III's aunt).

Another official occasion in Paris included a visit to Les Invalides. Originally commissioned by Louis XIV in 1670 as a hospital and retirement home for military veterans (and the inspiration for the Chelsea Hospital, London), it had also become the resting place of Napoleon I. Beneath the centre of the dome of the Cathedral de St Louis lies the grand but austere tomb of the great hero – in spooky similarity to the resting place of Horatio Nelson at St Paul's. At night and by torchlight, Napoleon III led the royal family to the crypt where his uncle lay in silence while old veterans of Russia and Waterloo silently stood guard looking on. The young Prince of Wales, Bertie (Edward VII), while adorned in Highland dress, apparently knelt at the coffin as a great sign of respect. The experience must have been eerie to the young Victoria. As the party began to leave the cathedral, the silence was only broken by a pianissimo 'God Save the Queen' on the organ. The Franco-British Alliance seemed cemented. Later that year, British and French forces were victorious in capturing Sebastopol.

A few years later, Napoleon and Eugenie would be invited to Osborne House in the Isle of Wight. A sketch of Eugenie drawn by Victoria herself survives. The empress had given birth to their only child in 1856, a son, another Napoleon – The Prince Imperial. Arguably, this was a high-point for the second empire and for Napoleon III. The successes in the Crimea and alliance with Britain had given France newly recovered prestige on the world stage. Indeed, for many Frenchmen, the military triumphs in the Crimea put to bed the ghosts of the fateful 1812 invasion of Russia by the first Napoleon. The Grande Armée was feeling grand again, and the empire had an heir. This may have given Napoleon enough feeling of security to engage in other foreign affairs projects – some of which were far less successful and ultimately disastrous for him. The new alliance was shaken, however, when assassins tried to bomb Napoleon and Eugenie's carriage while on the way to the theatre on 14 January 1858. Though they were unharmed, eight were killed and more than a hundred wounded. The ringleader, Ferlice Orsini, was an Italian revolutionary, but the bombs themselves were English-made which caused an international scandal. Many suspicious French politicians and veterans called for war against the old enemy. Napoleon attempted to mend bridges by inviting Victoria and Albert to Cherbourg; however, Albert did not help matters as he had made clear his intentions to draw closer family ties with Germany – he was expecting his first grandson (the future Kaiser Wilhelm II). Victoria also snubbed a popular member of the imperial court, Countess Marie Walewska (the famous former mistress of Napoleon I, by whom she had a son). Victoria did not like the company of those who lived, or had lived, in open 'sin'. Napoleon III calmed the British press and politicians that France was not about to invade England, and all was well again. He drew his attention to Italy, its independence and the wars that followed there.

The following years were an impressive roller coaster of politics, innovation and foreign affairs. Napoleon had reassured France's neighbours that, unlike his uncle, he would not wage war and extend territory in Europe; however, he did support the principle of nationalities – the creation of new states based on nationality, language or culture/national identity – such as Italy. Such new countries could be allies of France. This was contrary to the principles of the ancient Habsburg Empire. Napoleon had supported Italian independence as a youth and did not stop as a man. In 1859 came the Second War of Italian Independence. Napoleon, through his now solid relationship with Britain, was able to gain assurance of British neutrality from Prime Minister Lord Derby, although not all in the British government were comfortable. Napoleon helped pave the way for the eventual forming of the kingdom of Italy – under Victor Emmanuel II (king of Sardinia and Duke of Savoy). Napoleon surely could not escape the irony of this; his paternal uncle had made himself king of Italy, another was briefly king of Naples and Sicily. His maternal uncle had been viceroy of Italy and Prince of Venice. His cousin had been king of Rome, and his paternal aunts had been Grand Duchess of Tuscany, and Queen Consort of Naples respectively. The old policy of putting Bonapartes on various European thrones has not altogether been successful!

It was not repeated, although Napoleon did try to impose a European monarch on Mexico (Maximilian I, emperor of Mexico). Mexico was invaded by Spain, Britain and France in 1861 in order to force the republican government there to repay its vast debts to the three countries. Mexico City was captured by French forces in 1863. Napoleon invited

Maximilian (younger brother of Franz Joseph I of Austria) to form a pro-French monarchy. He arrived in 1864 with his wife Charlotte of Belgium (first cousin of Queen Victoria). The Mexico adventure ended in calamity. The French withdrew military support for the regime, partly due to pressure from the US, but also a need to deal with matters at home – such as the threat from Prussia. As a result, Maximilian was captured by Mexican republican forces, sentenced to death, and executed by firing squad.

Napoleon was direct in his colonial ambitions across the world. He had seen first-hand, as a younger man, the advantages Britain reaped from its far-flung empire. France herself had its own territories, and Napoleon sought to expand her influence internationally. He doubled the area of French colonial possessions such as Cambodia, New Caledonia and Cochinchina. He sent an army to support the British in the Second Opium War in 1857. The war resulted in the British securing possession of Hong Kong, and both France and Britain maintaining control of Canton for several years. The colonial period of Napoleon's reign pushed France's interests (not always successfully) in Japan, Korea, Senegal, Thailand, Vietnam, Laos, Algeria and the Pacific. Though the Cobden-Chevalier Treaty of 1860 had led to closer times of free trade between Britain and France, this imperial period of empire was politically opposite. Britain wished to maintain the 'balance of power in Europe', which rarely meant backing the Second French Empire in continental feuds. Indeed, Lord Palmerston's government regarded France with suspicion, especially since the sabre rattling of the French in the wake of the Orsini assassination attempt which led to (slightly unfounded) fears of possible invasion. Abroad, however, Britain helped France with its overseas territories, giving, or helping to obtain, territories in the Mediterranean: Syria, Algeria, Morocco. It was seen as important by the British government to have a close ally and fellow colonial power – albeit a lesser partner!

Prince Albert's death in 1861 caused a surprising turn in fortunes of Napoleon's foreign affairs – and his relationship with Britain. As Victoria plunged into her unstable grief, she ardently declared that she would see Albert's wishes and plans (for Europe) come to fruition. This meant that the queen became more pro-German, more prudish and judgemental – particularly of her son (Edward VII) whom Albert had regarded as a lazybones, womaniser and cunning sexual philanderer.

Napoleon had been regarded in a similar light by Albert, who had been suspicious of him from the beginning. The queen also 'adopted' Albert's strong dislike of the Catholic Church – a strong contrast to Eugenie, who was a devout Catholic.

The slight severing of the ties with the Coburg-Hanovers came at the beginning of a decline in the second empire. Uncle Jerome, former king of Westphalia, died in 1860, and was afforded a state funeral and interred near to his titanic brother. The now ageing Napoleon III seem to change his pace from here on, governing more slowly – after all, he had seen and done far more in his lifetime than many of his fellow rulers of the day. He loosened his grip, enacting decrees that began what is now known as the Liberal Empire – which gave more freedom of debate and a free(er) press. However, his age and illnesses (of the kidneys and bladder), were changing him. No longer the gay, suave adventurer, he became more silent and pensive. Some have argued that he lost his common touch. A typical man, he put off doctors' appointments or pain relief often until it was almost too late. Bad health, rather like his 'immortal' uncle, plagued his later years – and surely affected at least some of his decision making.

Clouds began to gather as Otto von Bismarck appeared on the scene in Paris as the ambassador from Prussia. The 'iron chancellor' and nemesis of the second empire, as he would become, was originally greeted with all the usual charm and courtesy of the day. He was well known to be a man who liked the ladies; however, Queen Victoria explained that this was because his own wife was ghastly and 'masculine'. He, like many, was captivated by the wit and charms of Eugenie, but, as a consequence, was often on his guard around her. Not averse to a practical joke, she once put a plaster cast of Bismarck's head (asleep) on the pillow of a lady of the court who clearly had a crush on the big German. When she retired to her chamber she screamed away in embarrassment, causing much mirth for those in on the prank; however, the plaster cast had also fooled a footman, who discreetly left the chamber and spread rumours of the Prussian being in a bed not his own, below stairs! Despite the close shave with scandal, Eugenie and Otto had a liking and a respect for each other. The imperial couple invited him to stay at Biarritz, but Eugenie, and others, identified that Bismarck was potentially a threat.

The threat of the rise of Prussian, and subsequently German, power was made obvious in the war for Schleswig and Holstein – buffer territories between Denmark and German states. Napoleon's most effective move should have been a consultation with Great Britain, but Victoria remained deep in grief and could only channel her pro-German husband. British ministers, however, offered aid to France to jointly assist Denmark – the homeland of Alexandra the then Princess of Wales. Napoleon missed his opportunity to put the Prussians in their place. He declined the offer. Denmark was therefore abandoned and lost the war that launched the beginning of a Prussian–German Empire and the imminent decline of the French Empire, and French political dominance in Europe.

In the last years of the empire, before the military and political disasters, came one of Napoleon's petit triumphs: The Paris Exhibition of 1867. The first world exposition had been at the Crystal Palace in London, and this was now Napoleon's second attempt at outshining it with over 52,000 exhibitors. Eighty sovereigns were invited; only Pope Pius IX and Queen Victoria declined. Bertie, the Prince of Wales was sent instead, giving him another opportunity to unleash his charm on Paris – charm he would later be famous for. Victoria did not wish Paris to surpass Albert's great efforts of the 1850s so she stayed away, although she did invite the Bonapartes to Osborne. Napoleon could not make it but the empress was happy to make a repeat visit – though owing to the queen's moping, it was rather a dull and difficult visit with only a visit to the church and the Swiss Cottage on the agenda. Many topics of conversation would have been prohibited, no doubt, such as Albert, Catholicism, Prussia, and the lecherous behaviour of Napoleon and the Prince of Wales. What a weekend that must have been!

The Osborne trip perhaps helped the relationship with Victoria. She was a jealous woman. In the years after her husband's death, she had watched with interest as the imperial couple rose to glittering stars of Europe. In her opinion, they owed much of their status to her and her recognition. In 1868, Victoria intended to holiday in Switzerland, and she was offered the imperial train for her transport across France. She travelled under the name 'the Countess of Kent' – though it is possible that did not fool everyone. Victoria snubbed the imperial couple by not paying a call on them on the return journey, which was especially rude as they had just named a boulevard after her in Paris and had lent her the train. The French press showed their anger and turned their attentions on her Scots' servant/companion, John Brown. All this did nothing to stop the decline in the Windsor–Tuileries friendship.

Meanwhile, in sunnier parts of the world, the Anglo-French Suez Canal Company had been busily constructing the Egyptian waterway that had been thought of by Napoleon I, when he had been on his campaigns there over half a century earlier. Frenchmen believed they had discovered ancient canals extending north from the Red Sea to the Nile. This idea was expanded to an even greater canal connecting the Red Sea with the Mediterranean. Ferdinand de Lesseps set up the company in 1858, with the waterway complete by 1869. The company was mostly the property of private French investors together with shares allotted to the Khedive of Egypt; however, these shares were eventually sold to the United Kingdom in 1875. De Lesseps was himself from a very ancient French family, and was a successful diplomat. He was made a Knight Grand Commander of the Star of India in 1870. (In later years, 'Ferdinand de Lesseps' were the key words used in President Gamal Abdel Nasser's speech which were the signal for Egyptian forces to immediately seize control of the canal from British and French authorities in the Suez Crisis of 1956.)

It was decided that the opening of the canal would be undertaken by Empress Eugenie on behalf of her husband, who was by now too frail owing to his rheumatism and bladder stones. After all, she was a cousin of de Lesseps. Taking the imperial yacht, *L'Aigle*, Eugenie set sail across the Mediterranean with a sizeable entourage. She stopped by Venice and was received by King Victor Emmanuel and then travelled to Greece to be given a tour by the new king of Greece, George I – who was the brother of the Princess of Wales. George had been elected to the throne of Greece in a referendum in 1862 where the Greeks chose a new head of state. Queen Victoria's son, Prince Alfred, received 230,016 votes; the Prince of Leuchtenberg (grandson of Napoleon I's stepson, Eugene) received 2,400 votes; Napoleon III himself received two votes; and his cousin Prince Plon-Plon Bonaparte got 345 votes. Nevertheless, the Greek Assembly gave the crown to Prince William of Denmark (George I) – who got just six votes!

After Greece it was on to Constantinople briefly – where the Sultan Abdul Aziz nearly killed Eugenie's American dentist, a Dr Thomas Evans, by colliding with his fishing boat. But for the empress's interference, he might have died.

From Cairo, the imperial yacht led a procession to Suez, accompanied by the yachts of the Khedive (viceroy) of Egypt, the Crown Prince of

Prussia (Victoria's son-in-law), Prince Louis of Hesse, Prince Henry of the Netherlands, and the emperor of Austria. Queen Victoria, perhaps still bitter about the French press and John Brown, had no wish to send any royal representation out to Suez. Britain was represented by a mere foreign office official. It was a true moment of greatness for France and the Bonapartes – realising a dream of the family's greatest son, which, in his day, had seemed nearly impossible. Now so much more was possible because of the canal. Christian and Muslim blessings upon the canal were performed, followed by celebrations, illuminations and fireworks. Eugenie always considered it one of the pinnacles of her career as empress.

The bright sunny days of Egypt were followed swiftly by the dark clouds of Prussian bullets. In June 1870, Lord Clarendon, British foreign secretary, one of the greatest diplomats of Europe, passed away. He had spent much of his career keeping peace between Paris and Prussian Berlin. Bismarck saw this as the last obstruction to a French/Prussian war. It is considered by many that Napoleon was tricked or manoeuvred into war by Bismarck. On 19 July 1870, a very reluctant Napoleon III declared war on Prussia. This was the Franco-Prussian War.

The war was disastrous for France, the second empire and especially Napoleon III. Bismarck and the Prussians had been preparing for such a fight for years. They were generally better equipped and better at mobilising – using modern technology. The Prussians conducted a campaign that even Napoleon I would have been impressed by. Napoleon III was no great military commander like his uncle and he was finally defeated at the Battle of Sedan on 1–2 September 1870. When news reached Paris of his capture, the empire immediately collapsed and a Government of National Defence was formed. The Prussians lay siege to Paris and occupied Versailles where, in the Hall of Mirrors – where Napoleon had danced with Victoria only fifteen years earlier – the German Empire was proclaimed. One empire had fallen, another was born.

As chaos mounted in Paris, Eugenie had had the foresight to get a British passport. With the help of Dr Evans, who owed her his life, she secretly journeyed through France to the Channel at La Toques. There, Evans and his associates, at great personal risk of arrest, searched for a vessel and skipper willing to smuggle the empress to England. Like a good novel or good period drama film, a willing English toff was close to hand. Sir John Burgoyne Bt, had sailed his yacht to La Toques to collect his wife. Sir John, an ex-Guardsman, a county Sheriff, Carlton and Travellers Clubs' member and 10th baronet, was reluctant at first but in comic cliché was persuaded by Lady Burgoyne – who was no doubt delighted to have an empress, albeit an ex-empress, on board. Sir John was aware there was a search for the empress and that the emperor's relatives were being arrested. Narrowly avoiding French police, the party sailed across the Channel in a violent storm, nearly capsizing. At last, they made it to Southampton. News in papers reported that the Prince Imperial, Eugenie's son, may have made an escape to Hastings – the Marine Hotel in fact. Eugenie travelled to Southsea, then Portsmouth and via train headed to Brighton, St Leonards, then Hastings for a tearful reunion with her boy.

The birds of British gossip press began their tweeting at the newly arrived 'frogs'. They received a mixed press but not a great deal of sympathy. The Duke and Duchess of Hamilton, the emperor's relatives, immediately offered their Scottish country homes, and the Prince of Wales offered up Chiswick House – for which he was scolded by his mama as a brash action. Princess Mary of Teck (later Queen Mary), who seems to have managed to catch a glimpse of the empress, reportedly found her quite changed and worn down. Not surprising – it had been a mighty fall from splendour. The dank and smelly Marine Hotel was a testament to it, yet, perhaps showing an element of Scottish grit and determination, Eugenie did not complain. They were not on the breadline, however, and she asked the dentist, Dr Evans to find a suitable country residence for them to rent. Meanwhile, Napoleon III was a 'guest' of the Prussian forces as the war continued in France.

Camden Place, Chislehurst, the old haunt of Napoleon III, where he had courted Emily Rowles, was selected. It seems unlikely that this was a mere coincidence. Emily married an Italian antiquities collector and archaeologist, Giampietro Campana, Marquis di Cavelli. He fell from grace when he was accused of embezzling public funds in order to subsidise his collecting. The collection was seized and put up for auction, and much of it went to some of the world's best museums such as the V&A. Napoleon III acquired some of the artefacts for France. Emily had sent parcels to Napoleon when he was imprisoned at Ham and later helped him escape to England. Another former mistress, Elizabeth Howard, who had financially backed Napoleon's plots, had a son. Though not his own, Napoleon settled property on mother and boy (he at least owed them that) held in trust by a Mr Nathaniel Strode. Strode bought Camden Place in 1860 and began renovating it into the style of a French chateau. Along with rumours that Strode had actually received money from Napoleon, it seems very possible that Chislehurst had long been developed as a bolthole or escape pod should things get ugly for the imperial family in France.

The three-storey Kentish house set in a beautiful park (now a golf course), about half an hour by train from London, soon became the centre of hopes the Bonapartists had of restoring or rescuing the regime. Bonaparte sympathisers regarded Eugenie as a sort of regent, but she lacked any real power over events in France. Bismarck too would have preferred to have dealt with Eugenie acting as a kind of regent rather than a series of republicans. The empress needed advice. Letters from the emperor were, of course, tame as they were read by the enemy. Representatives of the new French government told her she would be arrested if returned to France to rally Bonapartists' support. When her lack of power became apparent to everyone, including her, coupled by the French army's defeat at Metz, she suffered something short of a panicked breakdown – understandably. With the state of Napoleon's health being made clear to her, she decided to travel to his gilded cage in Wilhelmshöhe for a brief visit – permitted by his captors. It is difficult to imagine what they must have said to one another, but both were likely in need of emotional support. It had been a meteoric rise for both of them and they were on the start of a no less meteoric fall. Eugenie returned to Chislehurst, after a few days with him.

Queen Victoria, though torn between her Prussian son-in-law and French friends, paid a courtesy call on the diminished Eugenie and Louis-Napoleon the Prince Imperial, at Camden Place a few weeks later. She was accompanied by her youngest daughter, Princess Beatrice. Victoria must have delighted in the possibility of a 'connection' being formed between the teenagers. Unsurprisingly, the queen found the visit sad and decided to invite mother and son to Windsor just days later. The royal children gave Louis-Napoleon a tour of the castle, while Eugenie was given a tour of Albert's mausoleum. A few months later, the war was finally over. The Empire of Germany had been declared, their soldiers marched in the streets of Paris, France was very much a conquered state, and Napoleon was permitted to join his family.

Napoleon's captors had treated him well. Unlike his poor and glorious uncle, there was no ignominious captivity on St Helena. Indeed, it must have helped Napoleon to some degree that the son of his enemy, Kaiser Wilhelm I, was Crown Prince Frederick, who had Victoria, the Königin von Großbritannien, for a mother-in-law. Bismarck would also have been sympathetic to Eugenie's desire for her husband back. The ex-emperor was permitted to travel to Dover. He was welcomed like a celebrity hero by the public and local officials. The British had mixed views of the Franco-Prussian War, but most thought the imperial couple hard done by. Days later he too was invited to Windsor by the old widow. Not such a glamorous affair as it had been in 1855, but nonetheless he was very welcome as a former sovereign and old friend (and knight of the Garter let us not forget!).

The possibility of his becoming emperor or even president again was by no means extinct. He returned with his family to Camden Place and quietly pondered and plotted a possible return to power. But, as was his way, he did this stealthily and subtly. In fact, he was a regular in the local village shop at Chislehurst and was known to stroll around and he even took a great interest in the local cricket. This may have just been a ruse to throw republican spies off the scent; it is difficult to imagine a Frenchman taking any delight in cricket! He had not given up hope, but he knew these things took patience and time.

Eugenie, used to more action in her life, escaped the dreariness of Chislehurst and went to Spain to visit her mother. Napoleon and the Prince Imperial used this opportunity for a chaps' holiday – to the West Country – to Torquay. There is a legend that, while at the Imperial Hotel he wished to congratulate the chef on the menu. When the chef presented himself, it turned out to be one of Napoleon's old chefs from the Tuileries Palace. A delightful yet probably humbling moment for both men. While in Devon, father and son travelled as far south-west as Plymouth Sound – perhaps to visit the location where the first emperor had been greeted by such enthusiastic crowds earlier in 1815. Guides at Mount Edgcumbe House (now on the Cornish side of the Sound) maintain that when Napoleon III visited, the Countess of Mount Edgcumbe was rather 'unimpressed' by him. Her husband, the 4th Earl, had won a French yachting medal at Cannes from the emperor in 1869. While on the Edgcumbe estate, it may have made Napoleon III smile to see so many small forts around the Sound such as Cawsand, Picklecombe, and Drake's Island (Palmerston Forts) – all built (*c.*1860) as a direct response to the strength and growth of the French navy – his navy! Upon leaving Mount Edgcumbe, Napoleon narrowly missed, by a few days, an awkward encounter. The next group of royal visitors to the house were the Crown Prince of Prussia and his son, the future Kaiser Wilhelm II. One can assume the Bonapartes made a swift departure from Plymouth Sound. Not for the first time!

In February 1872, after Bertie Prince of Wales had narrowly escaped death by typhoid, a grand thanksgiving service was held at St Paul's Cathedral. Victoria invited the Bonapartes to Buckingham Palace to watch the procession and cheering crowds. They were hosted by Princess Beatrice. That summer, full of hope with news of French plebiscites in favour of his restoration, Napoleon decided he needed to get his ailing health back on track. To do this, he took the waters of Bognor and Brighton. Somehow, these restored him a little and the family rented a property at Cowes and sailed with old friends, Sir John and Lady Burgoyne, and new friends, Jennie Jerome – Winston Churchill's mother.

By the end of autumn that year, many predicted and anticipated the return of Napoleon III. The only obstacle was his health. He planned to undergo an operation, after which he could convalesce at Cowes; however, from there he would slip away to Belgium and then France where loyal French troops waited to greet his return.

These hopes were forlorn. The queen's doctor, Sir William Gull, and urologist Sir Henry Thompson, attendant on the emperor, were doubtful that any operations would result in complete success. After two operations, Napoleon deteriorated rapidly. The last rights were given by Father Goddard from the local Roman Catholic Church. His last words were 'we weren't cowards at Sedan?' His last action was to blow a kiss to Eugenie. He died five minutes later on 9 January 1872. With things in France still politically uncertain, and the possibility of returning his body to Paris impossible, Napoleon was buried at St Mary's Catholic Church in Chislehurst, where the family had lately been attending mass. (Years later, he would be moved to Farnborough.)

As the funeral preparations got underway, politics haunted the proceedings. Bertie, the Prince of Wales, who had looked up to Napoleon, and was indeed similar to him in so many ways, wanted to attend the funeral. Both his mother, the queen, and the foreign secretary advised against this. There were concerns that the Bonapartists present would make the event political and proclaim the Prince Imperial as Napoleon IV.

Agreeing not to be a part of petty dynastic politics, Bertie instead visited the Bonapartes the day before the funeral. Napoleon III lay in state at Camden Place. On the day of the funeral, mass crowds of well-wishers, ex-pats and curious Britons gathered on Chislehurst Common to watch the procession. The funeral itself was reportedly very plain, the sort of affair you would expect for a local old gent – certainly not an emperor and knight of the Garter. There was no insignia or heraldic displays, just a lot of plain black drapery – little to suggest this was an emperor. The Prince Imperial, walking behind the coffin, in a plain black coat, wore the star and scarlet sash of the *Legion d'honneur* – the only streak of colour at an otherwise dark ceremony. The bells of the local Anglican parish church tolled as a sign of respect during the funeral march.

A strange end for a man who had come so far in life. Unlike his uncle, fate did not allow Napoleon III a second attempt at being emperor of the French. Though both died and were buried on British soil, their predicaments were very different. The last emperor of France was no captive but a welcome, respected, even loved guest of Britain. He in turn must have had great affection for the country that had offered him a temporary home on more than one occasion when the continent was too dangerous for him, and had worked hard to forge strong links between it and France. In death, however, England became the permanent home of Napoleon III – a French emperor but an English gentleman.

Armorial bearings of Napoleon III as a Knight of the Most Noble Order of the Garter, painted by Alison Hill, heraldic artist at HM's College of Arms, London. The emperor was invested with the insignia at Windsor in 1855 by Queen Victoria. A stall plate in the Garter Chapel at Windsor also bears these arms.

Chapter 7

Eugenie and her Boy: An Officer and a Dame of the British Empire

From Camden Place, Eugenie and Louis-Napoleon (le petit prince) continued their lives rather like English gentlefolk. It is especially surprising to think that Louis-Napoleon, the Prince Imperial and heir to the French Empire, gained a commission in the British army, and served in the far-flung British Empire in Africa. He was possibly romantically entangled with one of Queen Victoria's daughters and has a tomb-like monument dedicated to him in St George's Chapel, Windsor – a burial place usually reserved for British royalty. Following the collapse of the Second French Empire, and the death of Napoleon III, Eugenie and her boy lived the rest of their lives as exiles from France and seem to have become Anglophiles, perhaps by predicament or perhaps by choice.

As we have seen, Eugenie had some British roots and was briefly educated in England. Her Scottish maternal grandfather, William Kirkpatrick of Closeburn, near Dumfries, was an immigrant to Spain who became a wine merchant and US consul in Malaga. Eugenie was known to dress in the Kirkpatrick tartan occasionally and greatly enjoyed her various trips to Scotland. There were, however, further family links to Britain.

Both Eugenie and her sister were daughters to Cipriano de Palafox, 8th Count of Montijo, 15th Duke of Penaranda and a grandee of Spain (1785–1839). A soldier who fought on the side of Joseph Bonaparte (while king of Spain) in the Spanish wars, he lost an eye in battle and was honoured for his service by Napoleon I. He married Maria Manuela Kirkpatrick de Grevignée; daughter of the aforementioned William Kirkpatrick and his wife, a French noblewoman, Marie François de Grevignée. Her sister, Catherine (Eugenie's great-aunt), married Mathieu de Lesseps and had a son; Ferdinand de Lesseps – making Eugene a first-cousin-once-removed of the creator of the Suez Canal – which she opened in his presence in 1869.

Maria Manuela (1794–1879) had what one might call a colourful past and had one or two gentleman admirers. Amongst her close friends was Prosper Mérimée. She was his inspiration for his novel *Carmen* – which Bizet later turned into the famous opera of the same name. Manuela was perhaps more worldly than her daughters. As a young woman, it is thought that she 'entertained' the customers at her father's winery. It was scandalous rumours such as this which lost her the coveted position of head of the household to Queen Isabella of Spain. Manuela also formed an 'intimate' friendship with a young Lord Clarendon (the great British foreign secretary). It is possible that they were lovers, and it was in fact he who had arranged that Eugenie and Napoleon should meet in secret for the first time – to give the two a chance to get to know one another. It is nice to know that an Englishman helped facilitate the imperial couple's happiness.

Eugenie's older sister was born Maria Francisca de Sales Portocarrero y Kirkpatrick, but was affectionately known by many as Paca. She was born in Granada in 1825. When she was a teenager, her father died. Having no sons, his many titles were divided between his two daughters. Paca, being the elder, received the majority; Paca gained a duchy together with five marquisates, five countships, a viscountcy and became a grandee of Spain. With such a grand position, albeit not a wealthy one, she was sure to gain a marriage of good standing. She married another Spaniard of Scottish descent, Jacobo FitzJames-Stuart, in 1848. Jacobo was the direct male-line descendant of King James II of England (James VII of Scotland). From around 1665, King James (at that time the Duke of York) began a long affair with one Arabella Churchill – sister of the future Duke of Marlborough and three times great-aunt of Prime Minister Winston Churchill. Their son was given the name James FitzJames and created Duke of Berwick (as in Berwick-upon-Tweed), Earl of Tinmouth and Baron Bosworth. In England, the titles were considered forfeit after James II's enforced exile. Nevertheless, Jacobo and Paca were recognised by the Spanish court as the 15th Duke and Duchess of Berwick (though usually known by his Spanish title: Duke of Alba). The Berwick link and strong Jacobite connections in Eugenie's family must have amused her while on her tours of Scotland now ruled by her Hanoverian friend, Victoria.

With the splendours of the Tuileries and Versailles behind them, the exiled Bonaparte family, cousins, retainers, servants et al., began

Family Tree

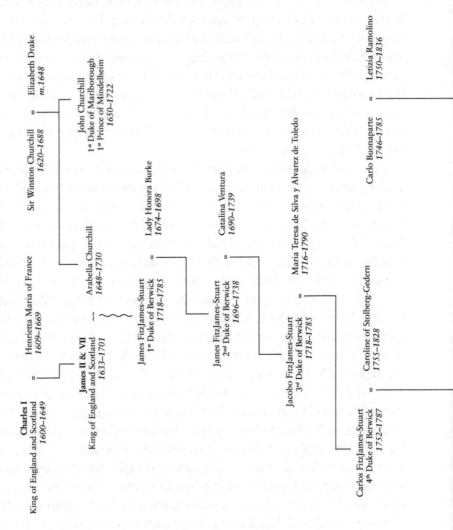

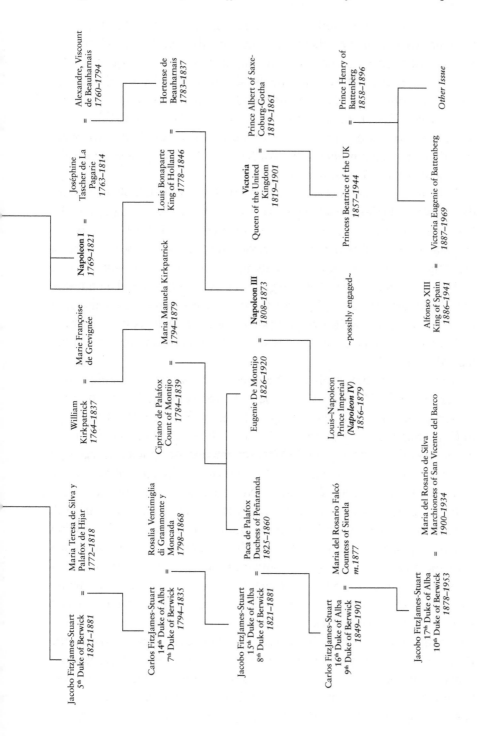

to settle in at their humble country house in Kent. From the first time the empress had arrived there, after her speedy and daring flight from France, Camden Place had been moulded into a small caricature of a French imperial court, with all the usual forms of address and courtesy observed – but in far quainter surroundings than anyone was used to. Veteran servants of the imperial household, with illustrious titles, who had been used to having a small office and staff of their own, were slightly diminished in that they now had to roll up their sleeves for the occasional bit of manual labour.

It should be remembered in these early days of the telephone that all the London telephone exchanges were named. This was usually just the first three letters of the exchange, for example 'CHI' for Chiswick. To avoid a clashing of names, however, the exchange name for Chislehurst was changed. It was named after its most prominent residents. It was 'IMP' – for imperial. This little legacy survives to this day. The number for Chislehurst is 020 8467. The Imperial Arms pub in Chislehurst is but a few minutes' walk from Camden Place too. Allegedly, one of the exiled emperor's many mistresses was lodged there, and now has a bar named after her!

The death of her husband, Napoleon III, brought Eugenie much closer to Queen Victoria. When the dust had settled after the funeral, Victoria, together with her youngest daughter, Princess Beatrice, went to Chislehurst to meet mother and son. Victoria and Eugenie formed a lasting sisterly friendship for the next several decades. Victoria, who was prone to be jealous of women who had men to cuddle up to at night, was rather short of feminine friendship. Now she had a 'captive' audience in Eugenie. Both were widowed with young unmarried children; both were empresses. (Victoria was made empress of India in 1876.) Being of near equal rank certainly helped the friendship. There was much enjoyment and mirth from the problem of precedence and which one of them should enter a room first. Eugenie certainly benefited from being so very close to Victoria – who acted very much like the older, wiser sister. In turn, Eugenie was the mischievous younger sister, who was not beyond making fun of Victoria behind her back. Victoria visited the Roman Catholic chapel in Chislehurst to pay her respects to her late old friend the emperor. It is possible that she felt a sense of duty to Napoleon to look after Eugenie and Louis-Napoleon. She certainly took on that position and was a great advocate and imperial protector to the boy.

Before Napoleon III died, and after the holiday together at Cowes, the Prince Imperial joined the Royal Military Academy at Woolwich – which in those days trained British army officers for the Royal Artillery or Royal Engineers. (Sandhurst trained officers for the cavalry or infantry.) His father wanted him to continue the Napoleonic tradition of being an artillery man – as Napoleon I had been. Young Louis-Napoleon, now 16, had been preparing for this. In the months running up to Woolwich, he had attended King's College, London, in the Strand, and studied physics. The boy's meddlesome, jealous cousin Prince Napoleon, known as Plon-Plon, son of Jerome Bonaparte, and technically the heir presumptive to the dynasty, wished to take the boy out of Woolwich, probably so as to lead the boy to stray into plots and schemes that would in fact discredit him. It was Plon-Plon who had stormed into Camden Place after the emperor's death and torn the emperor's desk apart looking for papers – he claimed there had been another will (in which, of course, he believed he was a beneficiary).

Aside from his mother, Prince Louis-Napoleon now had a new protector who shielded him from such creatures as Plon-Plon. Victoria took him under her wing. She was like a second mother or godmother. They were quite close and his intimacy with her was only really equalled or surpassed by John Brown or members of her immediate family. The idea of a Bonaparte restoration and a third empire was not yet extinguished, and Victoria believed that it would be good for Britain, France and Europe if the boy did become Napoleon IV one day. As such, he was virtually a member of the extended royal family – regularly visiting Windsor and Osborne. Owing to who he was, he was far more used to the grandeur and splendour of places such as these, than the rather twee Camden Place; he was more at home in the royal residences. Sadly, Victoria could not protect him from the French republican press – who would spread lies about his lack of ability at the academy, effectively claiming that he was a simpleton with deformities, in an attempt to discredit him and the Bonapartist party in France. The opposite was in fact true. He loved the academy; he was the best horseman of his year and he did well in the exams – considering English was a second language.

In truth, many Bonapartists on both sides of the Channel, particularly the common folk, saw him as a bright young star, and a possible future liberal ruler of France. This was apparent on his eighteenth birthday.

Many French made the journey across the sea to Kent to see the coming of age of their prince, and so did many Londoners hoping to attend what would be a very French event. Thousands descended on the Kentish village of Chislehurst for the ticketed event. In fact, there were not enough tickets to go round. Train companies had even put posters up advertising the occasion, hoping to cash in on the excitement. The village locals had put the bunting out and the bands played – though this was a certainly more than the annual village fête. Louis-Napoleon gave a speech thanking the well-wishers, in a marquee on the lawn of Camden Place, holding 3,000 people. He spoke rather well. The shouts, standing ovations and cries of support were reportedly overwhelming. He got a taste of his own power and public enthusiasm for him as emperor-in-waiting for the first time – but, in a tent – on a lawn – in Kent! It was not France.

Louis-Napoleon 'passed out' of Woolwich in February 1875 in the presence of his mother and the commander-in-chief of the British forces, Field Marshal Prince George, The Duke of Cambridge, KG. The same scandalous cousin of Victoria who had been sent to 'interview' Napoleon III prior to the state visits of 1855. It is not as uncommon as one might think to have a foreign prince being trained in or by the British army. To this day, there are always a great number of foreign princes (and sometimes princesses) training as cadets at Sandhurst, usually from Arabia or Asia. Indeed, it is donations from these foreign royal families that pays for some of the facilities there – which sometimes means the royal cadets merely skim through the course. The Prince Imperial, however, shirked none of his training. He came seventh in his year overall, taking first place in riding and fencing. Queen Victoria was so very proud, particularly as he had conducted himself so well. Victoria compared the prince to her own son Bertie and his scandalous liaisons and affairs while he had been in military training. He had disgraced himself with a woman who had been smuggled into barracks, but so far, it seemed that Bertie was much more like Napoleon III, as indeed was the case, and the Prince Imperial had sensible traits that would be more in line with Prince Albert (or so Victoria perhaps thought).

Eugenie was worried that Louis-Napoleon, now a grown man and a dashing British officer, might begin to take up the pursuits of his late father Napoleon, or of his honorary uncle-like figure, Bertie Prince of Wales, namely: chasing skirts and generally being lecherous or taking up foolhardy plots and coups across the water in France. All of which would probably lead to failure, humiliation and probably imprisonment like his papa. Perhaps from strength of character, or from the Victorian principles shown to him by his mother or the queen, Louis-Napoleon did not take that path. He understood that he needed an exemplary record and reputation if he was ever to succeed in returning as France's emperor. He knew he must bide his time carefully. For now, he accepted his posting at an artillery battery at Aldershot.

That said, the apple never falls far from the tree, try as we might to change that. Napoleon III's boy was, of course, not without an amusing social life. He was very much taken under the wing of the Prince of Wales. Though over ten years younger than Bertie, Louis-Napoleon and he had a mutual sense of humour and love of practical jokes. Lillie Langtry, Bertie's sometime mistress, reported that at a house party at Cowes, several such pranks authored by the two princes occurred: one involving dressing a donkey in lady's clothes and placing it in someone's bed; the other, showering Bertie in flour. Also involved in their shenanigans were other royal chums such as Prince Leopold (the haemophiliac son of Victoria) and Prince Louis of Battenberg (the future First Sea Lord, father of Earl Mountbatten of Burma, and grandfather of Prince Philip the Duke of Edinburgh). These sorts of antics were kept hidden from the queen – for obvious reasons. Rather like boys' relationships with their mothers today, it must have been difficult for Bertie. In the eyes of his mother, he was an adulterous lazybones, whereas his friend Louis-Napoleon was the golden boy. Why do mothers foolishly believe their son's friends are always so much better behaved than their own?

The British press, always keen for gossip and royal matchmaking, were snooping around to find out if there were any rumours of an intended bride for the young French prince. Victoria's youngest child, Beatrice, was unmarried. Since Albert's death, it was probably the queen's intention, like many Victorian mothers, that her youngest daughter should not fly the nest but remain with her as both a companion and a secretary. A rather boring prospect for any young girl. Unsurprisingly, because of their proximity in age, their mothers' close friendship, and public sightings of them together, the papers were awash with rumours of an imminent engagement between the Prince Imperial and Princess Beatrice of the United Kingdom. Victoria, uncharacteristically, did nothing to quash these rumours, which many be interpreted as evidence that she was not wholly opposed to the idea and that it may have been on the cards, or at least in discussion. Certainly Louis-Napoleon fanned the flames by publicly riding alongside Beatrice and her entourage in parks and chatting at great length. There were rumours that he had picked up girls on his train rides between Chislehurst and London; however, these were unlikely and ignored by Victoria anyway. Despite the little problem that he was Roman Catholic, it is easy to see the positives for all concerned in the match. Beatrice would gain some freedom from her mother. The prince would have a match that would constitute a powerful alliance and backer in the British royal family. Victoria's daughter would be married to the son of her beloved 'captive friend' Eugenie and, for now at least, would not be far away – probably living at Windsor or nearby for the foreseeable future. Beatrice, Louis-Napoleon and their progeny, would be members of the British and French royal/imperial families. A state of affairs which had not happened since the Middle Ages.

Youth is not congenial to wisdom though. The prince indicated he was not yet ready to be tied down by marriage. To be fair, he had great ambitions for himself on the path to becoming emperor; he was not going to get there by quietly sipping tea on the lawns at Windsor. The two clearly liked each other and it is generally accepted that they were romantically entangled. Sadly, for the time being, it seems he shelved marriage. Louis-Napoleon wanted adventure and some military glory. He needed that Napoleonic 'tick in the box' of military accomplishment, bravery or glory – which was the starting point in the political career (and legend) of his great-uncle Napoleon I. Like many young gentlemen of the previous fifteen or so decades, he wanted a bit of army, a bit of action, a bit of glory which would set him up for a good career on the political stage. (Not unlike other young Victorian men, such as Winston Churchill.) The prince searched for any opportunity to get stuck in – and maybe win some laurels.

His prayers were answered in 1879. At Isandlwana in Zululand, the Zulu army of King Cetshwayo overran and massacred British forces on 22 January. Over 1,300 soldiers and personnel were killed by a Zulu Impi force of around 20,000 warriors, and the Queen's Colours were captured. It was a humiliating disaster for the British in South Africa. Some face was saved by the heroic defence of Rorke's Drift – where a small British force of 150 or so successfully took a defensive position against 3,000–4,000 Zulus. (Eleven Victoria Crosses were awarded for valour.) Nonetheless, it was an overall embarrassment that could not go unanswered by British might. Reinforcements were prepared to be sent to quash the Zulus. Louis-Napoleon's own battery was to be sent and he hoped to go with them but he was refused permission by the commander-in-chief, Prince George Duke of Cambridge. The Prince Imperial was furious and very upset.

Eugenie, like a twenty-first-century headstrong mother off to school to give the football coach a piece of her mind, went to Horse Guards in person to do the same to George. With her beauty, charm and the backing of his cousin Queen Victoria, George was inclined to give in, but he had misgivings. The prime minister too, Benjamin Disraeli, former boating companion of Napoleon III, was not in favour – and one cannot blame him. There were political aspects to be considered. How would it look if Britain used the heir to the French Empire as a serving officer in its army to lead British men? If the prince was killed in battle, the French people might say that Britain had conspired to get rid of the one of the Bonapartes yet again – like the alleged poisoning of Napoleon I on St Helena. Despite the obvious concerns, both Cambridge and Disraeli were wise enough not to go up against two old empresses' wishes. The Prince Imperial was allowed to go, but as a civilian. While in the territories, he would be attached in the capacity of observer to the staff of the commander, General Lord Chelmsford, a friend of Queen Victoria. She left instruction to Chelmsford that the prince be careful and not exposed to too much adventure.

As one can sympathise, Chelmsford was not overcome with delight to be saddled with this young petulant, keen and green 'observer'. He had much responsibility and did not want the task of babysitting a foreign princeling or making sure he did not get killed at least. The 'petit prince', though a trained officer, was new to war. He was, of course, a little pampered. He had suits and uniforms from Henry Poole on Savile Row and a monogrammed travelling tea set from Leuchars & Son on Piccadilly, probably a leaving gift from his mama. But what of it?! Lord Cardigan had travelled to the Crimea in style with his private yacht before the great charge at Balaklava in 1856. Though fresh and privileged, the prince wanted nothing more than to get stuck in and to be where the danger was. Chelmsford passed him off on to the staff of Colonel Richard Harrison of the Royal Engineers. Harrison was responsible for reconnaissance and for the column's transport on its way to the Zulu capital, Ulundi. The theory was that this would allow the prince to be active, see some sights, but be relatively safe. Louis was ultimately to be accompanied at all times by an escort for his protection – which must have frustrated the young man as well as any officers set to watch over him. Such responsibility was given to Lieutenant Jaheel Brenton Carey, a Devon vicar's son who came from a Guernsey family and had been educated in France – and therefore was an excellent French speaker. Reports that the Prince Imperial had been gallivanting off into the hills while on mounted patrols, following any Zulus he caught sight of – a perfect way to get killed – infuriated and terrified Lord Chelmsford to the point that he effectively forbade such activity. This was a difficult position for a young British officer to be in. The prince had a rank in the British army, but not strictly recognised on this campaign; he was the prince and heir to a foreign empire, was friends with the sovereign, the commander-in-chief, the Prince of Wales and many senior British officers. Carey, a humble vicar's son, was arguably out of his depth when it came to Louis-Napoleon's commanding and brash nature. There was an ambiguity of social deference that clearly jeopardised the chain of command. This meant Napoleon could persuade or run rings around his 'supervisors'. It was difficult to tell who was giving the orders.

On 1 June 1879, Lieutenant Carey agreed that the prince could accompany an eight-man mounted patrol. Allegedly, the prince effectively took command. At 3 p.m., the order was given for a brief coffee break at a deserted kraal – a cattle enclosure. After an hour or so respite, the prince gave the order for things to be packed up in preparation for leaving. One can imagine the men packing away the tea set. Around this moment, a scouting party of approximately forty Zulus stumbled upon them. Louis-Napoleon quickly gave the order to mount up and retreat to safety. An excellent horseman, his favourite trick was to vault into the saddle of his horse while it was moving – a skill that was no doubt impressive at Woolwich and won him great acclaim. Tragically, this time, the one time it actually mattered, a strap broke. He fell and clung on to a holster on the saddle as the horse ran. The holster broke and the prince fell, and his right arm was trampled. As he got back to his feet, he attempted to make a run for it, but the Zulus were faster. He was speared in the thigh, but he pulled out the assegai and turned. His right arm wounded, he fired his revolver with his left hand into the approaching enemy three times and was speared in the shoulder. He attempted to fight on using the assegai which he had pulled from his leg. Outnumbered and weakened he was overwhelmed. The Zulus quickly finished him off. His body later revealed more than fifteen assegai stab wounds including one in the head through the right eye. Two of the escort were killed and one went missing. In the panic and flight from the kraal, it had been impossible to rescue the prince. Carey and the others came together some distance from Louis-Napoleon's last stand. The events all happened so quickly. His quest for a bit of military adventure and glory had gone disastrously wrong. Arguably, he had gambled away the future of the French Empire, and his life, on a chance of British colonial adventure. The escort had consisted of men of the 17th Lancers, whose motto was 'Death or Glory'. The prince had got a lot of the former, and a soupçon of the latter. He was just 23.

Unsurprisingly, there was an inquiry and a court martial. Carey was eventually acquitted. It was apparent to most that the circumstances regarding the care of the prince were difficult and ambiguous to say the least. A storm started in the French press. As Disraeli had feared, Britain was accused of wilfully 'disposing of' the young Bonaparte. Queen Victoria was even accused of having a hand in it by French writers – which was nonsensical – although other groups were blamed, such as ardent French republicans or even the Freemasons. Regretful of the incident, the Zulus later claimed that had they known he was a prince, they would not have killed him. Some, if not all, of the Zulus involved in his death died a month later at the Battle of Ulundi, the Zulu capital, and its subsequent destruction. An unfortunate rumour went around that the Prince Imperial had been wearing the *Epée d'Austerlitz* and that it had been lost – either to the Zulus or a plucky British soldier. (This was the sword his great-uncle had worn when commanding his greatest victory at the Battle of Austerlitz, 1805.) Fortunately, this was not true. Since 1824 it had been kept at Les Invalides in Paris – but the rumour was ultimately symbolic of the tremendous loss facing the Bonapartists and Imperial France. Coincidentally, the new king of the Zulus, Dinuzulu kaCetshwayo, was captured by the British in 1890 and, like Napoleon Bonaparte, was exiled to the island of St Helena. Arguably, it was poetic justice for the tragic death of Louis-Napoleon.

The prince's remains were returned to Woolwich on 11 July 1879. The Empress Eugenie had been told and was never the same again. Grief had hit her twice. Camden Place became her place of grief. Living in rooms so dark it was difficult to see, she barely moved. The body itself was kept from her; the mutilation marks and the month of decomposing in the African heat did not need to be witnessed by a mother. Eugenie's old friend and saviour (and dentist), Dr Evans, identified the body from the teeth. When Princess Beatrice was informed of Louis-Napoleon's end, she wept uncontrollably and needed much consoling – evidence again that they had probably been nearing an engagement or an understanding.

The funeral of the Prince Imperial at Chislehurst took place six years after his father's. Unlike then, engagement from the royal family was turned up a gear. Victoria and Beatrice came down to Camden Place and consoled Eugenie. Bertie, Prince of Wales, and George, Duke of Cambridge were pall bearers. As an artillery man, the prince's coffin was borne on a gun carriage and his horse walked behind – an ancient custom. In what was to be a nearly unique happenstance, the coffin was adorned in both the French flag and the British flag – he was, after all, a British army officer, and British troops are buried with the Union flag when buried with honours. After he had been lying in state at Woolwich, the funeral procession travelled from there to St Mary's Catholic Church, Chislehurst. One can only wonder what the original Napoleon, Britain's greatest enemy, would have made of the scene – his great-nephew and heir to his legacy being carried to his tomb as a British officer, draped in the three crosses of England, Scotland and Ireland, by the Prince of Wales himself and the commander of the British army.

The Prince Imperial was one of the great 'what ifs' of the nineteenth century. If he had lived, it is quite possible he would have returned to France as emperor. If that had happened, it is quite likely that he would have tried to marry Princess Beatrice. If that had happened, Queen Victoria would have had another one of her children on the many thrones of Europe. If that were the case, Louis-Napoleon (Napoleon IV) would have acquired Kaiser Wilhelm II as his nephew-in-law (they were only three years apart) and might have been able to avoid another even more terrible war between France and Germany – The First World War – which brought an end to many other emperors and kings.

A grand and impressive memorial statue of the Prince Imperial was erected at the Woolwich Academy. Sculpted by Count Gleichen, the monument was paid for by subscribers from the armed forces. Twenty-five thousand officers and men of the British army raised the funds for a statue of Louis-Napoleon Bonaparte, dressed in Woolwich uniform, standing atop polished granite and surrounded by four bronze imperial eagles. The Woolwich Academy eventually merged with Sandhurst in 1947. The statue currently stands at the Royal Military Academy Sandhurst near New College. The subscriptions and the monument are testimony to the high regard and affection in which the prince was held by soldiers of the British army. No such monument was built in France.

Naturally, there had been scandal and rage in France at the news of the prince's death; in Britain too, there was public outcry at the tragedy and the fact that it had been allowed to happen. There was an element of national guilt that the imperial princeling had been killed on Britannia's watch. Senior officials believed that, owing to the gravity of the situation, an official monument with royal support should be created. However, there were problems over where that should be. The Dean of Westminster briefly took things into his own hands and sought permission for there to be a monument at the abbey. Dean Stanley was eventually overruled by the queen's private secretary, Sir Henry Ponsonby, GCB, who, with the consent of Victoria, arranged for the monument to be built and placed in the Bray chantry chapel at St George's Chapel, Windsor Castle in 1881. It was felt that this was more appropriate because of the prince's closeness to the royal family and the special affection Queen Victoria had for him – not to mention the guilt she must have felt for persuading Cambridge and Disraeli to let him go to Zululand. Westminster Abbey had of late become a place of monuments to British heroes of arms, science and literature (as well as English monarchs). A Bonaparte monument was arguably inappropriate. Though only an exiled prince, the late Prince Imperial was very nearly a member of Victoria's family, therefore a monument to him in a chapel which was also the resting place of seven English monarchs (at that point), and the site of his father's greatest personal triumphs – being admitted to the Order of the Garter – did not seem so outlandish. The irony of the Prince Imperial's effigy being in the same building as the tombs of kings George III and George IV, the great enemies of 'old Boney', should also be noted. At its most positive, this may be seen as another step on the road towards the *entente cordiale*. At the negative end of the scale, it illustrates what disrepute the second empire and the imperial family were held in by the French. No grand monument was erected in Les Invalides, near to the other great Bonapartes. The St George's monument of white marble was moved to the south side of the nave in 1985.

But what of Eugenie? Understandably, she confessed that she did not wish to go on living, but her staunch Catholicism prevented her taking any measures in that direction. The empress, who had lost her throne, her husband and her only child in quick succession, instead lived the life of the merry widow and went on another forty years. She decided to address her grief head on. In March of 1880 she made a pilgrimage to Zululand, to visit the site of her son's death. This was no easy journey; it included an 800-mile horse-drawn carriage ride through the difficult terrain of South Africa. She slept either under canvas or the stars. Eugenie and her small party made their way to the kraal where, on direct instruction from Queen Victoria, British soldiers had already erected a stone cross on the spot of Louis-Napoleon's demise. On the anniversary of that fateful tea-break-ambush, Eugenie spent a day and a night at the foot of the cross in silence. She then returned to Kent. Unlike Victoria, she did not dwell on her grief. In a style perceivably Spanish, she grabbed life by the horns and pressed on.

Eugenie bought property on the French Riviera, and acquired new friends. She became a collector of the young and beautiful – perhaps as a distraction from her grief or to remind her of her son. That said, there may have been more primal motives behind the selections of young bachelors. Either way, Eugenie took pleasure in fun, and this may have been the reason for her long life. Putting fun to one side, her mind drew towards a more fitting resting place for her imperial husband and son. The Catholic church in Chislehurst was rather dank and twee. After her return from South Africa, the empress bought Farnborough Hill in Hampshire, along with nearly 300 acres of park and woodland. She came to greatly admire the Hampshire countryside. Here, in her new-found peace and tranquillity, she designed a special mausoleum and church for her man and her boy. This being a Roman Catholic foundation, it would also house several monks who would pray for the souls of deceased. The Priory of St Michael was built by French architect Hippolyte Destailleur, in the neo-gothic style reminiscent of some of the fine medieval priories and monasteries of France – typical of the Victorian era. Destailleur had also worked on Waddesdon Manor in Buckinghamshire, a chateau-style house for the Rothschild family. England being an ardently Protestant country, it was difficult to get priests or monks to come and live there;

eventually, priests were obtained from France, and the Pope promoted the building to an abbey in 1903. The bodies of the emperor and Prince Imperial were reinterred in the crypt of St Michaels by the Royal Horse Artillery. To this day they rest in tombs of Aberdeen granite – a personal gift from Queen Victoria. Farnborough Hill (House) became like a museum to the Second French Empire with knickknacks and souvenirs from various famous members of the Bonaparte clan. Like Victoria had done for Albert, there was a study where Eugenie had all of her son's possessions laid out – as though he may return tomorrow.

For her pleasure, she once again turned to her Scottish cousins-in-law, the Hamiltons. From the Duke of Hamilton, she bought a small yacht named *Thistle*. With it she was able to accept invitations (about twice a year) from Victoria to visit Osborne in the Isle of Wight and, ever a fan of Scotland, she was occasionally included on royal trips north. Eugenie formed a friendship with Victoria's special servant and confidant, John Brown. She more than most must have understood the relationship between the pair as a fellow empress-widow in need of a little companionship. The friendship between the ex-empress of France and the empress of India had its ups and downs. Victoria liked to remind other women of her place in the world, and would not brook a challenge of any kind, however small. This must have rankled Eugenie's temperament as a vivacious, outdoors and humorous character. Eugenie easily bored and made no attempts to hide it. Like Queen Elizabeth II, she was reportedly good at impressions and aired them in front of those whom she did not like or found boring. She was quick to anger and had almost Plantagenet-like mood swings and tempers; many staff at Farnborough bore the brunt.

Eugenie, perhaps not surprisingly, formed a close bond with Princess Beatrice. After all, had it not been for the Zulus, Eugenie might have been Beatrice's mother-in-law. Eugenie must have been a loving and welcome relief for Beatrice who had to bear the austere nature of her mother, Victoria. The princess had had a difficult existence in her role as perpetual companion and secretary to her mother. When the Prince Imperial was killed, she was heartbroken. This was made worse because it also must have seemed that her opportunity to escape her mother had been extinguished. Opportunity came again, however, when she met Prince Henry of Battenberg at a family wedding in 1884. Prince Henry's elder brother, Prince Louis of Battenberg, married Beatrice's niece, Princess Alice of Hesse (the grandparents of Prince Philip, the Duke of Edinburgh). Beatrice fell wildly in love with the handsome, moustached Prince Henry; it was clear that the two wished to marry. Naturally, Victoria felt threatened and betrayed by her youngest (and captive) child. There followed a period where mother and daughter did not talk – having servants pass notes instead. The Empress Eugenie was key in bringing Victoria round to the idea of the marriage and interceded on behalf of Beatrice. A compromise was agreed upon. The couple could marry but on the condition that they made their home with the queen. Henry and Beatrice were married at St Mildred's Church, Whippingham, Isle of Wight in 1885. Every silver lining has a cloud! In honour of their friendship (and the empress's diplomacy in making the marriage happen), Henry and Beatrice named their daughter Princess Victoria Eugenia Julia Ena of Battenberg. The Empress Eugenie stood as godmother. Little Victoria Eugenia eventually became queen of Spain in 1906. More recently, in 1990, Queen Elizabeth II's granddaughter, Princess Eugenie of York (now Mrs Jack Brooksbank), was named after Victoria Eugenia and therefore indirectly named after the Empress Eugenie.

Prince Henry of Battenberg mirrored the Prince Imperial in character: he was handsome, dashing and had a lust for adventure and military exploits. The Battenberg newlyweds, though in close proximity to the queen, enjoyed a happy marriage, producing four children; however, the wheel of (mis)fortune came around again. Henry, rather like the Prince Imperial, wanted to go on a British military campaign in Africa – Ashanti. Princess Beatrice, ever supportive of her husband, persuaded the military and the queen (who was against it) to let him go as a secretary to the commander-in-chief. Though in a relatively safe job, Prince Henry caught malaria and died in 1896 on ship near Sierra Leone.

The now twice-bereaved Beatrice had lost the two men she had loved. Both were foreign princes. Both serving under the British flag in Africa. The loss brought Beatrice and Victoria closer to Eugenie – they had all been through so much together. Soon after, Eugenie managed to get Victoria to visit a Catholic monastery in Spain – the first Protestant woman to be received there. The deep family friendship between the empress and royal family was illustrated by the regular holiday visits made to Eugenie's villa at Cap Martin, near Monte Carlo. As well as Victoria, the Prince of Wales, the Duke of Cambridge, Tsar Nicholas II of Russia and his wife, Empress Alexandra Feodorovna (Princess Alix of Hesse and by Rhine) – a favourite granddaughter of Victoria – were all guests.

With the death of Queen Victoria in 1901, one might have anticipated a lessening of Eugenie's station or influence over the royal family. On the contrary, it only increased. She was a senior member of the sovereigns' club of Europe; at 75 she was older than most. Bertie, now King Edward VII, adored her, looked up to her and valued her counsel. If Victoria was the 'grandmother of Europe' and Edward the 'uncle of Europe', Eugenie might be described as the 'honorary godmother of Europe' at that time. She was consulted by many Europeans in matters of politics, diplomacy and royal matchmaking. As Germany began the slow waltz towards war, Eugenie, with her first-hand experience in dealing with Bismarck, the Prussians and their army, was often asked her opinions by both French and British politicians. One of these was the then foreign secretary the Marquess of Lansdowne – himself a half-cousin of Napoleon III via the emperor's mother, Queen Hortense, and her lover, Charles de Flahaut. In the royal marriage market, Eugenie was instrumental in in finding a match for the Spanish king, Alfonso XIII. She had been asked because of her status in Europe and her Spanish background. After hosting her god-daughter, Princess Victoria Eugenia, at Farnborough Hill for a talk on the subject of marriage, and a meeting with the Spanish king in London, Eugenie's god-daughter was the successful candidate. The king proposed and they were married in 1906. A British princess on the throne of Spain thanks to a French empress. (The fury of English Protestants at a British princess marrying a Catholic was mercifully minor.)

King Edward often sought the advice of the empress, and they met on many occasions, one of which was on the royal yacht named *Victoria and Albert* at Cowes. However, the now elderly empress had forgotten she had given her yacht's crew the day off to attend a funeral. She had no way of getting to the royal party. Alone on the *Thistle*, she signalled with her handkerchief to Frederic Ponsonby, the king's assistant private secretary – who by chance happened to be passing on the water in the royal yacht's pinnace. He was shocked to find the empress of France all alone. She asked for a lift to the royal yacht. In order to get her from vessel to vessel, he practically had to carry her – much to her amusement. Her prized yacht, *Thistle,* also had an encounter with Kaiser Wilhelm II of Germany in Bergen Harbour. She had turned him down several times but finally allowed him to call on her for tea on board. We can only guess what they must have talked of; however, as a mark of respect to her, following the meeting, the passing German flotilla sailed past her yacht displaying the flag of France. Not bad for a Prussian – Napoleons I & III would have been amazed.

The death of Edward VII in 1910 brought with it the end of the Edwardian period during which harmony had been established between England and France, partly thanks to the jolly British monarch – often known as 'Mi Lord' due to his frivolous social life in the clubs of Paris and elsewhere. Edward was succeeded by George V. There could not have been a more different king. He was the opposite of his father in some ways. He was shy, lived frugally, collected stamps, and spoke no other languages than English. He had neither French nor German. Where his father had without a doubt been a European monarch, George was very British and concerned only with empire. Eugenie was not to have the same camaraderie with the new king as she had had with his livelier predecessor. She retreated to Farnborough Hill where she entertained members of her late husband's extended family. One such relative was Prince Victor Napoleon, whom her son had named as successor to the Bonaparte dynasty. Although a charming man, Prince Victor lacked the determination, panache and willpower to be a realistic contender in French politics; nevertheless, Eugenie treated this cousin-in-law as though he was in fact the emperor of the French, observing every courtesy and precedence. The imperial legacy really lived through her continued existence. She later sheltered Victor and his family during the First World War after they fled Europe for their safety. There were other more awkward family callers to Farnborough, such as the illegitimate offspring of her husband – mostly coming in the hope of support or patronage from the dowager empress. Eugenie bore these with great dignity. Napoleon III had spread his 'generosity' widely throughout Britain, France and Europe. One can only imagine how many characters came out of the woodwork in the years following his death.

Britain declared war on Germany on 4 August 1914. A few days earlier, Eugenie had just returned from a tour of her former residences in France, such as Fontainebleau and the Malmaison. Perhaps she felt she knew it would be her last opportunity to go to these places before the clouds of war encircled France. The *entente cordiale* was now in full swing and locked in perpetual battle against the goose-stepping enemy; an enemy which, arguably, Britain had inherited from the Bonapartes – the Prussians and Germans.

Eugenie, like many royals in Britain, flung herself into War Effort mode. She donated her precious yacht *Thistle* to the admiralty – no doubt taking great delight in the irony that it had once hosted the Kaiser! At her own expense, she turned a large part of Farnborough Hill into an Officers' Hospital. She was hands-on. Eugenie was no stranger to life on the wards. She had tended the wounded in the hospitals of the Tuileries during the Franco-Prussian War. The empress was full of positivity and bravado – encouraging happiness as a further antidote to pain. Impressed with the progress at Farnborough Hill, George V and Queen Mary visited the hospital; they were also present at Eugenie's ninetieth birthday in 1916. Perhaps in gratitude for the hospital's work, or her friendship and advice to the British royal family over the many decades, she was made an Honorary Dame Grand Cross of the Order of the British Empire. Presenting the insignia to her were George's sons: the Prince of Wales (Edward VIII) and the Duke of York (George VI). The last empress of the French was invested with the Order of the British Empire by the last emperors of India.

When the war was finally over, and her patients moved to Aldershot, Eugenie insisted that they all return to Farnborough for a visit when they were recovered – which many men did. However, as a continental woman in her nineties, Eugenie could bear the dull weather of England no more. She travelled to France and then to her homeland of Spain via Gibraltar – the last piece of Britain she would see. In Spain, Eugenie returned to the style of an empress. She entertained and was entertained. Her god-daughter, Victoria Eugenia, the queen of Spain, and her husband the king, hosted her with great pageantry. However, Eugenie's health was failing and she had trouble with her sight. An operation was performed with some success. Afterwards, while staying in Madrid, she was visited by her great-nephew, Jacobo, Duke of Alba and Berwick (grandson of her sister, Paca). One of her last acts was to insist that his upcoming marriage take place in England – preferably at Farnborough Hill. A few days later, before she could leave for Britain to attend the wedding, she caught a cold, took to her bed, and died in Madrid on Sunday morning, to the sound of church bells, 11 July 1920. She was 94.

Eugenie was interred beside her husband and son at St Michael's Abbey, Farnborough; the mausoleum she had designed for them. The funeral was attended by George V, Queen Mary, and Queen Victoria Eugenia. She left her home, Farnborough Hill, and various Bonaparte collections to her son's appointed heir, Prince Victor. The house is now a Roman Catholic school for girls. That would probably delight Eugenie. Her Spanish assets were left to the grandchildren of her sister including Jacobo, 17th Duke of Alba and 10th Duke of Berwick. Jacobo, as his great-aunt had hoped, was married later in 1920. He and his wife, Maria, were leading guests at the wedding of Princess Elizabeth and Prince Philip, the Duke of Edinburgh, twenty-seven years later in 1947.

Rather like Queen Elizabeth the Queen Mother, Eugenie was one of the great dowagers of the nineteenth and twentieth centuries. She lived long enough to see enormous changes both politically and technologically. When she was born, the map of Europe was very different. She had seen empires rise and fall – mostly fall. The French, Mexican, German, Austrian, Ottoman and Russian empires had all lost their imperial standing. Her life had not been without its adventures. Though it must have been pleasing for Eugenie to see Germany's greatest humiliation (so far) take place in the same room as France's humiliation earlier in 1871, she had the intelligence to predict that the 1919 Versailles Peace Treaty would not be the end of the matter for Germany. After the deaths of Napoleon III and the Prince Imperial, Eugenie had a second life, the highlights of which seem to have centred around her interactions with the British royal family – of which she was certainly an honorary and appreciated member. The motto of the Order of the British Empire she received is: *For God and the Empire*. Perhaps this is appropriate for a woman who was so devoted to her God, and to the memory of her emperor and empire – The Second French Empire. Nevertheless, in a crypt of Scottish granite, there rests the hopes of imperial France, but surrounded by English countryside.

Chapter 8

Lucien et al.: The Serpentine, a Clitoris and a Bath Companion

Lucien is sometimes known as the brother who stood up to Napoleon – or at least embarrassed him. Though he was one of the key people in helping his brother gain/seize control of the French government in 1799, he was far more of a revolutionary than Napoleon. This caused friction and clashes of views between the two men – the one not willing to follow commands or suggestions from the other (especially with regards to marriage) – all of which led to estrangement. This separation resulted in Lucien's awkward capture by the British in 1810 and subsequent exile in England for almost the rest of the Napoleonic Wars. The two men were only reconciled during the short-lived 'Hundred Days'. However, it is Lucien's offspring who possess some of the most surprising links to the shores of Britannia. He had by far the highest number of children of any of the Bonaparte siblings – there's not much else to do in exile – but, due to the disagreements with Napoleon, Lucien and his family were barred from the official line of succession to the throne (and headship of the Bonaparte family). This did not mean, however, that this revolutionary brood of Bonapartes led any less-interesting lives. From royalty, to High Sheriff; from studying Cornish, to almost disrupting the coronation in 1952, the family of Lucien appears remarkably diverse, and surprisingly British.

Like his older brother Napoleon, Lucien was born in Corsica, in 1775, and was educated in France. His return to Corsica coincided with the French Revolution and he joined the local Jacobins in Ajaccio. He was an excellent orator and advocate of the Revolution. At this time, he preferred to be known by his more republican name: Brutus Bonaparte. He was welcomed into the circles of key revolutionary men such as Maximilien Robespierre. He was a local revolutionary dignitary in his village of Saint-Maximin and showed little mercy by having dozens of

Family Tree

The British Bonapartes

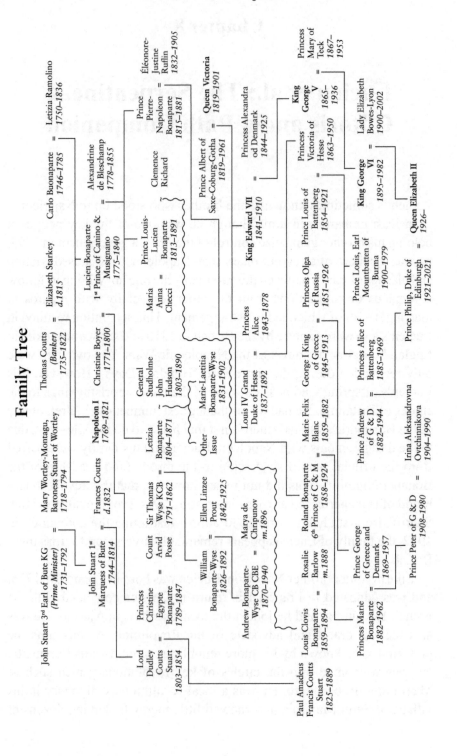

villagers imprisoned for unrevolutionary activity. Though Lucien's older brother had been a revolutionary in his youth, Napoleon was furious at Lucien's very democratic choice of wife – the local pub landlord's sister, Christine Boyer. She had neither money nor literacy. As the bloody Reign of Terror came to an end, on 23 July 1794, Robespierre and many of his allies were arrested, beheaded or imprisoned. Eventually, Lucien and even Napoleon himself were briefly imprisoned. Returning to politics, Lucien eventually succeeded in being elected the president of the Council of Five Hundred, the lower house of French legislature under the time of the Directoire. With his new-found authority, the perceived rising star of his brother Napoleon, the inefficiency of the Directoire and the perceived threats from royalists abroad, Lucien was able to be instrumental in devising a coup d'état to bring Napoleon into power. The coup of 18 Brumaire (19 November 1799) – where Lucien persuaded the grenadiers guarding the Assembly to invade it while pointing a knife to his brother's chest claiming he would put it through Napoleon's heart if he suspected him of violating rights and liberties of Frenchmen – brought General Bonaparte to power as the first consul of France. Five years later he would crown himself emperor of the French.

The new citizen First Consul, General Bonaparte, made his younger brother Minister of the Interior. Though this should have been a great honour and opportunity for Lucien, he remained the young revolutionary. He reportedly got civil servants to do all his work, and was often critical of Napoleon and his policies. When Christine died in 1800, he shut himself away for days – refusing to deal with any state papers. Lucien published a pamphlet comparing Napoleon to both Julius Caesar and Oliver Cromwell – two men who turned their republics into dictatorships. The furious first consul had him moved to Madrid as French ambassador; however, Lucien further provoked his brother by making suggestions that Napoleon divorce Joséphine de Beauharnais and marry one of the Spanish princesses. This sowed yet more seeds of discord in the Bonaparte clan, and Joséphine and Lucien were certainly bitter enemies. Meanwhile, Lucien had amassed a great fortune during his diplomatic tenure on the Iberian peninsula, mostly from bribes and backhanders from the Spanish and Portuguese courts.

Though in possession of pretentions of grandeur, and a meddler in his family's affairs (he had told his younger brother Louis that his wife to be, Hortense, was actually already pregnant by her stepfather, Napoleon!), he managed to slot himself into yet another unsuitable marriage. Despite his brother's offer of the throne via marriage to the queen of Etruria (Tuscany and Parma), Lucien married Alexandrine Jouberthon, daughter of a Normandy tax collector and 'widow' of dodgy banker who had fled to San Domingo, probably to avoid his debts. His death had not been completely confirmed, therefore to add to her unsuitability, there was a possibility of bigamy. Napoleon's rage and despair at his younger brother deepened. After Napoleon became emperor in 1804, and the Bonaparte family started putting on more imperial graces and titles. Lucien was not recognised as an imperial prince owing to his common marriage. His other young brother, Jerome, received the same treatment owing to his marriage to the American, Betsy Patterson.

Napoleon continued to try and break up the marriage of Lucien and Alexandrine. Though quite brash, Lucien was handsome and intelligent (in his own way) and he would make a useful dynastic match with a Royal House of Europe both for Napoleon and for France. However, Alexandrine was charming, red-haired and beautiful; Lucien ardently stood by her. He even turned down the viceroyship of Italy which Napoleon had offered him, yet he continued to insist that he and his wife be recognised as part of the imperial family, and he and his heirs be added to the succession. Napoleon did not give way and Lucien retreated to Rome to sulk. The new viceroy of Italy was Napoleon's stepson, Eugene, whom he adopted and made Imperial Highness and heir presumptive to the throne of Italy, later creating him Prince of Venice – much to the annoyance of Lucien. Lucien, despite refusing the opportunities his brother had gifted him, had the gall to ask his brother for the Grand Cordon of the *Legion d'honneur*. He was refused. Napoleon (and their mother Letitia) continued to insist that Lucien repudiate his wife in favour of an alliance with a more appropriate European royal princess.

Lucien and Alexandrine decided that, in order to avoid separation, they should escape to the New World across the Atlantic, along with their children and the children from Lucien's first marriage. (By this point he had six from Alexandrine and two from Christine.) In August of 1810 they went to Naples to seek passage to America. Naples was by now ruled by Napoleon's friend and brother-in-law, Joachim Murat – married to Caroline Bonaparte. Napoleon had made this innkeeper's son-come-dashing-cavalry-commander king of Naples in 1808. Since his elevation to kingly status, Murat's loyalty was not as reliable as it had been. Murat assisted Lucien and his family in boarding the American ship *Hercules* which was in port and bound for home. However, the transportation had barely got underway, when it was interrupted by storms; the *Hercules* had to take shelter off the Sardinian coast. They were intercepted by a British warship' and Lucien, the whole family and retinue, numbering about forty, were taken as prisoners of war. They boarded HMS *Pomona*, commanded by Captain Sir Robert Barrie, KCB, KCH, and were taken to British-held Malta. Captain Barrie explained the situation to the British commissioner of the island, Sir Hildebrand Oakes Bt. Oakes, who was rather alarmed at Boney the Ogre's brother suddenly appearing, and what it could mean for British rule on the island, promptly informed London. Meanwhile, the captured Bonapartes were held in relative comfort compared to the usual prisoners of war of the day. They were housed in the Palace of St Antonio, formerly the residence of the Grand Master of the Order of Malta – that ancient Catholic order derived from the crusader Knights Hospitaller.

It was felt by London, namely by the Secretary of State for War, Lord Liverpool, that the Bonapartes' presence on Malta might be a threat to peace and stability on the island, since there was still a small French faction there. Oakes, who had served in the American Wars of Independence under Lord Cornwallis, had reservations. After all, Malta had only been taken from the French a few years earlier in 1800. Sir Hildebrand was also concerned that Lucien was corresponding with parties hostile to Britain on the island. Furthermore, Lucien had sullenly refused the offer of dinner with Sir Hildebrand, asking instead to be given permission to go to America and to stop being treated as a prisoner of war. Of course, these decisions were not Hildebrand's to make. Like a good civil servant, he passed the problem up! The foreign secretary, Lord Wellesley (older brother of the Duke of Wellington), wrote to Lucien refusing permission for him to travel to America, instead offering asylum in England. It was felt that Lucien might be troublesome for Britain if allowed to meddle in US politics. Very reluctantly, Lucien had to accept the offer. The frigate, ironically called HMS *President* – which had been captured from the French fleet (and originally called *Minerve*), collected him and his family and made the winter sea crossing to England. It was yet another embarrassment to his brother Emperor Napoleon.

The exiled/captive Bonapartes arrived in Plymouth Sound in December (the same place Napoleon would be brought when he was captured by the British five years later in 1815). They were not to disembark for some days, however. A letter from Lord Wellesley explained that they could not go on shore until preparations for Lucien's accommodation had been made. Meanwhile, Lucien and the captain of the *President,* Captain Warren, exchanged gifts. Warren received a gold pocket watch. Lucien received a double-barrelled pistol. Coincidentally, Warren (later Rear-Admiral Sir Samuel Warren, KCB, KCH) had previously commanded the HMS *Bellerophon* in action – the ship that Lucien's brother Napoleon would finally surrender himself on and be taken to Plymouth effectively as a prisoner.

The family Bonaparte eventually disembarked at the Victualing Office in Plymouth. Lucien's standing in the British public's eye, who knew of his fallouts with Napoleon, was that he was anti-Bonapartist and against tyranny and dictators. Large crowds of people gathered on shore to welcome Lucien as a fellow struggler against the tyrant Napoleon. Though this was well meant, the top brass of England worried that these sentiments were only a hop, skip and a jump from republicanism and anti-monarchism. Lucien would have to be watched lest he fan the flames of an imagined possible British revolution. In true British glamour and style, the Bonapartes were extracted from the port to the nearby Kings Arms pub, where the possessions and carriages were sorted. They were accompanied by the Port Admiral, Sir Robert Calder, and various senior naval dignitaries for good measure. Before proceeding onwards, Lord Wellesley sent an official with papers of parole, a promissory note acknowledging capture and promise not to escape, which Lucien, somewhat deflated, duly signed.

Where was this interesting prisoner to be housed? The Earl of Powis (son of Robert Clive of India) placed his country seat, Dinham House, near the town of Ludlow in Shropshire, at Lucien's disposal. Lucien was to travel ahead of the family with some of the servants, the rest would follow. Despite Lucien's vast fortune and valuable items in his baggage (including art and antiquities), it was agreed that the travel costs would be met by HM's government. After waiting several days for his things to clear the Plymouth Customs House, Lucien left Plymouth on 23 December. Amidst his shame, he still had the cheek to write to his mother asking her to persuade Napoleon to arrange a prisoner exchange as soon as possible so that he and the family could continue to America in spring! Unsurprisingly, this did not happen.

The public and press followed Lucien's progress with much interest as he travelled, staying at Chudleigh, Exeter, Taunton, Old Down, Ston Easton (future home of Lord Rees-Mogg), Bath, Gloucester and Tewkesbury on his way north. He had a deep interest in history and architecture and visited the cathedral at Gloucester and possibly Tewkesbury Abbey too. Large crowds gathered to welcome him at the inn where he lodged in Worcester. The people were very curious to get a glimpse of Lucien to see if he resembled the amusing caricatures of his brother they were so used to seeing in the British press. Of course, Napoleon was represented as a short, stroppy, almost goblin-like figure, so Lucien was a great improvement in the crowd's eyes. It was certainly a nice Boxing Day activity, to go and see a 'Boney' down the pub! He later attended a festive dance, much to the amusement and mutterings of the locals. Finally, once at Ludlow, the party rested at the Angel Inn and waited for Lucien's wife and children to catch up from Plymouth. She too was greeted by curious crowds on the way. In January 1811, the family and its retinue, with the blessing of Lord Powis, moved into Dinham House.

At Dinham, Lucien began to transition most agreeably from upstart French revolutionary to English country gentleman. He began to rub shoulders with the local aristocracy and gentry – who found him rather impressive. Visitors in the area went out of their way to stop off in Ludlow in the hope of catching a glimpse of him. Lucien's daily walk around Ludlow Castle was the key opportunity. There are stories of Lucien being greatly amused by gentlemen travelling great distances in the hope of just catching sight of him. He would often invite them for a drink instead. The new squire of Dinham, Mr Bonaparte, Esq, held dinner parties and small concerts, and began to write. Lucien lived like one of the gentlemen from a Jane Austen novel – whose work he probably read during the years of his English stay. The French gentleman attended hunt balls and local assembly rooms in the same way one might have found characters in various novels by Austen.

Local affection eventually began to wear off. It seems that curiosity turned to slight hostility in Ludlow. The Bonaparte family, including the children, were subject to sly and unpleasant remarks and the throwing of stones from the occasional ruffian child. The mild hostility was understandable – Lucien was, after all, brother of Britain's most ardent enemy who was threatening invasion and was already responsible for the death of many servicemen. Two of Lucien's servants were even arrested in a brawl with some locals – something short of a lynching. Mr Bonaparte grew to loathe Ludlow, and hoped to move soon. He wrote to ask Lord Wellesley if he might find new lodgings in the countryside or if he could travel to the US, promising he would avoid international politics. Of course, this was refused. Furthermore, Lucien wrote a letter to the Prince of Wales congratulating him on his elevation to Prince Regent, probably in the hope of finding favour or even being granted an audience to plead his case. It backfired. All his correspondence was supposed to go through Wellesley's office, who was furious. It is strange to think that while Napoleon was master of Europe, his little brother was sucking up to the ruler of his most generous of enemies, the Prince Regent and the British government. Around this time, Lord Powis began to change his tune. He now demanded rent and back-rent from the Bonapartes lodging in his property. It is possible that he slowly realised that Lucien was by no means poor and that it was not right for an Englishman/Welshman to be so accommodating to the brother of the nation's enemy. Though Lucien had understood that the accommodation was to be a rent-free gift, he duly paid the Clive family off. It was time to leave Ludlow for good.

Having already dipped into his cash, Lucien soon grabbed another handful in order to buy his own residence – free from unreliable aristocratic landlords. He purchased Thorngrove in Worcestershire, a 130-acre [small] country estate, for the not inconsiderable sum of £9,000, eventually moving to the property around June 1811. From Thorngrove he continued to correspond with his mother Letizia, still hoping in vain for an intervention from his brother in his passage to America or return to France. Lucien furnished the house with all his collections from Italy and used a cottage on the grounds as his writing studio. Invitations from local county gentry were forthcoming; however, Lucien could not accept them all as he may have been observing a 10-mile curfew limit laid down by the authorities. An accomplished writer as he was, he visited Stratford-upon-Avon, the home of William Shakespeare, though there is some debate as to the timing of this visit. At one time, a plaque commemorating Lucien's visit to the bard's shrine existed.

While at Thorngrove, Lucien entertained yet more important aristocrats such as Lord Holland (nephew of the great Whig orator, Charles James Fox MP, and great-great-great-grandson of King Charles II), Lord Brougham (MP and eventual Lord Chancellor), and the Marquess of Lansdowne (whose family would be oddly connected to the Bonapartes in future years). Thorngrove is also where Lucien completed his epic poem on Charlemagne – a fitting topic for the brother of the new 'master of Europe'. It was published in England, first in French and then English in 1814 and 1815 respectively, by Longman & Co. It is highly possible that, during this golden age of literature happening in England at that time, Lucien crossed paths with Lord Byron. Though no record of a meeting exists, Byron held Lucien and his works in very high regard. The English translation of the epic work was undertaken by one of Byron's friends, Francis Hodgson, and the headmaster of Shrewsbury School, Samuel Butler. The publishers had originally approached Sir Walter Scott Bt, but, perhaps as an ardently patriotic Scot, or perhaps sensitive to his reputation, he found the idea of working on a piece by a member of the Clan Bonaparte abhorrent and turned down the offer. Time has been kinder to Scott's literary efforts than to Lucien's.

The year 1814 brought with it the defeat of the Emperor Napoleon in Europe. After his disastrous retreat from Moscow, from 1812 on, Napoleon's fortunes faded. The War of the Sixth Coalition (against France) ended in the capture of Paris and Napoleon's abdication from the throne. He was sent into exile on the Isle of Elba off the coast of Italy. No longer a 'guest' of the His Majesty's government, Lucien on the other hand was free to return to the continent; he prepared to leave Thorngrove. By now he was a popular resident of Worcestershire and many well-wishers followed his departure to Dover in the same way that his arrival from Plymouth had been followed. Upon his return to Rome, Pope Pius VII made him a Roman prince and Prince of Canino. He had finally been given a title and rank worthy of his brothers and sisters – all of whom were (ex) kings, queens and princesses. Meanwhile in Worcestershire, the contents of Thorngrove were being auctioned off. Lucien evidently had no need of it and no real desire to return to England. A great collection of furniture from cushions to conversation-chairs were sold. Even the cellar contents were up for grabs – over 200 bottles of port! The house itself did not go on the market for another year.

Lucien was finally reconciled with his brother Napoleon after the latter's escape from Elba and retaking of power as emperor of the French in 1815. Napoleon made Lucien a prince of France; however, the reunion did not last long. Napoleon's reprise as emperor lasted 100 days; he was defeated at Waterloo and sent into exile on the island of St Helena in the South Atlantic. It is here that he finally had time to read his brother's epic poem of which he was so proud. Napoleon found it dull beyond measure and believed that it would only ever collect dust on eclectic bookshelves. He was not wrong. The book was not the triumph Lucien had expected. He retired to Italy and lived rather as he had done previously: an academic, eccentric, enthusiastic aristocrat. Like many collectors of the day, he became interested in archaeology and excavated the Tusculum bust of Julius Caesar in 1825 – the first Roman general to invade Britannia. Lucien, 1st Prince of Canino and Musignano, died on 29 June 1840 of stomach cancer – the same illness that took his brother, Napoleon, as well as his father and sister.

Lucien and his immediate family had lived through much of the Napoleonic Wars in the enemy camp – England! Despite being VIP prisoners of war, it had been their home for nine years. Indeed, some of his children and descendants would return to Britain to make it their home.

While at Thorngrove in 1813, a British-born Bonaparte arrived. Lucien's third son, Louis-Lucien Bonaparte, was born at Thorngrove on 4 January. He was probably named after the only brother Lucien was still in contact with at the time. French royalty born in Worcestershire! That same year, Arthur Wellesley (then Marquess of Wellington), defeated Lucien's brother, King Joseph of Spain, at the Battle of Vitoria. Louis-Lucien was quite possibly an Anglophile. He certainly spent most of his life in Britain, both early and late. He returned to France following the Revolution of 1848. By now, his first cousin, Prince Louis-Napoleon, also a former resident of England, had become the first president of the Second French Republic – the self-styled 'prince-president'. For many Bonapartes, however minor, scattered across Europe, it was a chance to return to France and seek positions through the tried and tested policy of nepotism. Louis-Lucien was appointed to the Assembly as representative for Corsica in 1848 and the Seine Departments in 1849. Louis-Lucien did not directly take part in his cousin's coup d'état to become emperor of the French in 1851 – perhaps, like his father before him, he had reservations about democracy being circumvented. Napoleon III made him a senator and recognised him as a prince of France, yet Louis-Lucien seems to have been less involved in politics than other members of the clan. Returning to London, he became a philologist – a scholar of ancient languages. Originally, his chief subject was the Basque language, but, probably through living in Britain, this grew into a study of Celtic languages: Breton, Gaelic, Welsh and Cornish as well as Sardinian and Italian dialects. Prince Louis-Lucien became a leading scholar of philology.

Perhaps thanks to his princely status, or perhaps owing to his academic status, Louis-Lucien moved in the upper circles of London society, he counted amongst his acquaintances Alexander Graham Bell and William Gladstone. Sometime after the fall of the second empire, and Eugenie and Napoleon III's exile to Chislehurst, Louis-Lucien become friends with their son, his cousin-once-removed, the young Prince Imperial. Prince would visit prince in the glamorous surroundings of Bayswater! It is perhaps through this friendship he was able to dine with Queen Victoria a few times. He is known to have made at least two tours of Scotland in order to improve his fluency in Gaelic. Over time, he was a respected authority on many languages and amassed an important collection of books on philology – some were the only publications in known existence – and wrote extensively himself.

Louis-Lucien was particularly fascinated by the wealth and diversity of English dialects. Indeed, it is surprising that such a small country can have so many different accents surviving up to the present day. Using the *Song of Solomon* from the Old Testament as crib, he compiled twenty-four translations of it in twenty-four different dialects of both England and Scotland. It was published in 1862. After the fall of his cousin and the second empire in 1870, Louis-Lucien's income undoubtedly decreased. He was granted a civil list pension in 1883, presumably in gratitude for his work on British dialects, though his political and royal contacts should not be forgotten. A Bonaparte – the nephew of 'old Boney' – receiving a British pension less than fifty years after Waterloo!

Prince Louis-Lucien died while in in Italy in 1891. He had once been married there but had been estranged from his first wife since 1850. During the separation he fathered a son in 1859 with one Clemence Richard; they named the boy Louis Clovis Bonaparte. When his first wife died in 1891, Clemence and Louis-Lucien were finally married in London in June 1891, but in November, Louis-Lucien died. His affection for his home, London, endured. His remains were brought back to England. He was buried at Kensal Green Roman Catholic cemetery. The funeral was well attended. Although Queen Victoria did not attend, she was well represented. Louis-Lucien's personal library of around 25,000 books were mostly sold to the Newbury Library in Chicago. Louis Clovis (not quite a prince due to his being born illegitimately) married into the English gentry – Rosalie Barlow, a descendant of King Edward III and of John Brydges 1st Baron Chandos (the Lieutenant of the Tower of London who was jailer to Lady Jane Grey and Queen Elizabeth I). Louis Clovis died aged 35 in in 1894 with no legitimate issue. Clemence outlived both her husband and son, dying in 1915 in London and is buried next to them at Kensal Green.

Politics was a recurring theme in Lucien's family, with several being involved in legislative or diplomatic posts on both sides of *La Manche*, sometimes by choice and sometimes by marriage. One such marriage was to one of Britain's first-division families and to a bright young thing in the Parliament of Westminster.

Lucien's second surviving child from his first marriage to Christine Boyer, was Christine Charlotte Alexandrine Egypte Bonaparte. Born in 1798, she, along with her father and other siblings, had been made a Princesse Française during Napoleon's Hundred Days (22 March 1815). After the family's return to Italy following the disastrous Waterloo campaign, Christine Egypte married the Swedish-born Count Arvid Posse in Rome in 1818; it was not a happy marriage. Posse reportedly abandoned her in favour of chasing skirts. His fate is unknown but it probably ended in the US. It was during these marital issues that Christine Egypte met a young dashing and handsome (by many accounts) Scottish aristocrat, Lord Dudley Coutts Stuart.

Born in 1793, Lord Dudley was the youngest son of John Stuart, 1st Marquess of Bute, and Frances Coutts, daughter of Thomas Coutts the banker and founder of Coutts & Co bank. Dudley's paternal grandfather, the 3rd Earl of Bute, had briefly been prime minister in 1762–3, and the Bute Stuarts belonged to the noble House of Stuart which had once ruled Scotland, England and Great Britain. The first Stuart king had been Robert II of Scotland, whose maternal grandfather was Robert the Bruce. The Stuarts of the Isle of Bute were neighbours in the Isles to the Hamiltons of the Isle of Arran and therefore of Napoleon III's cousin – Marie Amelie, the Duchess of Hamilton. Lord Dudley was brought up by his mother in Naples where he acquired liberal views and ardently opposed oppression of different peoples. His education continued at Cambridge with a plan to eventually go into politics. He was British yet rather continental in outlook. Not short of wealth or powerful connections, he would have certainly been an attractive prospect (or temptation) to any young woman of the day.

Temptation and opportunity manifested itself when Dudley and Christine Egypte met in Italy. By now she had been estranged from her husband for five years. There had been some failed attempts at acquiring an annulment. She was older than Dudley by a few years but no doubt this young adventurer thought the prospect of a liaison with a princess – and a niece of 'old Boney' to boot – was too tempting. They married secretly (probably bigamously) in a Roman Catholic ceremony in Rome, in 1824. Their son, Paul Amadeus Francis Coutts Stuart was born the following year. When news of the death of Christine's first husband came, another marriage was performed in an Anglican service in 1826. Time and money were spent on lawyers who sought a formal papal annulment from the mysterious Count Posse, which did not come until 1828.

The Stuart-Bonaparte marriage received mixed reviews in London society. To begin with, the problem of religion was raised. The Stuarts were Protestant and the Bonapartes were Catholic. Both sides' families wished for one or the other to convert. Dudley's family were reportedly disappointed in his choice of bride. It is possible that he had originally been betrothed to his cousin Lady Georgina North. The Coutts family were about to make Dudley a partner in the bank but now saw him as wayward and reneged on the offer. Despite this setback in his fortunes, Dudley returned to England with his wife and was elected Member of Parliament for Arundel in 1830 (unopposed). This was because he was sponsored by his Whig patron and chief local landowner, Bernard Howard, 12th Duke of Norfolk. The duke was an ardent supporter of Catholic emancipation. For centuries, Catholics were barred from holding various public offices – they could not even matriculate from Oxford or graduate from Cambridge universities. The unfairness irritated the duke immensely, so much so that he was known as the grumpy duke. The Howards were one of the oldest and most prominent Catholic families in the land at that time. Perhaps Lord Dudley's wife, being a Catholic princess, was of some help in acquiring this particular seat which was under the gaze of Arundel Castle – the Howards' ancestral home.

Lord Dudley continued his political career adopting liberal, progressive policies, such as the enfranchisement of the middle classes. He sometimes strayed from the views of the Duke of Norfolk and was regarded by some as a potential revolutionary, albeit a mellow one. This must have been exacerbated by the fact that his father-in-law had been so fervent a supporter of the French Revolution and took an active part in the Reign of Terror. That said, this son-in-law of a Jacobin, and husband of a Bonaparte princess, found himself returned for the seat of Arundel in the election of 1832 and he appears in the 1833 painting of the members of the House of Commons by Sir George Hayter, now in the National Portrait Gallery, along with many great statesmen of the day such as Field Marshal the Duke of Wellington – who became prime minister the following year. Dudley continued as MP for Arundel, strongly opposing proposed boundary changes which would merge it with nearby Littlehampton. Dudley lost his Arundel seat in 1837 but would be returned for Marylebone in 1847. His replacement in Arundel was the Duke of Norfolk's eldest son. Nepotism was not just a Bonaparte policy!

As a supporter of people's struggles against larger oppressors, Dudley became an ardent supporter of Polish independence, which, curiously, Napoleon himself had been an advocate of. Could this have been an influence from Princess Christine, Lady Dudley? He also lamented the struggle of Eastern European peoples against Russia. Lobbying attempts were made for him to acquire the role of British ambassador to Warsaw, but this did not happen. In keeping with his support of the oppressed, Lord Dudley received the exiled governor-president of Hungary, Lajos Kossuth, whose country had just lost its revolution and bid for independence from its Austrian rulers. Kossuth's journey to England had been delayed because his crossing through France had been forbidden by Dudley's cousin-in-law, Emperor Napoleon III of France.

The controversial marriage between the French princess and the dashing British lord began to fall apart. It is perhaps because of this awkward alliance that Lord Dudley's career did not take off as it might have. His having a Bonaparte for a wife would certainly have been a problem if he wanted to be an ambassador abroad. It seems that Dudley would be barred from high office owing to the awkward history of his wife's family. It is not difficult to imagine that this sowed the seeds of bitterness in the relationship. In around 1840, the couple separated and Christine returned to Italy. The whirlwind romance had not worked out – perhaps they had read too many novels. She died there in Rome in 1847, seven years after her father. Lord Dudley Stuart died in 1854 in Sweden – which has a touch of irony to it. The couple's 'legitimised' son, Paul Amadeus, joined the British army and became a captain in the 68th Regiment of Foot (which eventually became the Durham Light Infantry). This regiment served in the Crimean War, most notably at Inkerman. However, there was to be no Stuart-Bonaparte dynasty. Paul Amadeus, who had suffered head injuries from a riding incident, died unmarried and childless in 1889 and was buried with a grand monument at St Peter's Church, Petersham. A Scottish aristocrat with an important French heritage, his monument gives top billing to Christine and Lucien. Lord Dudley is almost a footnote.

Christine Egypte was not the only one of Lucien's children to marry a British politician, nor the only one to return to the place of their former exile. Her younger half-sister, Laetitia, was born in Italy in 1804 a few weeks after her uncle's coronation as emperor of the French. At the tender age of 16 she married an Irishman thirteen years her senior, in March 1821 in her father's fief of Canino. Her husband was Thomas Wyse, a scholar and politician educated at Stonyhurst and Trinity Dublin. He met her while on a ten-year grand tour of Europe. He had become a frequent guest of Lucien Bonaparte, who must have liked Wyse, as he suggested he marry Laetitia. Unlike Lord Dudley Stuart, Wyse was not from a prominent aristocratic family, but he was a Catholic, and his chief calling was the cause of Catholic emancipation in Britain and Ireland. A reduction in the restrictions laid on Roman Catholic persons in the kingdoms was a view which gained much support through the century. Through this, and his liberal, progressive Whig leanings, Wyse was able to have a successful career. He helped set up one of the first teacher training colleges in Battersea, became MP for Waterford, Lord of the Treasury, Secretary to the Board of Control, and British minister to Greece. He was made a Knight Commander of the Order of the Bath in 1857. In contrast to Dudley, an alliance with a Bonaparte princess did not seem to hinder Wyse's career.

The romance, however, between the princess and the Irishman was short-lived. From 1824 onwards they had been on troubled waters. They reportedly fought a lot; this featured shouting matches and the slamming of doors. They managed to produce two children; Napoleon Alfred (in 1822) and William (in 1826). But the couple's love developed into a form of mutual loathing and they separated in 1828. An uninterested father, Wyse was mostly estranged from his children. They took the hyphenated name Bonaparte-Wyse. Laetitia, in a possible fit of grief or stress, attempted to commit suicide by drowning herself in the Serpentine in London's Hyde Park. (The same stretch of water her cousin, the future Napoleon III, would row Mr and Mrs Disraeli in a rowing boat.) Laetitia was reportedly rescued from death by a passing gallant gentleman. With this rescue she was reborn, promptly fell in love with her rescuer, and the two became lovers. The man was a British army officer, Captain Studholme John Hodgson. He later became a general. From a proud military family, Hodgson's brother and father had also been army generals, and his grandfather, Field Marshal Hodgson, served as aide-de-camp to the Duke of Cumberland at the Battle of Culloden.

This steamy dalliance with dashing hero Hodgson went on for many years. Laetitia may have regarded Hodgson as her saviour. Their romance produced three children. To avoid scandal, each child was legally the offspring of Sir Thomas Wyse and were given the surname Bonaparte-Wyse, but most of society knew very well that they were not his. Many turned a blind eye. Laetitia lived long enough to see the second empire rise and fall. In its early years, all members of the extended Bonaparte clan benefited in some way – Napoleon III turned few away. Princess Laetitia was recognised as Her Imperial Highness in 1853 together with many of her siblings and cousins. Princess Laetitia outlived her estranged husband, Sir Thomas Wyse, KCB, who had died while minister in Athens; she died in 1872 having returned to Italy.

Laetitia's children (and love-children) lived remarkable lives – considering the scandal surrounding their existence – and, unsurprisingly, Britain was a key part in their lives. The second (actual) son of Sir Thomas and Laetitia, William Bonaparte-Wyse (1862–1892) partially followed his father into Irish politics. He was made High Sheriff of Waterford in 1855 – an annual appointment. As part of his role, the young William was briefly the sovereign's chief judicial representative in the area – a real Bonaparte ceremonially governing Britons and Irishmen – for one year! Like many gentlemen of his day, this Irish Bonaparte gained an army commission in the 9th Wiltshire Rifle Volunteer Corps. As with some of his relatives, William was interested in language and joined a society for the protection of the Provençal language and culture. During his membership, he invented the famous dish of *Les Figues aux Whiskey* – a culinary combination of France and Ireland brought together in a dessert.

William Bonaparte-Wyse married and had four sons. One such son, Andrew (born 1870), took the path of his grandfather Sir Thomas as a pioneer educationalist working for the Commissioners of National Education. He was a noted Irish Unionist, despite being Roman Catholic, and reportedly commuted to Belfast from the suburbs of Dublin every week – even after the 1922 partition. He was appointed Private Secretary to the Northern Ireland Ministry of Education and continued to work as a civil servant until his retirement in 1939. By the end of his career, he had been made a Commander of the Order of the British Empire, and a Companion of the Bath – an order which at one point had been Britain's answer to Napoleon's *Legion d'honneur*. There is a touch of irony about a Bonaparte being the recipient of the same order bestowed upon both Nelson and Wellington. Andrew Bonaparte-Wyse was only the second Bonaparte to become invested in the Order of the British Empire; his cousin's wife Empress Eugenie was made a GBE during the First World War. Andrew died in 1940. His only son, no doubt to honour his ancestry, volunteered for the Free French Navy during the Second World War.

Of Princess Laetitia's other three children by Captain Hodgson, Lucien Louis Bonaparte-Wyse (1845–1909) joined the French navy and became a notable engineer – primarily owing to his involvement in the installation of the Panama Canal. He rubbed shoulders with Suez Canal pioneer, Ferdinand de Lesseps, a relative of the Empress Eugenie. Laetitia's youngest daughter, Adelina Bonaparte-Wyse married a Hungarian revolutionary; however, her eldest daughter and namesake is more widely remembered. Marie-Laetitia Bonaparte-Wyse was a successful author and infamous salon hostess. In Paris, she hosted the likes of Victor Hugo, Alexandre Dumas junior, Lajos Kossuth and her cousin the Emperor Napoleon III. She was chased out of Paris by Empress Eugene when rumours were widely circulating that the emperor was regularly visiting his pretty (bastard) cousin on evenings. She continued the family tradition of having affairs and produced a bastard son, a legitimate daughter and adopted two others. The Lucien side of the family certainly gained an 'interesting' reputation for a touch of scandal throughout the nineteenth century.

Scandal continued to dog the family via Lucien's fifth son, Prince Pierre Napoleon Bonaparte. Born in 1815 after the fall of uncle Napoleon, he did not miss out adventure. As a teenager he was involved in an insurrection in Italy, travelled to New Jersey to visit uncle Joseph and went to Colombia to join General Santander who was involved the independence wars of New Grenada. On Pierre's eventual return to Rome, the Pope gave special instruction that he be arrested – there was talk of his having murdered a policeman; an escape was needed. Pierre bolted. Like his cousin, Napoleon III, he retreated to England. With his cousin's eventual election to president and later as emperor of the French, Pierre was able to ride on the coat-tails of Bonaparte success. Though he had always been a socialist, he was more than happy to accept the title of prince and be made a deputy for Corsica.

Pierre followed adventure. He fought alongside the Foreign Legion in Algeria and was present at the Battle of Zaatcha. But scandal always persisted on his side of the family. He was certainly a debauched gentleman, but also in possession of a violent streak. When two disgruntled journalists met with him and took him to task – hoping to provoke a duel, Prince Pierre declined the duel but was riled with anger. He slapped the journalist, pulled out his revolver and shot him dead. He was arrested soon after. In the inquiry that followed, the (probably biased) courts naturally acquitted the troublesome cousin of the emperor, but from then on, he lived in obscurity, shunned by the imperial court. He died, hidden away at Versailles with a mistress, in 1881.

Probably because of his socialist leanings, Pierre had married the daughter of an out-of-work plumber working as a doorman in 1853. Pierre and his wife, Éléonore-Justine Ruflin, were scandalous, low-born and extremely out of favour; however, they were to produce a granddaughter who would become not only entwined with some of the grandest families in Europe, but leave an important mark and contribution to history.

Owing to all the other elder male-line descendants of Lucien dying out, Pierre's son, Roland, inherited the papal titles as 6th Prince of Canino and Musignano in 1899. Roland was the last to hold these titles, which had been created for his grandfather, Lucien, by the Pope back in 1814. On Roland's death in 1924, the titles became extinct and the senior (primogeniture line) of the Bonapartes died out. The last male-line descendants of the Bonaparte brothers became those descended from the youngest brother of Napoleon, Jerome (former king of Westphalia).

During his lifetime, Prince Roland was a celebrated patron of science. He was president of the French Geography Society as well as the Astronomy Society. Roland also took an interest in anthropology and indigenous peoples of all kinds. Bonaparte Point in Antarctica is named after him as well as Bonaparte Lake in Norway. Roland made a particularly advantageous marriage. At San-Roche in Paris, in 1880, he married Marie-Felix Blanc, daughter of wealthy businessman François Blanc. Mr Blanc founded and owned the Monte Carlo Casino as well as other investments and real-estate in Monaco. He had also made a name for himself by establishing the casino at the spa town of Bad Homburg in Germany. To compete with the more popular casino spots of Europe, Blanc introduced a roulette wheel with one 0 pocket instead of the more common 0 and 00 pockets. His mastery of the casino industry was thought of as spooky – owing to the fact that the numbers on his roulette wheels added up to 666, 'the number of the beast'. François Blanc died in 1877 when his daughter Marie-Felix was just a teenager, leaving her an immense fortune of around 10 million francs plus other investments. Seeing an opportunity, Prince Roland, who was of a similar age, swooped in and won the beautiful heiress – despite the objections of his new bourgeois mother-in-law. In 1882, the couple produced their only child: Princess Marie Bonaparte – (technically the end of the legitimate Bonaparte line from Lucien).

Marie grew up fairly secluded, heavily influenced by her father's scientific research and lectures. She too developed an interest in science and the understanding of people. At this point one might wonder, how this girl is relevant to Britain, but it was her scientific interest and particularly her marriage which brought her to the shores of old Britannia. As an only child set to inherit a large fortune, there was no shortage of suitors for her hand from the royal families of Europe – most notably Prince Herman of Saxe-Weimar, and the family's Monegasque neighbour, Louis II Prince of Monaco. However, at what we might assume was a very boozy lunch in Paris, Prince Roland agreed with King George I of Greece that Marie would marry his second son, another George – Prince George of Greece and Denmark.

King George I was originally just a Danish prince. He was known as Prince William, the second son of King Christian IX of Denmark. However, in October 1862, the Greek people rose up against their king (Otto) in a popular revolt. Although they had deposed their monarch, the Greeks were quite happy to find a new royal family for their country from existing stock of European royals. Diplomatically speaking, it was an opportunity to gain closer ties with strong countries such as Great Britain. The Greeks invited Queen Victoria's second son, Prince Alfred, to take the throne. They may have hoped that a union with Britain might result in the return of the Ionian islands which were under British control. Victoria did not support the idea and Alfred was barred from accepting the offer. Still determined, the Greeks held a public referendum so that the people could vote for their new monarch. Naturally, Prince Alfred acquired the most votes – about 95 per cent. The runner-up, the Prince of Leuchtenberg, was the grandson of Napoleon Bonaparte's adopted son, Eugene de Beauharnais. Many other princes of Europe were on the list, including Emperor Napoleon III, but most only received a handful of votes.

Despite overwhelming support for Prince Alfred of the United Kingdom, the Greek government and the 'Great Powers' (Britain, Austria and Prussia) had to settle for one of the more suitable runners-up. Most were unsuitable due to being either too French or too Russian. They settled upon Prince William of Denmark – who had received only six votes in the referendum! The Greeks may have invented democracy, but they were not yet able to implement it. William became King George I of the Hellenes on 30 March 1863. Six years later, his fourth son was born: Prince George of Greece and Denmark.

Prince George, obeying his father, began to court Marie over the next few weeks. He was tall, attractive but emotionally distant. After about a month of courtship, he gallantly waived any money he might receive from her fortune and promised that only she and any children they might have would have access to her wealth and trusts – much to the surprise of both fathers. Cordially, the couple were married firstly in Paris and secondly in a Greek Orthodox ceremony in Athens in 1907.

Marie (Princess George), who was a mere offshoot of the jumped-up clan of Bonaparte, now found herself connected to some of the most senior royal families of Europe. Her husband's aunt, Alexandra, another Danish princess, was married to Bertie, by then King Edward VII,

Emperor of India. Marie's sister-in-law, Sophie, was the sister to Kaiser Wilhelm II. Another sister-in-law was married to the uncle of Tsar Nicholas II, and her husband's brother, Andrew had married a Battenberg princess, Alice – a great-granddaughter of Queen Victoria. Andrew and Alice's four daughters were Marie's nieces; their only son, Marie's nephew, had a successful career in the navy and would go on to make the most important marriage of the twentieth century. His name was Philip – but more on that later.

Princess Marie's personality, life and times were complex, and she is really worthy of a book and film in her own right. (Indeed, a French television film of her life was made in 2004.) She and George produced two children in 1908 and 1910 respectively, but there were sexual troubles in their marriage. Firstly, George had a close and strangely deep relationship with his uncle, Prince Valdemar, who was a father-like figure as well as an intimate, passionate friend. When parting from each other they would become incredibly emotional and sob. Prince George and Marie were possibly not sexually compatible; there are reports that she enjoyed intimacies with Andrew's same uncle Valdemar – Andrew was content to be a spectator. Unsurprisingly, Marie ended up conducting numerous affairs but remained 'unfulfilled'. During the First World War, she entered into an affair with the French prime minister, Aristide Briand. The affair went on for several years and created political tension. Greece remained a neutral state during the war. Nations on both sides of the conflict believed that Briand's affair with King Constantine I of Greece's sister-in-law was an attempt by the allies to bring Greece into the war on their side and possibly replace Constantine with George as king. Certainly, the affair may have helped bring Greece into the war via the Macedonian front which the allies had opened up in an attempt to aid Serbia against Austria.

A good-natured person, Marie worked on hospital ships in Athens during the war, but the affair with Briand continued even after the conflict. Prince George was jealous but retained his emotional distance and did little about it. The affair seems to have ended in 1919.

Marie was plagued by the fact that she could not seem to achieve vaginal orgasm with a man – it became an obsession. She began to do her own research into the problem. Like her botanist father, she approached the issue with scientific fervour. While having an affair with one of Sigmund Freud's followers (among others), Marie conducted her research in to her self-diagnosed sexual dysfunction – her orgasmic quest. She interviewed 243 women, discussed their sexual history and measured the distance between the clitoris and vagina of each of them. Her findings seem to have revealed that the greater the distance (say, over 2.5cm), the less likely orgasm would be during intercourse. Based on her findings, she decided to undergo a surgical operation to move her clitoris closer to her vagina. The first operation not having provided the fulfilment she sought, a second operation was performed. Her quest for an orgasm continued.

She published some of her research in 1924 – under a pseudonym, of course. But in 1925 she took her research further and met with the father of psychoanalysis, Sigmund Freud. She had a great fascination for his new science and formed an intimate friendship with him. Though her troubles were not necessarily the norm for Freud to deal with, he was no doubt grateful for the wealthy and beautiful patroness. From his treatment of Marie and discussions surrounding her frigidity, Freud suggested that it might be the case that it was merely that the missionary position was not a good position for Marie to achieve orgasm.

Female sexuality and psychoanalysis became a lifelong passion of Marie's and she would go on to produce a book on the subject in 1953. There are stories that Freud confessed to Marie that, despite his career and research, he never worked out what a woman wanted.

Marie used her wealth to help set up a psychoanalysis school in Paris. She took her own patients and, like Freud, would treat them by talking with them. Quite an active and outdoors woman, she preferred the garden to an office. Marie liked to crochet during the treatment or while listening to her patients' troubles. Many have agreed that it is in part thanks to her money and interest in psychoanalysis that the new science became as popular as it is.

Princess Marie took particular interest in her nephew, Philip, and at one time gave him and his family a home at Sainte-Cloud. More crucially, as Philip's father was not adept with money, Marie paid for much of Philip's schooling, which included Gordonstoun School in Scotland. When Philip's mother, Princess Alice of Battenberg, became unwell and was diagnosed as a paranoid schizophrenic, it was Marie who arranged for her to receive treatment at a specialist centre in Switzerland. Marie was most likely best placed to ask Sigmund Freud to treat Alice. The doctors consulted with Freud who believed that the illness was caused by unfulfilled sexual desires or frustration. His recommendation was to X-ray her ovaries, killing off her sex drive. Despite her protestations, the operation was carried out, and Alice tried to flee the institution/asylum several times. However, it is Freud who was soon in need of more help than many others.

On 10 May 1933, students outside the State Opera in Berlin began burning books as a show of loyalty to the Nazi cause. Among the various works written by Jews were books by Freud. Five years later, Nazi-German forces occupied Freud's home town of Vienna in the Anschluss. Freud remarked that Austria was now finished. Where the Nazis led, antisemitism followed, and before long Freud's own daughter was arrested and interrogated by the Gestapo. Horrified, the Freud family realised the writing was on the wall. They attempted to leave the country, but the movement of Jews was strictly governed by the Nazi authorities and exit visas were nearly impossible to come by. As a member of a reigning royal family with diplomatic immunity, wealth and connections, Freud's former patient and fan, Princess Marie, was able to help the family and exit visas and passage to London were arranged. Thanks to Marie's bribes and persuasion of key Nazis and Gestapo officials, Sigmund and his family were able to get away from the Nazis along with many of his letters, writings and antiquities, and importantly, his famous couch. Sadly, his sisters were too infirm to travel. They perished in concentration camps. Freud and his immediate family might well have shared that fate; however, because of Marie effectively paying the Nazis' ransom, the legacy of Freud's work was saved. The house where he lived near Primrose Hill in London is now the Freud Museum and his couch is on display. Freud's ashes are kept in a fourth-century BC Roman vase – a gift from Marie Bonaparte.

During the Second World War, the Greek royal family were exiled to Crete, Egypt and then Britain. Like many men from the Greek royal family, and like his uncle Lord Mountbatten, Marie's nephew Philip entered the navy – the (British) Royal Navy. He had the mark of an excellent naval officer and served with distinction during the Second World War. Philip won the heart and affection of his third-cousin, Princess Elizabeth, first in line to succeed to the throne of the United Kingdom. (Both descend from Queen Victoria as well as Christian IX of Denmark.) The couple were married in 1947; Marie was present at the wedding.

In 1953, as senior members of the Greek royal family, and as Philip's aunt and uncle, Prince and Princess George, were invited to the coronation of Elizabeth II at Westminster Abbey. They were officially representing their other nephew, King Paul of Greece. Now an elderly lady, the great pageantry of the day bored Marie, and for those sitting in the abbey there was famously a lot of waiting around. She decided to psychoanalyse the man sitting next to her for the duration of the coronation service. The man agreed. Marie missed most of the ceremony as she was locked in conversation with her new 'patient'. Both were more interested in their discussions than the pomp. The patient in question turned out to be François Mitterrand – he would later become the longest serving president of France. Despite her lack of interest in the service, Marie received the 1953 coronation medal – another Bonaparte receiving honours from the British Crown. A future president of France and a Bonaparte ignoring the pageantry at a British coronation – how very French!

Having translated some of Freud's works into French, she continued as a psychoanalyst right until her death from leukaemia in Saint-Tropez in 1962. Marie had witnessed two world wars and seen the destruction of most of the royal houses of Europe. But amid the chaos of the twentieth century, she saved the father of psychoanalysis and helped bring him to England. Perhaps, just as importantly, she had helped set up a young man on his way through life to become the consort to the queen of the United Kingdom.

By poetic coincidence, at the funeral of HRH Prince Philip the Duke of Edinburgh in April 2021, the Royal Marine buglers sounded the last post in an empty nave of St George's Chapel, Windsor, standing alongside the memorial sculpture of Napoleon, the Prince Imperial – Napoleon III and Eugenie's son – which had been created in 1881. It serves as a reminder of Prince Philip's proximity to the Napoleonic dynasty, and the Bonapartes' closeness to the royal family of Great Britain.

It is worth mentioning that the whiff of scandal attached to the Bonapartes of Lucien's line did not end with Princess Marie Bonaparte. She did not pass on the name of Bonaparte, but she did perhaps pass on the rebellious, passionate streak, and the close association with Britain.

Marie's son, Prince Peter of Greece and Denmark (1908–1980), continued two family traits of his branch of the 'Lucienic' Bonapartes. Firstly, like his father and mother, he was interested in the study of people – anthropology – specialising in both Tibetan culture and the practice of polyandry (when a woman takes two or more husbands). Secondly, as per tradition in his family, he made a scandalous marriage. To the frustration of many of his family, Prince Peter married beneath him – a Russian commoner named Irina Ovtchinnikova. The marriage took place while the couple were on an anthropological research trip to Asia in 1939. He did not inform the Greek authorities or his family – they only found out via the press. Though Irina had formerly been a marchioness via her first husband, the Marquis de Monléon, the fact that she was twice divorced and not of noble birth was unsavoury to Peter's family – especially in the wake of abdication crisis in Britain a few years earlier. The Peter/Irina match outraged the Greek royal family so much that Prince Peter was barred from the succession to the Greek throne, and his father, Prince George, disowned him. Princess Marie, however, continued to give him money. Prince Peter's exclusion from the succession actually brought Prince Philip Duke of Edinburgh much closer to the throne.

After the Second World War, and after the Greek monarchy's restoration, Prince Peter declared himself heir presumptive to the Greek throne. In other words, first in line. His young cousin King Constantine II had succeeded as king in 1964 and at that time had no children. However, in order to avoid Prince Peter and his Russian wife from getting anywhere near the throne, Constantine II's parliament changed the laws of succession from agnatic-primogeniture to male-preference-primogeniture, similar to the UK system at that time. This meant that a few princesses stood between Peter and the throne. Ultimately, Greece abolished the monarchy becoming a republic again. Had Prince Peter not made such an ill-advised marriage, he may well have succeeded the throne of Greece or might have been offered it by alternative governments. Another Bonaparte (half at least) on another European throne.

Peter and Irina moved to London and Copenhagen, and he continued his Tibetan and Asian studies. He made some use of the connections of his relative Lord Mountbatten (the last Viceroy of India) in the area. The couple, both childless, eventually separated, and Prince Peter took up with an English woman but there was no divorce. Irina was buried with him in Denmark; both were ostracised by the royal family and neither was permitted a burial in Greece.

Lucien Bonaparte and his descendants, though known as both papal and French aristocracy or royalty, were far more than that. In some cases, they were clearly world citizens. Many of them were intelligent, revolutionary and clearly prone to passion. It is interesting that this side of the family was formed in the crucible of the Napoleonic Wars and on the shores of England.

During the 1800s, there had been many male Bonaparte descendants of Lucien's line. Arguably this was the senior primogeniture line of the Bonaparte family. Napoleon died in 1821 and his only legitimate son followed him in 1832. His older brother, Joseph, had only two daughters, making Lucien and his descendants the next most senior line. However, in accordance with Napoleon's will, Lucien and his progeny were barred from the succession, so the seniority passed to Louis and his son – who became Napoleon III. This line in turn died out with the death of the Prince Imperial in 1879 in Zululand. The headship of the House of Bonaparte then passed to the male-line descendants of the youngest of Napoleon's brothers: Jerome.

Chapter 9

Jerome & Co: Money, Americans and Advantageous Marriages

Fans of C. S. Forester, and of the *Hornblower* ITV television series will remember an episode (*Loyalty*, 2003) in which the freshly promoted young Captain Hornblower encountered a newly married couple whom he saved from shipwreck. The couple were Jerome Bonaparte, Napoleon's youngest brother, and his American wife, Betsy Patterson. The couple were hoping to reach America to make a life away from Europe. After much drama, discourse and adventure, Hornblower, under the advice of his superiors, transported Jerome back to France, persuading him to part with his wife, and sent a furious Betsy to her homeland across the Atlantic. Though this tale is historically inaccurate, it is a slight amalgamation of the true stories of Lucien and his family being captured by the British in the Mediterranean on route to America in 1810, and of the elopement between Jerome and his first wife in 1803.

Jerome was the youngest of the Bonaparte brothers. In any other ordinary middle-class or noble family of that day, the outlook for a fifth son was not rosy. Not destined to inherit a fortune, and running on hand-me-down items and connections, the best they could hope for might be the Church or, God forbid, a job. Not so for Jerome. Despite being the baby of the brood, he too was briefly a king for a time: king of Westphalia, thanks to his elder brother Napoleon. Though his reign was short, he left his own mark on continental Europe. He eventually proved his loyalty to his brother the emperor by renouncing his American wife and entering into a more politically beneficial marriage. In fact, Jerome was arguably the most successful of all of his brothers, if only from a dynastic point of view. He was the only brother to marry into royalty and successfully form a dynasty from it, although none of his progeny ever got to rule France. To this day, direct male-line descendants of Jerome carry the headship of the House of Bonaparte – many of whom have

Family Tree

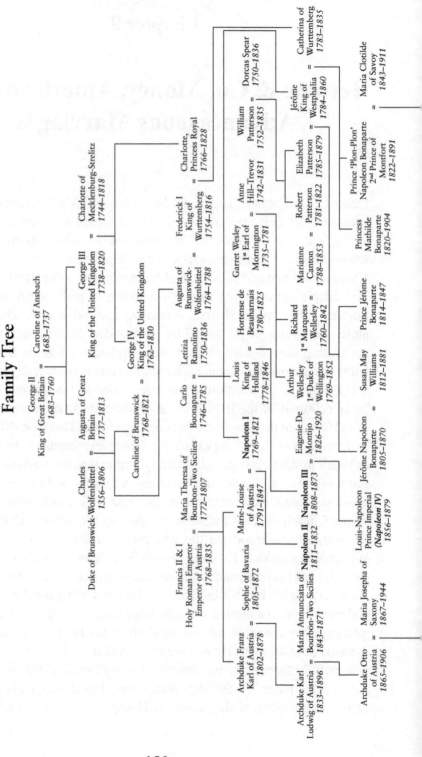

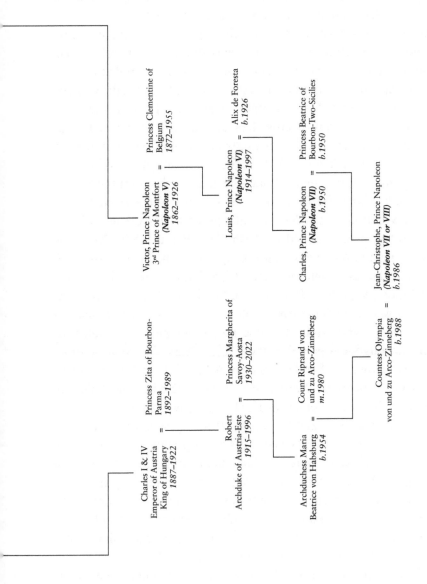

surprisingly British connections. Furthermore, Jerome's family, in yet more contrast to their other Bonaparte cousins, continued to make 'good marriages' for many generations to come, even into the present century. Unlike his brothers and nephews, Jerome did not spend long stretches of time in exile in Britain, but many of his descendants did.

Jerome was born Ajaccio in 1784, the eighth and youngest child of Carlo and Letizia Bonaparte. At 15 years old, he was barely a man and still at his studies when his second-eldest brother Napoleon seized power as first consul. Part of his education was conducted at the College of Juilly in Paris which had originally been founded as a medieval orphanage for the children of crusaders by Queen Blanche of France (granddaughter of King Henry II of England). Joan of Arc is rumoured to have been nursed back to health there following one of her skirmishes with the English or Burgundians. It later became a school for the French nobility, a rank which the Bonapartes had narrowly achieved shortly before the Revolution. Later, Jerome entered the Irish College in Paris. The Irish College was founded by Irish Catholics in 1578. Monastic schools and institutions were later suppressed in Ireland by both Elizabeth I and James I, therefore many Irish Catholics travelled abroad for their religious education. Jerome acquitted himself adequately at the school. A fellow student at the Irish College was Eugene de Beauharnais (Joséphine's son), who would become his step-nephew, and later his brother-in-law. Eugene was in fact about three years older than Jerome.

History has shown us that the Bonapartes had little luck where boats or navies were concerned. Napoleon was humiliated at the Nile and Trafalgar (as well as many other places) by the Royal Navy. Lucien was captured by a British ship, and Napoleon III nearly accidently drowned Benjamin Disraeli in a rowing boat on the Serpentine! All too often, ships and the Royal Navy were regularly the Achilles heel of the First French Empire. Perhaps in the hope that the family might produce an admiral as well as a general, Jerome was sent into the French navy; he even gained the rank of lieutenant. No doubt the emperor had high hopes for his younger brother's naval career; however, fortune and the sea did not go together where Napoleon was concerned.

In 1801, Napoleon, having had his great European triumph against the Austrians at the battle of Marengo, was able to concentrate on France's internal matters as well as problems in the wider empire. In French-held Saint-Dominique (now Haiti), a rebellion led by Toussaint Louverture was underway. He was a former slave who, after the Revolution and the republican abolition of slavery, became French Governor General of Saint-Dominique; however, he later advocated a separate constitution and effectively became a national leader. He sought help from both Britain and America – who were happy to help weaken the French in the Caribbean – and he produced a constitution in 1801. This was effectively a declaration of independence from France, and Louverture appointed himself governor general for life. When Napoleon was delivered this constitution, he was unamused and had the messenger sent into exile on the Isle of Elba. One wonders if he saw the irony in that years later.

To 'deal with' the situation in Saint-Dominigue, Napoleon sent his brother-in-law, General Charles Leclerc. Lieutenant Jerome Bonaparte was to accompany him on this expedition with the hope of seeing some action and perhaps distinguishing himself. Leclerc was husband to Jerome's and Napoleon's favourite sister, Pauline. Despite being a famous beauty, and accustomed to the finer things, she agreed to accompany her husband on the Atlantic voyage and the expedition. In the end, however, misfortune struck. Despite some initial success, such as the capture of Louverture, Leclerc succumbed to yellow fever and the expedition was an eventual failure. The 19-year-old naval lieutenant Jerome had not acquitted himself in the way his brother had hoped. During the expedition through Caribbean waters, he allegedly fired a warning shot at a British naval ship, but it overshot and hit the rigging. To avoid an international scandal, he was told to lie low for a while. Perhaps as part of his lying low, he was sent on a dispatch mission to Martinique on the French brig *Epervier* (hawk) in 1802. At some point during (or just after) the mission, Jerome abandoned the ship and made his way to the US initially under a pseudonym. In true Napoleonic naval luck, *Epervier* was actually captured by the British a year later, in another vessel captured from the French. She became HMS *Epervier* and captured several more French prizes during the wars.

It is unknown how, but while in the US, Jerome met Elizabeth 'Betsy' Patterson. Possibly on the advice of a friend, he headed to Baltimore where America's most beautiful women were believed to dwell. Their first acquaintance was probably at a ball or a polite social gathering, and the two teenagers fell for each other. She was a Grecian beauty, wild (American), and certainly seemed exotic to a minor European aristocrat. He was good looking, charming, well connected and an escape from a predictable life in Baltimore society. Betsy, born in 1785, came from a wealthy Maryland merchant family, who like many similar families had prospered owing to their support of the American War of Independence. Her maternal grandfather was an Irish immigrant from Donegal who had become extremely wealthy in the US, having backed the winning side in the Revolutionary War. Betsy's father, William Patterson, was also Irish-born and had been a gun-runner for the revolutionary army. Following the Revolution, he too had a successful career in business becoming a founder of the Baltimore Ohio Railroad, and first president of the Bank of Maryland. He was reputedly one of (if not, the), richest men in the area. For that reason, Betsy was a high prize indeed for any young up-and-coming American man. Indeed, this was probably the path she was prepared for.

Jerome was captivated by Betsy, or at least he certainly must have lusted after her. For Betsy, Jerome was a sort of escape. He could offer all sorts of opportunities in Europe that were not open to American ladies. The attraction quickly blossomed into a lusty romance which was cemented by a marriage on Christmas Eve 1803, to the annoyance of the Patterson family, and to the rage of Napoleon when he found out. The brother of Napoleon himself was married to an American-born Irishwoman. Both must have shared a rebellious spark! However, Napoleon was on the path towards the height of his powers and was already planning for his family to be the founders of a great dynasty. He had already lost the use of his brother Lucien owing to his poor choice of wife; losing the only other single brother was a not inconsiderable setback. He wrote to demand Jerome return to France *sans* wife. Like a true Bonaparte, Jerome ignored the summons and would not abandon his woman. However, the following year, Napoleon was declared emperor of the French. Feeling that their status in the world had changed as brother and sister-in-law to the emperor, Jerome and the now pregnant Betsy boarded a ship bound for France. Jerome hoped the two of them could attend the coronation of his brother. After a difficult journey across the ocean, they disembarked at Lisbon. The plan was that Jerome would travel ahead to prepare the ground with his brother and persuade Napoleon to accept his pregnant wife as a family member. However, Jerome never returned. For want of a better word, he abandoned her. Betsy was not to see Jerome again for over thirty years.

Napoleon demanded Jerome get his marriage to Betsy annulled. While away from his wife and in the clutches of his ambitious family, and threatened with disinheritance – which would mean being barred from the succession like Lucien – Jerome was swayed. It was a difficult choice between passion or duty (and opportunity); Jerome chose the latter. A long period of silence existed between him and Betsy. He did not contact her. Stuck in a state of limbo in Lisbon, Betsy travelled (still pregnant) to London. At 95 Camberwell Grove (now between Camberwell and Peckham), Betsy gave birth to the first British-born Bonaparte, Jerome Napoleon Bonaparte, on 5 July 1805. It is very strange to think that the same year as the battles of Trafalgar and Austerlitz, Napoleon had a nephew born near Peckham!

It is by odd coincidence that Betsy, already very Irish by blood, would become loosely connected with the Anglo-Irish noble family, Wellesley (the Duke of Wellington's people). Betsy's brother, Robert Patterson (1781–1822) married Marianne Caton. But after he died, Marianne went on to marry secondly Richard, 1st Marquess Wellesley – the elder brother of the 1st Duke of Wellington. As the marchioness, Marianne was in the strange position of being able to claim both Wellington and Napoleon as brothers-law.

Napoleon, now with his youngest brother back under his wing, hurriedly did what he could to extinguish the marriage in the eyes of both the state and the Roman Catholic Church. With a child bearing the name Bonaparte that had technically been born in wedlock, Betsy was in a strong position to demand compensation from the now imperial family. Napoleon obliged in considerable sums after some considerable time. In America and elsewhere, she held on to the title Madame Bonaparte – as was her right – and, over many years, petitioned for her son to have a place in the line of succession. This did not materialise, however. In 1807, two years after their separation, Betsy learnt that Jerome had not only been made king of Westphalia in July but also married Princess Catharina of Württemberg in an arranged marriage, despite his first marriage not being strictly annulled yet – it took until 1815 to be properly finalised.

Betsy never remarried. It would have altered her position as the ex-wife of a king. But what of her son? The infant Jerome Napoleon returned with his mother to the US and lived in comfort. He was technically not permitted to use his family name of Bonaparte owing to Napoleon's ruling – though it was possible he would still receive the dignity of prince. Allegedly, owing to the possibility of him (as an American) receiving an imperial title, the US Congress proposed an amendment to the constitution in 1810 that would effectively strip any American of their citizenship if they were to accept a dignity or title of nobility from another nation. The amendment never received enough votes, and besides, Jerome Napoleon was also British by birth. The ruling on his surname was reversed decades later by his cousin Emperor Napoleon III.

As a young man he attended both Mount St Mary's and Harvard, and was a founding member of the Maryland Club and its first president. Like his father, he married an American heiress, Susan Williams, and produced two sons in 1830 and 1851. The first of these he named after himself and he bore the bizarre Americanism of having the number two after his name, but, considering that he was the grandson of a king – perhaps we can forgive this. Jerome Napoleon Bonaparte II followed in the tradition of his great-uncle (Napoleon) and entered the army – the US army. He enrolled at the Military Academy at West Point in 1848 and graduated four years later, commissioned as lieutenant, and served in Texas in the Mounted Riflemen Regiment. During this time, his cousin-once-removed had become president of France (and would soon be emperor). He left America to join the French army in 1854 where he served with distinction for many years. After serving in the Crimean War, he not only received the *Legion d'honneur*, but also the British Crimean medal in thanks for his service – another Bonaparte receiving British honours!

After the Franco-Prussian War and the fall of Paris, Jerome Napoleon II returned to America. He married the granddaughter of a US congressman and by her had two daughters. One daughter, Louise-Eugenie, married Count Adam von Moltke-Huitfeldt, a German/Danish noble. He was ironically from the same clan as the Prussian Field Marshal Helmuth von Moltke who had just defeated France in the recent war. (Helmuth's nephew, Ludwig von Moltke was the famous German Chief of Staff during the First World War.)

Lieutenant Colonel Jerome Napoleon Bonaparte, via his daughter Louis-Eugene (Countess von Moltke) has many living descendants in America. His younger brother, another grandson of King Jerome, died without issue. That said, he is certainly worthy of a brief note. Charles Joseph Bonaparte was born in Baltimore in 1851, while his cousin was president of France. Unlike his brother, he did not pursue a military career in France; however, he entered politics in his native US. In 1905, President Theodore Roosevelt appointed him secretary to the navy. Ironic given the family track record in boats! A year later he was appointed the

46th United States Attorney General. He also served as president of the National Municipal League and argued for the rights of black citizens. In 1908, he was a founder of the Bureau of Intelligence, later renamed the Federal Bureau of Intelligence (FBI). After a long and respected career, he died in 1921.

Though the descendants of King Jerome's first child were never truly accepted as full members of the clan, nor was their place in the succession confirmed, they bore the name of Bonaparte, became American, fought alongside the British, created the FBI, and had strong Irish roots. King Jerome's world, however, had further to go.

Shortly after his final farewell to Betsy in 1805, Jerome was sent by his brother the emperor back into the navy – where his performance remained patchy. Nevertheless, he was duly made a rear-admiral. Jerome also briefly entered the army and was appointed major general. Following Napoleon's victory at the battle of Friedland and the Peace of Tilsit in July 1807, Prussia ceded some of its territories in central Germany. That same month, Napoleon effectively gathered these lands and other captured territories to form the satellite state or buffer named the kingdom of Westphalia with his brother Jerome as king. Among the captured territories was the Electorate of Hanover – ruled by King George III of Britain at that time. Neither the British government nor the Hanoverian ministers recognised the French occupation, preferring to operate from London. It is bizarre to think that a country ruled by the British Crown was briefly ruled by a Bonaparte monarch.

To cement his place among the crowned heads of Europe, a political marriage was arranged for Jerome with the daughter of a fellow Germanic ruler, King Frederick I of Württemberg. Frederick had been the Elector of Württemberg, but that title was rather redundant following the collapse of the Holy Roman Empire in 1806. In exchange for providing France with military support, Napoleon recognised Württemberg as a kingdom, and Frederick as king. Added to the bargain was an alliance of marriage between Frederick's daughter Catharina and Napoleon's brother Jerome, the new king of Westphalia. Strangely, this family also had British connections. Catharina was descended from George II of Britain and was great-niece of George III – Napoleon's (mad) enemy. Catharina's mother was sister to Caroline of Brunswick (future queen of George IV), and, after her death in 1788, her father married Charlotte, the Princess Royal – fourth child of George III.

Though just a French/Corsican ruling an assorted group of German territories, effectively, Jerome Bonaparte's mother-in-law was the Princess Royal of Great Britain. King Jerome and Queen Catharina would go on to have two sons and one daughter – all of them were both simultaneously a Bonaparte and descendants of King George II of Great Britain.

As the years and campaigns rolled on in Europe, Jerome developed a reputation for spending and excessiveness. He spent lavishly on his court – beyond the country's means. Napoleon underwrote the bills, but at one point Jerome was spending the same money on his court as Napoleon who was ruler of a far larger and richer empire. Jerome was often reprimanded for this. During the 1812 campaign in Russia, he was effectively told off for wanting to travel in style with most of his court joining him on the campaign. He had to send them back; however, he rejoined them after being reprimanded again – this time for letting the Russian army, under General Bagration, escape following the Battle of Smolensk. Jerome left the campaign. A furious Napoleon had to lie through gritted teeth saying that the king of Westphalia was ill and had to go home!

Following the disastrous Russian campaign, Jerome was worried for his kingdom's future as coalition forces marched against France. The kingdom was bankrupt and Napoleon was in no position to bail it out. By 1813, it was overrun by Russian Cossacks and the territories went back to their former owners, although Prussia made some gains. Hanover was later elevated to a kingdom and it too increased its borders in 1814. George III could add another kingdom to his collection – despite the loss of America.

After the fall of the empire, the loss of his kingdom and his brother's impending exile to Elba, Jerome and his family retreated to the safety of his father-in-law's kingdom, Württemberg. As we know, however, Napoleon did not stay in Elba long. During the Hundred Days, Jerome returned to his brother's side – which was a gamble. Having fought well in Napoleon's army at Quatre Bras, when it came to Waterloo, he was given command of a division. On 18 June 1815, his division was part of the diversionary attack on the Hugermont farmhouse, planned by Napoleon to draw more of Wellington's forces into combat. True to form though, Jerome exceeded these orders somewhat. He committed more than he should have to the farmhouse siege and surrounding wood, which turned into some of the bloodiest fighting of the battle. It was one of the contributing reasons for French defeat on the day. At times,

Jerome was in danger from British fire. Napoleon, however, commended Jerome for his eager bravery at Waterloo. Following the battle, Jerome even attempted to regroup the remains of the French army for a potential further battle, but the game was up. Napoleon abdicated for a second time nine days later and within weeks was on a British ship bound for Plymouth.

Following the fall of the first empire (for a second time), the now embarrassed Jerome was eventually and, somewhat begrudgingly, accepted back into the Württemberg court. Now that all his titles and relations were meaningless (since the Bourbons had been restored and banned the Bonapartes from returning), it was difficult to know what to call him. King Frederick created Jerome the title of Prince of Montfort – if only for his daughter and grandchildren's sake. Like so many of the other Bonapartes, Jerome did not elect to keep his brother company in exile on St Helena, and entered a phase of exile and political limbo. Shortly after the young Napoleon II died in exile in 1832, Jerome reportedly attended the meeting of the brothers Bonaparte, as called together by Joseph at his house in Park Crescent by Regent's Park in London. Ultimately, as we have seen, very little action was implemented following these meetings. It is unclear how long he stayed in England although he, like Joseph and Lucien, rented an English country house. During the limbo years between the fall of the first empire and rise of the second, the Prince of Montfort reportedly rented Brettenham Park in Suffolk for a time – a curious building with a mix of styles. Decades later, it became a Preparatory School in 1956 and is now known as Old Buckenham Hall School. (Benjamin Britten was an old boy.) That said, Jerome and Catharina spent much of their time living in Switzerland. Catharina died there in 1835.

Having done his duty with a dynastic marriage, Jerome was now free to love whom he wished. Unfortunately, he had never been good with money. He had usually relied on his high-achieving relatives for that. The Prince of Montfort was broke. In 1840, he married a wealthy Italian widow, Giustina Pecori-Suarez, who had been married to the Marquess Luigi Bartolini-Baldelli. This does not seem to have been a love match. Jerome would not allow her to be recognised as a princess or use his surname and she was not liked by her stepchildren. In 1847, Jerome was permitted to return to take up residence in France by the now ailing July Monarchy. Giustina moved with him to Paris. But though her money had helped pay his debts and keep him in the style to which he had become accustomed, he soon exiled her. When Jerome's nephew Napoleon III restored him as an imperial prince, Giustina was packed off to a property in Florence amid accusations that she had made eyes at one of Jerome's (alleged) illegitimate children, Baron Jerome David (nominally the grandson of the great Napoleonic painter, Jacques-Louis David).

Jerome was the only one of Napoleon's brothers to live long enough to see the empire restored. His nephew Napoleon III poured honours on him: he was an imperial prince again, a marshal of France, governor of Les Invalides, president of the Senate, residency at the Palais-Royal and, more importantly heir presumptive to the throne. Napoleon III had no children yet. Were he to die without a son, the heirs to the empire would be Jerome and his offspring – Lucien and his descendants having been barred from the succession. Jerome was old though and was extremely unlikely to succeed to the title created by his older brother. He died aged 75 in 1860 and was buried in Les Invalides close to his brothers Napoleon and Joseph, his nephew Napoleon II, along with his eldest son, Jerome Napoleon Charles Frederic Bonaparte, a soldier who had predeceased him in 1847. It is fortunate for Jerome that he did not live to see the fall of the second empire a decade later.

Amongst a plethora of rumoured illegitimate children (as was the fashion), Jerome had three legitimate offspring with Catharina. As well as Jerome Napoleon Charles Frederic they had a daughter, Mathilde, who was initially in the running to marry her cousin Napoleon III but settled for a rich Russian aristocrat – a marriage which ended in separation and affairs with artists. She remained close to her cousin. Mathilde was such a close companion of the prince-president (Napoleon III) that she is sometimes regarded today as having been the first First Lady of France. She was present at the 1855 state visit to Versailles. She was particularly witty. The only Bonaparte permitted to stay in France following the collapse of the second empire, she kept a very popular salon frequented by many of the great French artists of the day. Mathilde is reported to have praised her great-uncle Napoleon I by saying that if it had not been for him, she would most likely be selling oranges in the streets of Ajaccio. Famously, in old age, she was invited to a national event at Les Invalides by the republican government. The invitation card was required to gain access. Mathilde pointed out that the card was redundant to her since she possessed the key!

Most prominent of the royal Westphalian children was Napoleon-Jerome Bonaparte (sometimes known as Plon-Plon). Born in 1822, he was still young man when his cousin became president in 1848 and then emperor in 1852. Nevertheless, he went on to be a senior character in the second empire and have several surprising links to Britain.

After his mother died in 1835, Napoleon-Jerome was welcomed by his aunt Hortense in Arnenberg, Switzerland, where he spent time alongside his cousin Louis-Napoleon, the future emperor. Napoleon-Jerome, known by the family as Plon-Plon, joined the military of Württemberg where he was an officer in the guards' regiment of his uncle King William I. Aged 22, he accompanied his friend Alexandre Dumas on a tour of Italy where the two visited the island of Monte Cristo together. Just two years later, Dumas published *The Count of Monte Cristo*. After the future Napoleon III escaped from the prison fortress of Ham in 1847, Napoleon-Jerome travelled to London to join his victorious cousin. During his brief time in London, he met and began an affair with the French actress Rachel Felix. Rachel is not only famous as a performer; she managed to have a relationship with Plon-Plon and also his cousins: Alexandre Walewski and Napoleon III (who was probably unaware of her other dalliances). It is likely she knew Bonaparte men better than any other that century.

Following his cousin's election to president of France and subsequent rise to emperor, Napoleon-Jerome was appointed to several high offices, including head of the French army of Italy (a role Napoleon himself had had), governor of Algeria and a general of a division in the Crimea. He commanded a division at the Battle of Alma in 1854, alongside the British forces commanded by Lord Raglan. With ties becoming ever closer between Britain and France, Plon-Plon was involved in the state visits of Napoleon III and Queen Victoria in 1855. The same year, he was invested as an Honorary Knight Grand Cross of the Order of the Bath. Though he was a Bonaparte receiving a very high honour from the British, we cannot ignore the fact that the Order (in its present form) was founded by Plon-Plon's great-great-great-great-grandfather, King George I of Britain. The Empress Eugenie was by this time pregnant with the Prince Imperial. After he was born, Plon-Plon's place in the succession slipped and he became irritable and less enfranchised with his cousin's rule.

Like his father had been, Plon-Plon was used as a bargaining chip in game of European politics. He too entered into an arranged marriage.

In 1859, as part of Napoleon III's policy with Italy, Plon-Plon married Princess Clotilde of Savoy. Her father, Victor Emmanuel II, and the House of Savoy, were soon to become the kings of a united Italy. Coincidentally, the last person to use such a title had been Napoleon himself. Through her mother, Clotilde was also half a Habsburg. But wealth or family does not necessarily equate to a happy marriage. Theirs was not a blissful union. She was only 15 at the time of their political marriage; custom dictated Plon-Plon wait for her to come of age, but he only waited a year before collecting her from Turin. He liked a fast life; she liked a quiet one. She was small, modest and pious. He was large and had neither of the other qualities. They were compared to a gazelle and an elephant. While Clotilde dedicated herself to charitable good works, Plon-Plon lived life to the fullest – with various partners.

Plon-Plon had several mistresses in his time but principal among these was an Englishwoman. Their relationship lasted nine years. Cora Pearl was another courtesan. Born in Plymouth in 1836, she was the daughter of a renowned cellist, Frederick Nicholls Crouch. A few years after Cora's birth, Crouch left his family in Plymouth, married bigamously, and travelled to Virginia. In the Civil War he joined the Confederacy. Nonetheless, Cora was sent to a boarding school in France for her education, but a disagreeable encounter on Jersey, where a man got her drunk, took advantage of her, and left her some money, led to her leaving her studies and heading for Covent Garden. It was not only flowers or fruit one could buy at the market. An ambitious girl, she set her sights far higher, and planned to become a courtesan – or kept woman. She soon moved to Paris. By the 1860s, she was one of the most celebrated courtesans of the day being mistress to the Prince of Orange, the Duke of Gramont and the Duke of Morny – Napoleon III's half-brother. Wealth swiftly followed and she was able to rent chateaux and keep horses.

Another Bonaparte relative, Achille Murat, was a 'friend' of hers. Plon-Plon joined the ranks of these men as her most dedicated patron and lover, while also providing her with gifts and even a small palace. Following the disastrous Franco-Prussian War and end of the empire, however, he regrettably had to end the affair as he could not shoulder the cost. Though Cora would eventually end her days in relative poverty, it is amazing to think that a young Plymouth girl rose so far in the court of France.

As we know, Napoleon III did have a son, the Prince Imperial, who became head of the House of Bonaparte following his father's death in 1873.

Tragedy followed when the Prince Imperial was killed in a Zulu ambush fighting for the British army in 1879. Despite Plon-Plon being alive, the prince had willed that the headship of the House should pass to Plon-Plon's son, Prince Victor. This created some friction between father and son.

Prince Victor (1862–1926), sometimes known as Napoleon V, continued his side of the clan's tradition of high-profile marriages. The politics of France in the late nineteenth century were still unsteady; a return to power for the Bonapartes could not be ruled out, and Victor had both Italian and German royal relations. Victor married Princess Clementine of Belgium in 1910. This was much more of a love match and it took some years for the couple to persuade her father King Leopold II to agree to their union – which he never did. Only after he died did the two finally marry. Clementine was from the House of Saxe-Coburg and was therefore a cousin to the late Prince Albert, Edward VII and George V of Britain. Her ancestry was also curious in that she was a great-granddaughter of King Louis-Philippe of France – the Orleanist king who had imprisoned Napoleon III and barred so many Bonapartes from entering France. The future heirs of the Bonaparte dynasty are, to this day, descended from this king.

Clementine and Victor's only son, Louis (1914–1997) succeeded as head of the dynasty in 1926 (Napoleon VI). As a child he had been able to visit the Empress Eugenie at her home in Hampshire before she passed in 1920. During the Second World War, Louis asked permission to join the French army but was refused, as heads of former French ruling families were not permitted. Under a false name he joined the Foreign Legion and then the resistance after the surrender in 1941. Louis hoped to join the Free French in London under de Gaulle, but was arrested by the Germans before he could make it. After release, he continued in resistance activities and was decorated for bravery. Perhaps in recognition of war service, in 1950 the government of France allowed the heads of the houses of Bonaparte, Bourbon and Orleans to return to their homeland to live.

The House of Bonaparte is now headed by Louis's grandson Prince Jean-Christophe (Napoleon VII) who was born in France in 1986 to Prince Charles Napoleon and Princess Beatrice of Bourbon-Two-Sicilies. The house of Bourbon-Two-Sicilies is a cadet branch of the Spanish Bourbons. In an historically amusing twist of fate, the head of the House of Bonaparte is half a Bourbon and direct descendant of Louis XIV and, more crucially, King George II of Britain.

Today the Prince Napoleon lives in London and works in high finance. He married in 2019, Countess Olympia von und zu Arco-Zinneberg. Through her Habsburg mother, Olympia is a great-granddaughter of Charles I, last emperor of Austria, and subsequently the four times great-grandniece of Marie-Louise of Austria – Napoleon's second wife.

The year 2015 was a particularly busy one for the head of the Bonaparte dynasty, with many official Waterloo centenary events to attend both in Belgium and in the UK. A sombre commemoration event took place at the site in Belgium attended by the heads of various families concerned (Bonaparte, Wellesley, von Blücher, and Orange), together with representatives of the governments and armed forces of the original protagonists. A moment of great significance in the history of Western Europe. There was also, inevitably, a large-scale re-enactment of the battle. Later that year, Prince Jean-Christophe was presented with the Freedom of the City of London in a lavish ceremony and grand dinner in the City.

In England, when we look at our history, we are fascinated by our military defeats and disasters. Many of them are more famous than our victories. Hastings, Bannockburn, the Light Brigade, Isandlwana, the Somme, the Dieppe Raid, the bridge at Arnhem, and even the *Titanic*. These are taught in schools and made into excellent motion pictures (sometimes). Culturally, we enjoy examining our hubris. Not so with the French and their history. An element of improving history is culturally common. Very few Frenchmen have been taught about Agincourt, Crecy, Quebec or Blenheim. Some French museums claim the French liberated Paris (without a nod to the Americans or Allies). Ohers claim that one of the beachheads at Normandy was invaded entirely by Free French forces, and that the Battle of Waterloo was … inconclusive! In fact, some French people have reported being taught in school that the Battle of Waterloo was either a draw or in fact a French victory.

In Prince Jean-Christophe's acceptance speech in London in 2015, he jokingly explained that when he first came to London, the Eurostar arrived at Waterloo Station. He thought: how odd! In Paris, stations are named after victories, but in London they are named after defeats. (This was met with much laughter by most of the room – with a few baffled British faces dotted around!)

As the current Prince and Princess Napoleon (as they are known) live in London, it is possible that there will be yet more *British Bonapartes!*

Chapter 10

Other British Links: The Barely British Beauharnais

It is worth remembering that, as well as many brothers, sisters, children, nieces and nephews, Napoleon also had his stepchildren. These were the family and children of his first wife, Joséphine, by her earlier marriage to Vicomte Alexandre de Beauharnais, who was guillotined in the wake of the (first) French Revolution, in 1794.

The Beauharnais family was a noble French family whose origins can be traced back to the days of Joan of Arc at Orleans (*c.*1429) and to Brittany. One member of the family, François (d. 1746), became a colonial administrator in French Canada. His title, that of Baron de Beauville was named after an estate he owned in the French colony of Acadia. His brother, Charles le Marquis de Beauharnais, was governor general of New France (Canada) from 1726 to 1746. Following the Seven Years War and the Battle of Quebec, much of New France was ceded to Great Britain in the 1763 Treaty of Paris.

Alexandre's father, another François, was the governor of Martinique and the French Antilles from 1757–1761. Both Alexandre and Joséphine were born in the French Caribbean (and probably both in Martinique) and had two children. Hortense born in 1783, became the queen of Holland and mother to Napoleon III. Eugene, born in 1781, became one of Napoleon's right-hand men. Both of these children were dear to Napoleon as well as important figures throughout the first empire. Eugene was in many ways the son Napoleon never had. As a young man he started his military career as an aide-de-camp to his stepfather General Bonaparte. Through many campaigns he distinguished himself as a leader. In 1805, having become the king of Italy, Napoleon made his stepson Eugene the viceroy of Italy as well as a prince of France. Eugene married the Bavarian Princess Augusta in 1806 and continued to be support his stepfather both as a military commander and a governor right up until Napoleon's eventual downfall

Family Tree

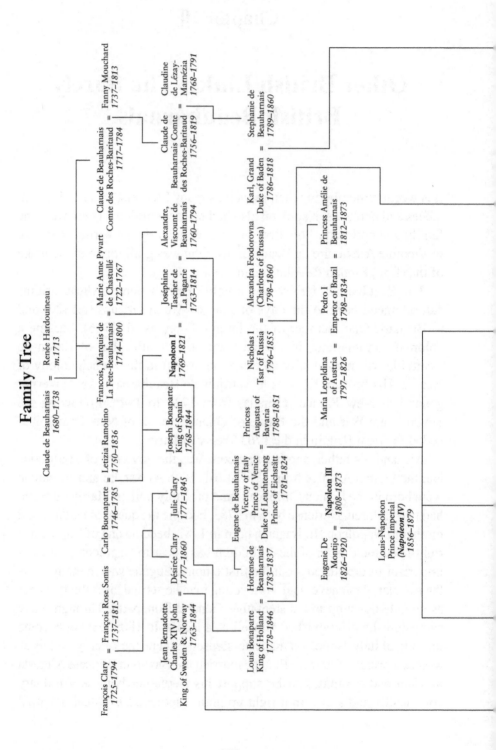

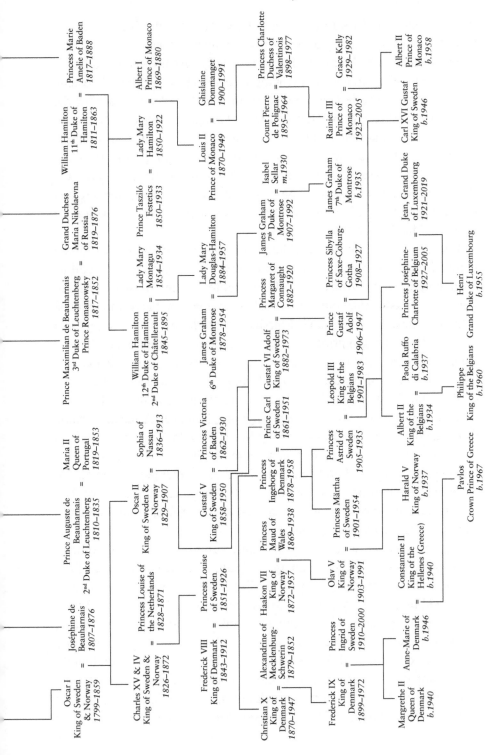

and abdication in 1814. Eugene had briefly also been the Grand Duke of Frankfurt but in name only as it was overrun by the allied powers in 1813. After the emperor's abdication, Eugene sensibly gave up politics and lived in the lands of his father-in-law, King of Bavaria, Maximilian I Joseph. Perhaps more sensible still, he did not rush to Napoleon's aid after the escape from Elba and the Hundred Days Campaign; besides, Napoleon was no longer married to Eugene's mother. In fact, when he returned to France following the death of his mother Joséphine, the Bourbon Louis XVIII welcomed him – after all, the Beauharnais had served the Bourbons for generations. Eugene was created Duke of Leuchtenberg and Prince of Eichstätt in 1817 by his father-in-law, perhaps as consolation for the loss of his French titles.

Eugene and Augusta's children's marriages certainly moved the family firmly into the first division of royal circles. A true roll call of nineteenth-century royalty. His eldest daughter, Joséphine, married King Oscar I of Sweden (he being the son of Napoleon's first love and greatest betrayer, Désirée Clary and Marshal Bernadotte). Other daughters became (by marriage) princess of Hohenzollern; empress of Brazil; and Duchess of Urach (Württemberg). Eugene's eldest son, Auguste, married Queen Maria II of Portugal in 1834, and thus became prince consort of Portugal. This would have been a prestigious moment where the Beauharnais dynasty would rule a kingdom; however, Auguste became ill and died only months after meeting Maria in 1835. The queen went on to marry a prince from another rising family – the Saxe-Coburg-Gothas. Incidentally, Auguste had been considered as a potential contender for the newly created position of king of the Belgians; however, he had been beaten to the post by another Saxe-Coburg prince, Leopold, Prince Albert and Queen Victoria's uncle.

Eugene's second son, Maximilian, inherited his father's and brother's titles as 3rd Duke of Leuchtenberg. In 1839, he married into one of the richest and most powerful royal families in the world: the Romanovs. The wedding ceremony between Maximilian and Grand Duchess Maria of Russia, daughter of Tsar Nicholas I, took place at the Winter Palace. A step-grandson of Napoleon's, and a son of French military commander became a son-in-law of the Tsar less than thirty years after the bloody 1812 campaign. As a member of the extended Bonaparte dynasty, the Tsar 'restored' Maximilian to the rank of Imperial Highness and the title of Prince Romanovsky. Over the many decades, this Russian branch of the Beauharnais family has died out, although there is a male-line descendant of Eugene's claiming the title of Duke of Leuchtenberg to this day, with many other living relatives.

How is any of this British? One might well ask. It all related to a small spa town in Germany: Baden-Baden.

In fairness, it is not so much Baden-Baden, but more the area of Baden from which the town takes its name. The Margraviate of Baden was a medieval fiefdom that was a domain of the Holy Roman Emperor. A Margrave was appointed to rule it in true feudal tradition as a military protector and governor, which soon became a hereditary position. In 1803, it was raised to the status of an Electorate by the Habsburg emperor. However, after the dissolution of the Holy Roman Empire, in part thanks to Napoleon, Baden became a sovereign independent state – becoming a Grand Duchy in 1806. The new Grand Duke, Karl Frederick, backed the French in the Napoleonic Wars, joining the Confederation of the Rhine and expanding its territories. To cement the alliance, the Grand Duke Karl and Napoleon agreed that a marriage between their two dynasties should take place. Karl put forward his grandson, Prince Charles. Napoleon on the other hand was short of legitimate descendants or unmarried or appropriate nieces.

Since the 'union' of the Beauharnais and Bonaparte families in 1796 via Joséphine and Napoleon's marriage, he had acquired not only two stepchildren but also an extended family who over the years began to benefit from his care and patronage. Stephanie de Beauharnais (1789–1860) was a second cousin of Napoleon's stepchildren. During the chaos of the French Revolution, her mother died when Stephanie was an infant and her father fled into exile. She was cared for by her godmother, an Englishwoman named Henrietta Laura Pulteney, Countess of Bath – a peeress in her own right. Pulteney was a wealthy English heiress who was raised partly in Parisian society, and had come into her inheritance. As such, she had endowed schools and good causes as well some godchildren. (Her titles of Baroness and Countess of Bath were effectively purchased for her by her father, Sir William Pulteney Bt, in 1792 and 1803 respectively. Henrietta's distant cousin, had briefly held the title Earl of Bath until its extinction in 1764.) Henrietta, a small town in Munroe Country, New York, is named after the countess. To some degree, Stephanie de Beauharnais benefited from an association with this wealthy, independent Englishwoman.

Sometime after Napoleon became first consul, he learnt of Stephanie's existence and decided to take charge of her welfare and upbringing – either out of kindness or calculation. Years later, in lieu of any daughters of his own and in need of political alliances, Napoleon hastily adopted Stephanie and she was married to Prince Charles of Baden in 1806. She was just 16. On the death of Charles's grandfather in 1811, Stephanie became the Grand Duchess of Baden. Despite a rocky start to the marriage, the couple became close and produced several children. The youngest of these was Princess Marie Amalie of Baden.

Marie was born in 1817 in Baden. By then, Napoleon's fall from power was permanent and Marie's mother was entirely reliant on the support of the Baden Grand Ducal court. In a post-Napoleonic world, Grand Duchess Stephanie walked a difficult road. She was an awkward reminder that Baden had allied with the losing side. Allegedly, in order to avoid a scandal involving her daughter Louise's failing marriage to the (Swedish) Prince of Vasa, Stephanie encouraged her youngest daughter into a hasty marriage with a dashing young man of 'lesser blood' – noble but not royal. A new marriage might draw gossips' attention away from the scandal of the other marriage – which did end in divorce (shortly after this new marriage). The chosen man in question was a British aristocrat holidaying in the Black Forest. He was William Hamilton, Marquess of Douglas and Clydesdale, son and heir of the Duke of Hamilton and Brandon, one of the premier families of Scotland and indeed Britain. That said, this was a morganatic marriage; they were not of equal rank. Permission, however, was given by the Grand Duke, and William and Marie were married in Mannheim in 1843. William had entered the Black Forest on vacation; he came away with a princess.

Suddenly a European princess, and granddaughter of Napoleon (on paper), was a senior member of the British aristocracy. The move to her new home in Scotland must have been a slight shock to Marie who was in her twenties and used to a royal court – not that the Hamiltons were without the finer things in life. They had been wealthy land owners for centuries. They had been lords in Scotland since the Middle Ages and held many peerages over the generations – too many to recount here. As Dukes of Hamilton, they were (and remain) the premier peers of Scotland, much like the Dukes of Norfolk are in England. Attached to the title came certain hereditary offices such as Keeper of Holyrood Palace in Edinburgh and bearer of the Crown of Scotland at official ceremonies – a tradition which was revived in 1999. William was the next-in-line and would become the 11th Duke.

All was not easy in the beginning. Today when we think of difficult marriages between the classes, we think of working class joined or locked in battle with upper-middle. In the nineteenth century, there was a similar jump between noble and royal. William's wife could boast royalty (and even Napoleon) in her family tree. He too, of course, had a gilded pedigree of English/Irish/Scottish nobilities, and with some connections to royalty, but only from earlier centuries. His ancestry was also peppered with untitled commoners such as William Beckford in his family tree. Beckford was a novelist and art collector and was the builder of Fonthill, a fanciful Gothic country house which later collapsed. The sticking point was at the court of Queen Victoria. If Marie was present, protocol dictated that she be received as royalty and as a princess of Baden. As Marie's husband, William was in an ambiguous position, not being quite royal himself. It would be grossly inappropriate for a British monarch to receive one of their subjects as a royal – even if that subject was the premier peer of Scotland. However, perhaps out of tact or as a dutiful wife, Marie often retreated from court to avoid embarrassment on any side.

It is perhaps for that reason that William decided to renovate one of their retreats: Brodick Castle. Brodick is on the Isle of Arran on the west coast of Scotland. William greatly increased the size of the castle and its accommodation. In an effort to make his princess bride more at home, he created the Bavarian summerhouse in the gardens. This was at the same time as Scotland was experiencing a revival both culturally and economically. That said, the couple spent much of their time in Paris and other parts of Europe over the years.

In the same year that William and Marie became Duke and Duchess (William's father having died), Marie's cousin, Louis-Napoleon, became emperor of the French. In 1852, Napoleon III merely replaced the word president for emperor before his name, and was now ruler of the French Empire. As we have seen, the 1850s were a time of courtship between France and England, between Napoleon and Victoria. He needed an alliance with England, and his cousin was a shoe-in to the British court and way of life. He had, of course, visited the couple in Scotland before, even attending the famous Eglington Tournament of 1839, but Napoleon had put away such childish things now he was a statesman. By an odd coincidence, Napoleon III, then Prince Louis-Napoleon, had used the surname 'Hamilton' to check into the Hotel Holland in Place Vendôme while travelling incognito with his mother in Paris back in 1831.

The ducal couple accompanied Marie's cousin on his triumphal entry into Paris as emperor in 1852. They were considered to be part of the extended imperial family – certainly Eugene would remain very close to the Hamiltons, visiting their Scottish estates even after the empire had fallen. With their proximity to the British royal court, Duke William and Duchess Marie may well have helped influence Victoria and Albert into agreeing to the 1855 state visits to London and then Paris – moments which sowed the seed of the future *entente cordiale*.

But, although not a full-blooded Bonaparte (only an adopted granddaughter of Napoleon), the family habit for scandal or mischief was ever strong, even around Marie. In the 1850s it was reported that she had converted to Roman Catholicism. This put her slightly at odds with Victoria and Albert and their court. She developed a coldness in her behaviour which her critics would later blame on her staunch Catholicism. For example, she did not visit the deathbed of her mother, sending her husband instead. The new queen of the Netherlands described her as bloodless and sick. Many may have also disliked her for her close relationship with the Empress Eugenie – who became a lifelong regular in Scotland, partly because it was one of the few places in Europe where it was politically neutral for the empress to take a holiday. Eugenie put many noses out of joint when she insisted that Marie be seated with the imperial family at the Prince Imperial's christening in 1856. In widowhood, Marie continued to have a black mark against her name. She retired to a villa in Baden where many royals and socialites would visit her, including Bertie the Prince of Wales (Edward VII) and his grandmother, the Duchess of Kent. However, Queen Victoria noted Marie and her offspring as the sort of disreputable people that Bertie was not to socialise with. Marie continued to live in Baden until her death in 1888, though she certainly left a little mark on a small island off the west of Scotland.

Marie's husband, William, the 11th Duke, had died in 1863 following what we must imagine was a gloriously large dinner at the famous restaurant Maison Dorée – a regular haunt of Edward VII, Rossini, and Balzac. After collapsing at the dinner, William died a few days later. He was succeeded by his and Marie's eldest son, another William, the 12th Duke of Hamilton and 9th Duke of Brandon. In a unique state of affairs, he was a British duke, but the great-grandson of Napoleon (by adoption) and close relative of senior European royals. His first cousins included the king of Romania, the queen of Portugal and the queen of Saxony. On top of this he was a distant cousin of the emperor of the French and was considered a member of the extended imperial family. So much so that Napoleon III revived a title for the young duke, which had previously been given to an ancestor.

The Duke of Châtellerault is a title that was created several times over the centuries by kings of France, usually for extended members of the royal family. In 1548 or 1549, its fifth creation was for James Hamilton (2nd Earl of Arran). He was the regent in Scotland for Mary, Queen of Scots during her minority. He had to navigate a difficult political world as England and France wrestled for influence in Scotland. In return for agreeing to Mary's marriage to the Dauphin (future Francis II), King Henry II of France made James the Duke of Châtellerault. Not a bad deal you might think, although owing to the politics of the Scottish reformation, it was promptly confiscated a few years later when he declared for the Protestants. At one point he petitioned to have his title reinstated, but this is unlikely to have happened. Despite this, claims to the dukedom have been made by many noble descendants of James Hamilton, including the Dukes of Hamilton. Napoleon III was able to settle any disputes by recognising/creating William the Duke of Châtellerault in 1864, though this did not do much good as he only had one child, a daughter. The title has occasionally been claimed by successive Dukes of Hamilton and also by the Dukes of Abercorn, but with little grounds.

William, though very titled, was not overcome with coin. His father had spent much of the family fortune on keeping his princess bride and had divided much of what was left between his offspring. A true gentleman of fortune, however, William was able to recoup much of the fortune when his Irish horse, Cortolvin, came in first at the Grand National Steeplechase at Aintree in 1867. Luck of the Irish, or luck of the Bonapartes/Beauharnais?

The 11th Duke and Princess Mary had a second daughter born in 1850: Lady Mary Victoria Douglas-Hamilton. Though born in Scotland and a Scottish aristocrat, she became part of the Bonaparte political marriage market. Thanks to the Treaty of Turin in 1860 between Napoleon and Victor Emmanuel, king of Sardinia (and later, Italy), the County of Nice became fully part of France. Nice is very close to Monaco, a small independent principality now surrounded by the French state. The emperor, led by Eugenie, sought to gain closer ties with Monaco's ruling Grimaldi family so that Monaco and France would be politically aligned. Not having many young female relatives, Napoleon III found himself in the same position as his uncle had been in with Baden. In a repeat of family history, he turned to the Beauharnais-Hamiltons and to Princess Marie to provide a sacrificial female cousin. In a strange twist, Lady Mary Douglas-Hamilton, a British noble and Napoleon's distant cousin, was dispatched to marry Prince Albert of Monaco. Today this would sound luxurious; however, at this time, Monaco was not yet the place it is today. It was anything but glamorous. In dire need of money, the Grimaldis had created a gambling den to create some income in the small principality.

The marriage did not go well. Mary had not been the Grimaldis' first choice. They had hoped for an alliance with the all-powerful British Empire. For the young Prince Albert, his family sought Princess Mary Adelaide of Cambridge, Victoria's cousin (and mother of Mary of Teck, the future British queen,). Queen Victoria, however, could not stomach the idea of a British princess marrying someone who made money from gambling! Napoleon swiftly suggested his cousin Lady Mary, herself related to many royal families, as a consolation. The Hamiltons initially looked down on the Grimaldis but soon recognised that their princely status was at least a step up for Lady Mary. The couple were cordially married in the south of France in 1869. A year later, their only child, Louis, was born in Baden. In the following years, Mary's relationship with her husband deteriorated. He was a keen oceanographer and often away on expeditions or experiments. It has been reported by a former mistress of his that he also suffered from erectile disfunction. It did not help that Mary did not especially like Monaco nor much of Mediterranean society – one can imagine her prudent Scottish sensibilities not mixing with the needlessly showy lifestyles of the titled and untitled rich that passed through Monte Carlo. The marriage was dissolved in 1880. Just days later, Lady Mary married a Hungarian aristocrat and lived a happier life in Budapest and on the shores of Lake Balaton where she was able to entertain visitors such as her brother, the Duke of Hamilton and the Prince of Wales (Edward VII). Albert also moved on quickly. He married an American heiress, the recently widowed dowager Duchess of Richelieu. Her late husband's family were connected to the famous cardinal of the same name. Prince Albert and Lady Mary's son became Louis II Prince of Monaco. Odd to think of a Monegasque monarch as half Scots. Louis II's grandson, Prince Rainier, married American actress Grace Kelly. Surprising marriages are almost a Monegasque tradition these days. To this day, the current Prince of Monaco, Albert II, can count Scottish and English aristocrats and gentry, Americans, and Napoleon's stepdaughter among his ancestors.

As we have seen, the Beauharnais family were not Bonapartes. Originally an ancient, minor noble family, they reached substantive heights of influence and nobility in the decades leading to the French Revolution. The family name (and some of its individuals) were met by Madame Guillotine; it could have ended there for the clan and its prospects; however, a certain marriage changed everything and increased their fortunes and potential. The union between Napoleon Bonaparte and Joséphine de Beauharnais (née Tascher de La Pagerie), brought position and influence to not just Joséphine's children but other members of the wider family. This naturally led to advantageous marriages, and alliances with great and powerful dynasties. Napoleon has no living legitimate descendants; however, the descendants of the wife he divorced in favour of a Habsburg match ironically include the crowned heads of many lands – such as the rulers of Sweden, Denmark, Norway, Belgium, Luxembourg, Baden, an empress of Brazil, a prince consort of Portugal, and, perhaps more crucially, the only other ruling emperor of the French, Napoleon III. Half-Bonaparte, half-Beauharnais; he was perhaps a little more than barely British!

Bibliography

Abbott, Joseph S. C., *The Life of Napoleon Bonaparte*, (London: Ward, Lock & Co.) 1900

angelfire.com/realm/gotha/bonapartedescendants Accessed: 2020

Apraxine, Pierre and Demange Xavier, *La Divine Comtesse – Photographs of the Countess de Castiglione*, (Newhaven and London: Yale University Press) 2000

Atteridge, Andrew Hilliard, *Napoleon's Brothers*, (London: Methuen and Co.) 1909

Begent, Peter and Chesshyre, Hubert, *The Most Noble Order of the Garter*, (London: Spink) 1999

Bonaparte, Prince Jean-Christophe Napoleon, Personal Correspondences 2020–2022

Caiani, Ambrogio A., *To Kidnap a Pope: Napoleon and Pius VII*, (Newhaven and London: Yale University Press) 2021

Connelly, Owen, 'Jerome Bonaparte, King of Westphalia', in *History Today*, Vol 14, Issue 9, 1964

D'Ornano, Count, *Life and Loves of Marie Walewska*, (London: Hutchinson) 1934

De Bourrienne, Louis Antoine Fauvelet (Napoleon I's Private Secretary) and Ramsay Weston Phipps, *Memoirs of Napoleon Bonaparte*, Vol.1, (New York: Charles Scribner's Sons) 1895

De Lano, Pierre, *The Emperor Napoleon III*, Translation by Helen Hunt Johnson, (New York: Dodd, Mead & Co.) 1895

De Soissons, Count, *The True Story of the Empress Eugenie*, (London: John Lane The Bodley Head) 1921

Duff, David, *Eugenie & Napoleon III*, (London: Book Club Associate with Wm. Collins, Sons & Co.) 1978

Fleischmann, Hector, *Napoleon III and the Women He Loved*, Translation by A. R. Rappoport, (London: Holden & Hardingham) 1915

Galloway, Peter, *The Order of the Bath*, (London: Phillimore) 2006

Galloway, Peter, *The Order of the British Empire*, (London: The Central Chancery of Orders of Knighthood) 1996

Geer, Walter, *Napoleon and his Family: Moscow to St Helena*, 1813–1821, (London: Allen & Unwin) 1929

Guedalla, Philip, *The Second Empire: Bonapartism, The Prince, The President, The Emperor*, (New York: G.P. Putnam's Sons) 1922

Harris, John Henry Edward Joseph, *Letters and Works*, Hadlow Castle, Kent

Hibbert, Christopher, *Napoleon: His Wives and Women*, (London: Harper Collins) 2002

Jourdan, Annie, *Louis Bonaparte, Roi de Hollande*, (Paris: New World) 2010

Le Petit Homme Rouge, *The Court of the Tuileries 1852–1870: Its Organization, Chief Personages, Splendour, Frivolity, and Downfall*, (London: Chatto & Windus) 1907

Leff, Lisa Moses, Rachel (Eliza Rachel Felix) 1821–1858, Jewish Women's Archive, jwa.org, accessed 2021

Lincoln, Margarette, ed., *Nelson and Napoléon*, (London: National Maritime Museum) 2005

Ludwig, Emil, *Napoleon*, Translated by Eden and Cedar Paul, (London: George Allen & Unwin) 1935

McAuliffe, Mary, *Paris, City of Dreams: Napoleon III, Baron Haussmann and the Creation of Paris*, (Maryland: Rowman & Littlefield) 2020

Normington, Susan, *Napoleon's Children*, (Dover: Alan Sutton) 1993

Oman, Carola, *Napoleon's Viceroy, Eugene de Beauharnais*, (London: Hodder & Stoughton) 1966

Palnert, Ute, ed., *Napoleon's Empire: European Politics in Global Perspective*, (London: Palgrave Macmillan) 2016

Pereltsvaig, Asya, *Napoleon Bonaparte: Frenchman, Corsican, Italian or Moor? And the last of the Romanovs*, Languagesoftheworld.info, 2015

Perrottet, Tony, *The Sinner's Grand Tour – A Journey through the Historical Underbelly of Europe* (New York: Broadway Paperbacks) 2011

Records and Manuscripts of HM's College of Arms, London

Roberts, Andrew, *Napoleon and Wellington*, (London: Phoenix Press) 2002

Roberts, Andrew, *Napoleon the Great*, (London: Penguin) 2015

Royal Collection Trust, *Crown and Camera: The British Royal Family and Photography 1842–1910, RCIN 2935077, The Royal and Imperial Visit to the Crystal Palace, April 20th 1855.*

Schom, Alan, *Napoleon Bonaparte*, (London: HarperCollins Publishers) 1997

Seward, Desmond, *Napoleon's Family*, (London: Weidenfeld & Nicolson) 1986

Smith, William H. C., *The Bonapartes: The History of a Dynasty*, (London: Hambledon and London) 2005

Strauss-Schom, Alan, *The Shadow Emperor: A Biography of Napoléon III*, (Stroud: Amberley) 2018

Stroud, Patricia Tyson, *The Man Who Had Been King: The American Exile of Napoleon's Brother Joseph*, (University of Pennsylvania Press) 2014

Stroud, Patricia Tyson, *The Emperor of Nature: Charles-Lucien Bonaparte and his World*, (University of Pennsylvania Press) 2000

Tucker, Spencer C., *500 Great Military Leaders*, (Santa-Barbara: ABC-Clio, LLC) 2015

Weis, René, *The Real La Traviata: The Song of Marie Duplessis*, (Oxford University Press) 2015

Williams, Roger L., *Gaslight and Shadow: The World of Napoleon III 1851–1870*, (New York: Macmillan) 1957

Williams, Roger L., *The Mortal Napoleon III*, (New Jersey: Princeton University Press) 1971

Wraxall, Lascelles, *Memoires of Queen Hortense, Vol 1 & 2, The Mother of Napoleon III* (Reprint) (London: Forgotten Books) 2018